Machine Learning Quick Reference

Quick and essential machine learning hacks for training smart data models

Rahul Kumar

BIRMINGHAM - MUMBAI

Machine Learning Quick Reference

Commissioning Editor: Amey Varangaonkar
Acquisition Editor: Porous Godhaa
Content Development Editor: Ronnel Mathew
Technical Editor: Sagar Sawant
Copy Editor: Safis Editing
Project Coordinator: Namrata Swetta
Proofreader: Safis Editing
Indexer: Priyanka Dhadke
Graphics: Jisha Chirayil
Production Coordinator: Shraddha Falebhai

First published: January 2019

Production reference: 1310119

Published by Packt Publishing Ltd.
Livery Place
35 Livery Street
Birmingham
B3 2PB, UK.

ISBN 978-1-78883-057-7

www.packtpub.com

`mapt.io`

Mapt is an online digital library that gives you full access to over 5,000 books and videos, as well as industry leading tools to help you plan your personal development and advance your career. For more information, please visit our website.

Why subscribe?

- Spend less time learning and more time coding with practical eBooks and Videos from over 4,000 industry professionals

- Improve your learning with Skill Plans built especially for you

- Get a free eBook or video every month

- Mapt is fully searchable

- Copy and paste, print, and bookmark content

Packt.com

Did you know that Packt offers eBook versions of every book published, with PDF and ePub files available? You can upgrade to the eBook version at `www.packt.com` and as a print book customer, you are entitled to a discount on the eBook copy. Get in touch with us at `customercare@packtpub.com` for more details.

At `www.packt.com`, you can also read a collection of free technical articles, sign up for a range of free newsletters, and receive exclusive discounts and offers on Packt books and eBooks.

Contributors

About the author

Rahul Kumar has got more than 10 years of experience in the space of Data Science and Artificial Intelligence. His expertise lies in the machine learning and deep learning arena. He is known to be a seasoned professional in the area of Business Consulting and Business Problem Solving, fuelled by his proficiency in machine learning and deep learning. He has been associated with organizations such as Mercedes-Benz Research and Development (India), Fidelity Investments, Royal Bank of Scotland among others. He has accumulated a diverse exposure through industries like BFSI, telecom and automobile. Rahul has also got papers published in IIM and IISc Journals.

About the reviewers

Chiheb Chebbi is a Tunisian infosec enthusiast, author, and technical reviewer with experience in various aspects of information security, focusing on investigations into advanced cyber attacks and researching cyber espionage. His core interests lie in penetration testing, machine learning, and threat hunting. He has been included in many halls of fame. The proposals he has put forward with a view to giving presentations have been accepted by many world-class information security conferences.

I dedicate this book to every person who makes the security community awesome and fun!

Dat Tran is currently co-heading the data team at idealo.de, where he leads a team of data scientists and data engineers. His focus is to turn idealo into a machine learning powerhouse. His research interests range from traditional machine learning to deep learning. Previously, he worked for Pivotal Labs and Accenture. He is a regular public speaker and has presented at the PyData and Cloud Foundry summits. He also blogs about his work on Medium. His background is in operations research and econometrics. He received his MSc in Economics from Humboldt University, Berlin.

Packt is searching for authors like you

If you're interested in becoming an author for Packt, please visit `authors.packtpub.com` and apply today. We have worked with thousands of developers and tech professionals, just like you, to help them share their insight with the global tech community. You can make a general application, apply for a specific hot topic that we are recruiting an author for, or submit your own idea.

Table of Contents

Preface

Machine learning involves developing and training models to predict future outcomes. This book is a practical guide to all the tips and tricks related to machine learning. It includes hands-on, easy-to-access techniques on topics such as model selection, performance tuning, training neural networks, time series analysis, and a lot more.

This book has been tailored toward readers who want to understand not only the concepts behind machine learning algorithms, but also the mathematics behind them. However, we have tried to strike a balance between these two.

Who this book is for

If you're a machine learning practitioner, data scientist, machine learning developer, or engineer, this book will serve as a reference point for building machine learning solutions. You will also find this book useful if you're an intermediate machine learning developer or data scientist looking for a quick, handy reference to all the concepts of machine learning. You'll need some exposure to machine learning to get the best out of this book.

What this book covers

Chapter 1, *Quantification of Learning*, builds the foundation for later chapters. First, we are going to understand the meaning of a statistical model. We'll also discuss the thoughts of Leo Breiman about statistical modeling. Later, we will discuss curves and why they are so important. One of the typical ways to find out the association between variables and modeling is curve fitting, which is introduced in this chapter.

To build a model, one of the steps is to partition the data. We will discuss the reasoning behind this and examine an approach to carry it out. While we are building a model, more often that not it is not a smooth ride, and we run into several issues. We often encounter overfitting and underfitting, for several reasons. We need to understand why and learn how to overcome it. Also, we will be discussing how overfitting and underfitting are connected to bias and variance. This chapter will discuss these concepts with respect to neural networks. Regularization is one of the hyperparameters that is an integral part of the model building process. We will understand why it is required. Cross-validation, model selection, and 0.632+ bootstrap will be talked about in this chapter, as they help data scientists to fine-tune a model.

Chapter 2, *Evaluating Kernel Learning*, explains how **support vector machines (SVMs)** have been among the most sophisticated models and have grabbed a lot of attention in the areas of classification and regression. But practitioners still find them difficult to grasp as it involve lots of mathematics. However, we have tried to keep it simple and mathematical too, so that you should be able to understand the tricks of SVMs. Also, we'll look at the kernel trick, which took SVMs to another level by making computation simple, to an extent. We will study the different types of kernel and their usage.

Chapter 3, *Performance in Ensemble Learning*, explains how to build models based on the concepts of bagging and boosting, which are ruling the world of hackathons. We will discuss bagging and boosting in detail. They have led to the creation of many good algorithms, such as random forest and gradient boosting. We will discuss each in detail with the help of a use case so that you can understand the difference between these two. Also, an important part of this chapter deals with the optimization of hyperparameters.

Chapter 4, *Training Neural Networks*, covers neural networks, which have always been deemed black box algorithms that take lots of effort to understand. We have tried to unbox the complexities surrounding NNs. We have started with detailing how NNs are analogous to the human brain. This chapter also covers what parameters such as weights and biases are and how an NN learns. An NN's learning process involves network initialization, a feedforward system, and cost calculation. Once a cost is calculated, backpropagation kicks off.

Next comes the challenges in the model, such as exploding gradients, vanishing gradients, and overfitting. This chapter encompasses all such problems, helps us understand why such challenges occur, and explains how to overcome them.

Chapter 5, *Time-Series Analysis*, covers different time series models for analyzing demand forecasting, be it stock price or sales forecasting, or anything else. Almost every industry runs into such use cases. In order to carry out such use cases, there are multiple approaches, and what we have covered is autoregressive models, ARMA, ARIMA, and others. We have started with the concepts of autoregression. Then comes stationarity, which is an important element of such models. This chapter examines stationarity and how we can detect it. Also, assessment of the model is covered too. Anomaly detection in econometrics is also discussed at length with the help of a use case.

Chapter 6, *Natural Language Processing*, explains what natural language processing is making textual data talk. There are a number of algorithms that make this work. We cannot work with textual data as it is. It needs to be vectorized and embedded. This chapter covers various ways of doing this, such as TF-IDF and bag-of-words methods.

We will also talk about how sentiment analysis can be done with the help of such approaches, and compare the results of different methods. We then move on to topic modeling, wherein the prime motive is to extract the the main topics from a corpus. And later, we will examine a use case and solve it with a Bayesian approach.

Chapter 7, *Temporal and Sequential Pattern Discovery*, focuses on why it is necessary to study frequent itemsets and how we can deal with them. We cover the use of the Apriori and Frequent Pattern Growth algorithms to uncover findings in transactional data.

Chapter 8, *Probabilistic Graphical Models*, covers Bayesian networks and how they are making a difference in machine learning. We will look at Bayesian networks (trees) constructed on conditional probability tables.

Chapter 9, *Selected Topics in Deep Learning*, explains that as the world is transitioning from simple business analytics to deep learning, we have lots to catch up on. This chapter explores weight initialization, layer formation, the calculation of cost, and backpropagation. And subsequently, we will introduce Hinton's capsule network and look at how it works.

Chapter 10, *Causal Inference*, discusses algorithms that provide a directional view around causality in a time series. Our stakeholders often mention the causality behind the target variable. So, we have addressed it using the Granger causality model in time series, and we have also discussed Bayesian techniques that enable us to achieve causality.

Chapter 11, *Advanced Methods*, explains that there are number of state-of-the-art models in the pipeline, and they need a special mention in this book. This chapter should help you understand and apply them. Also, we have talked about independent component analysis and how it is different from principal component analysis. Subsequently, we discuss the Bayesian technique of multiple imputation and its importance. We will also get an understanding of self-organizing maps and why they are important. Lastly, we will also touch upon compressed sensing.

To get the most out of this book

This book requires a basic knowledge of Python, R, and machine learning.

Download the example code files

You can download the example code files for this book from your account at www.packt.com. If you purchased this book elsewhere, you can visit www.packt.com/support and register to have the files emailed directly to you.

You can download the code files by following these steps:

1. Log in or register at `www.packt.com`.
2. Select the **SUPPORT** tab.
3. Click on **Code Downloads & Errata**.
4. Enter the name of the book in the **Search** box and follow the onscreen instructions.

Once the file is downloaded, please make sure that you unzip or extract the folder using the latest version of:

- WinRAR/7-Zip for Windows
- Zipeg/iZip/UnRarX for Mac
- 7-Zip/PeaZip for Linux

The code bundle for the book is also hosted on GitHub at `https://github.com/PacktPublishing/Machine-Learning-Quick-Reference`. In case there's an update to the code, it will be updated on the existing GitHub repository.

We also have other code bundles from our rich catalog of books and videos available at `https://github.com/PacktPublishing/`. Check them out!

Download the color images

We also provide a PDF file that has color images of the screenshots/diagrams used in this book. You can download it here: `http://www.packtpub.com/sites/default/files/downloads/9781788830577_ColorImages.pdf`.

Conventions used

There are a number of text conventions used throughout this book.

`CodeInText`: Indicates code words in text, database table names, folder names, filenames, file extensions, pathnames, dummy URLs, user input, and Twitter handles. Here is an example: "Now we will extract a bootstrap sample with the help of the `resample` function."

A block of code is set as follows:

```
#using "resample" function generate a bootstrap sample
boot_samp = resample(dataset, replace=True, n_samples=5, random_state=1)
```

Bold: Indicates a new term, an important word, or words that you see onscreen. For example, words in menus or dialog boxes appear in the text like this. Here is an example: "Select **System info** from the **Administration** panel."

Warnings or important notes appear like this.

Tips and tricks appear like this.

Get in touch

Feedback from our readers is always welcome.

General feedback: If you have questions about any aspect of this book, mention the book title in the subject of your message and email us at customercare@packtpub.com.

Errata: Although we have taken every care to ensure the accuracy of our content, mistakes do happen. If you have found a mistake in this book, we would be grateful if you would report this to us. Please visit www.packt.com/submit-errata, selecting your book, clicking on the Errata Submission Form link, and entering the details.

Piracy: If you come across any illegal copies of our works in any form on the Internet, we would be grateful if you would provide us with the location address or website name. Please contact us at copyright@packt.com with a link to the material.

If you are interested in becoming an author: If there is a topic that you have expertise in and you are interested in either writing or contributing to a book, please visit authors.packtpub.com.

Reviews

Please leave a review. Once you have read and used this book, why not leave a review on the site that you purchased it from? Potential readers can then see and use your unbiased opinion to make purchase decisions, we at Packt can understand what you think about our products, and our authors can see your feedback on their book. Thank you!

For more information about Packt, please visit `packt.com`.

1
Quantifying Learning Algorithms

We have stepped into an era where we are building smart or intelligent machines. This smartness or intelligence is infused into the machine with the help of smart algorithms based on mathematics/statistics. These algorithms enable the system or machine to learn automatically without any human intervention. As an example of this, today we are surrounded by a number of mobile applications. One of the prime messaging apps of today in WhatsApp (currently owned by Facebook). Whenever we type a message into a textbox of WhatsApp, and we type, for example, *I am...*, we get a few word prompts popping up, such as *..going home, Rahul, traveling tonight*, and so on. Can we guess what's happening here and why? Multiple questions come up:

- What is it that the system is learning?
- Where does it learn from?
- How does it learn?

Let's answer all these questions in this chapter.

In this chapter, we will cover the following topics:

- Statistical models
- Learning curves
- Curve fitting
- Modeling cultures
- Overfitting and regularization
- Train, validation, and test
- Cross-validation and model selection
- Bootstrap method

Statistical models

A statistical model is the approximation of the truth that has been captured through data and mathematics or statistics, and acts as an enabler here. This approximation is used to predict an event. A statistical model is nothing but a mathematical equation.

For example, let's say we reach out to a bank for a home loan. What does the bank ask us? The first thing they would ask us to do is furnish lots of documents such as salary slips, identity proof documents, documents regarding the house we are going to purchase, a utility bill, the number of current loans we have, the number of dependants we have, and so on. All of these documents are nothing but the data that the bank would use to assess and check our creditworthiness:

$$Creditworthiness = f(salary, no. of loans, no. of dependants)$$

What this means is that your creditworthiness is a function of the salary, number of loans, number of dependants, and so on. We can arrive at this equation or relationship mathematically.

A statistical model is a mathematical equation that arrives at using given data for a particular business scenario.

In the next section, we will see how models learn and how the model can keep getting better.

Learning curve

The basic premise behind the learning curve is that the more time you spend doing something, the better you tend to get. Eventually, the time to perform a task keeps on plummeting. This is known by different names, such as **improvement curve**, **progress curve**, and **startup function**.

For example, when you start learning to drive a manual car, you undergo a learning cycle. Initially, you are extra careful about operating the break, clutch, and gear. You have to keep reminding yourself when and how to operate these components.

But, as the days go by and you continue practicing, your brain gets accustomed and trained to the entire process. With each passing day, your driving will keep getting smoother and your brain will react to the situation without any realization. This is called **subconscious intelligence**. You reach this stage with lots of practice and transition from a conscious intelligence to a subconscious intelligence that has got a cycle.

Machine learning

Let me define machine learning and its components so that you don't get bamboozled by lots of jargon when it gets thrown at you.

In the words of Tom Mitchell, "*A computer program is said to learn from experience E with respect to some class of tasks T and performance measure P, if its performance at tasks in T, as measured by P, improves with experience E.*" Also, another theory says that machine learning is the field that gives computers the ability to learn without being explicitly programmed.

For example, if a computer has been given cases such as, [*(father, mother), (uncle, aunt), (brother, sisters)*], based on this, it needs to find out *(son, ?)*. That is, given son, what will be the associated item? To solve this problem, a computer program will go through the previous records and try to understand and learn the association and pattern out of these combinations as it hops from one record to another. This is called **learning**, and it takes place through algorithms. With more records, that is, more experience, the machine gets smarter and smarter.

Let's take a look at the different branches of machine learning, as indicated in the following diagram:

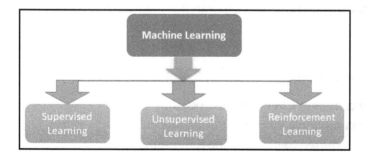

We will explain the preceding diagram as follows:

- **Supervised learning**: In this type of learning, both the input variables and output variables are known to us. Here, we are supposed to establish a relationship between the input variables and the output, and the learning will be based on that. There are two types of problems under it, as follows:
    - **Regression problem**: It has got a continuous output. For example, a housing price dataset wherein the price of the house needs to be predicted based on input variables such as area, region, city, number of rooms, and so on. The price to be predicted is a continuous variable.
    - **Classification**: It has got a discrete output. For example, the prediction that an employee would leave an organization or not, based on salary, gender, the number of members in their family, and so on.
- **Unsupervised learning**: In this type of scenario, there is no output variable. We are supposed to extract a pattern based on all the variables given. For example, the segmentation of customers based on age, gender, income, and so on.
- **Reinforcement learning**: This is an area of machine learning wherein suitable action is taken to maximize reward. For example, training a dog to catch a ball and give it—we reward the dog if they carry out this action; otherwise, we tell them off, leading to a punishment.

Wright's model

In Wright's model, the learning curve function is defined as follows:

$$Y = aX^b$$

The variables are as follows:

- Y: The cumulative average time per unit
- X: The cumulative number of units produced
- a: Time required to produce the first unit
- b: Slope of the function when plotted on graph paper *(log of the learning rate/log of 2)*

The following curve has got a vertical axis (*y* axis) representing the learning with respect to a particular work and a horizontal axis that corresponds to the time taken to learn. A learning curve with a steep beginning can be comprehended as a sign of rapid progress. The following diagram shows **Wright's Learning Curve Model**:

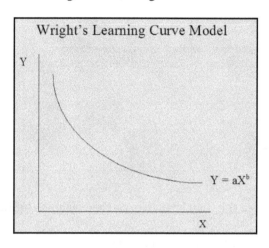

However, the question that arises is, *How is it connected to machine learning?* We will discuss this in detail now.

Let's discuss a scenario that happens to be a supervised learning problem by going over the following steps:

1. We take the data and partition it into a training set (on which we are making the system learn and come out as a model) and a validation set (on which we are testing how well the system has learned).
2. The next step would be to take one instance (observation) of the training set and make use of it to estimate a model. The model error on the training set will be 0.
3. Finally, we would find out the model error on the validation data.

Step 2 and *Step 3* are repeated by taking a number of instances (training size) such as 10, 50, and 100 and studying the training error and validation error, as well as their relationship with a number of instances (training size). This curve—or the relationship—is called a **learning curve** in a machine learning scenario.

Let's work on a combined power plant dataset. The features comprised hourly average ambient variables, that is, **temperature (T)**, **ambient pressure (AP)**, **relative humidity (RH)**, and exhaust **vacuum (V)**, to predict the net hourly **electrical energy output (PE)** of the plant:

```
# importing all the libraries
import pandas as pd
from sklearn.linear_model import LinearRegression
from sklearn.model_selection import learning_curve
import matplotlib.pyplot as plt

#reading the data
data= pd.read_excel("Powerplant.xlsx")

#Investigating the data
print(data.info())
data.head()
```

From this, we are able to see the data structure of the variables in the data:

```
<class 'pandas.core.frame.DataFrame'>
RangeIndex: 9568 entries, 0 to 9567
Data columns (total 5 columns):
AT    9568 non-null float64
V     9568 non-null float64
AP    9568 non-null float64
RH    9568 non-null float64
PE    9568 non-null float64
dtypes: float64(5)
memory usage: 373.8 KB
None
```

The output can be seen as follows:

```
      AT      V       AP      RH      PE
0   14.96   41.76  1024.07  73.17  463.26
1   25.18   62.96  1020.04  59.08  444.37
2    5.11   39.40  1012.16  92.14  488.56
3   20.86   57.32  1010.24  76.64  446.48
4   10.82   37.50  1009.23  96.62  473.90
```

The second output gives you a good feel for the data.

The dataset has five variables, where **ambient temperature (AT)** and PE (target variable).

Let's vary the training size of the data and study the impact of it on learning. A list is created for `train_size` with varying training sizes, as shown in the following code:

```
# As discussed here we are trying to vary the size of training set
train_size = [1, 100, 500, 2000, 5000]
features = ['AT', 'V', 'AP', 'RH']
target = 'PE'
# estimating the training score & validation score
train_sizes, train_scores, validation_scores = learning_curve(estimator =
LinearRegression(), X = data[features],y = data[target], train_sizes =
train_size, cv = 5,scoring ='neg_mean_squared_error')
```

Let's generate the `learning_curve`:

```
# Generating the Learning_Curve
train_scores_mean = -train_scores.mean(axis = 1)
validation_scores_mean = -validation_scores.mean(axis = 1)
import matplotlib.pyplot as plt
plt.style.use('seaborn')
plt.plot(train_sizes, train_scores_mean, label = 'Train_error')
plt.plot(train_sizes, validation_scores_mean, label = 'Validation_error')
plt.ylabel('MSE', fontsize = 16)
plt.xlabel('Training set size', fontsize = 16)
plt.title('Learning_Curves', fontsize = 20, y = 1)
plt.legend()
```

We get the following output:

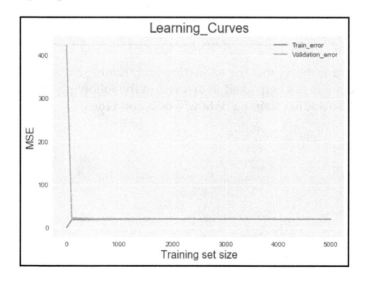

From the preceding plot, we can see that when the training size is just 1, the training error is 0, but the validation error shoots beyond **400**.

As we go on increasing the training set's size (from 1 to 100), the training error continues rising. However, the validation error starts to plummet as the model performs better on the validation set. After the training size hits the 500 mark, the validation error and training error begin to converge. So, what can be inferred out of this? The performance of the model won't change, irrespective of the size of the training post. However, if you try to add more features, it might make a difference, as shown in the following diagram:

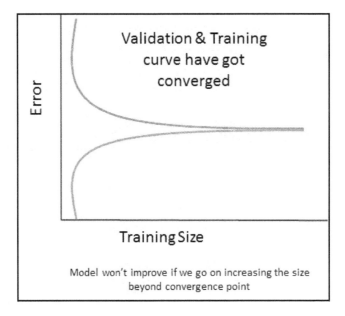

The preceding diagram shows that the validation and training curve have converged, so adding training data will not help at all. However, in the following diagram, the curves haven't converged, so adding training data will be a good idea:

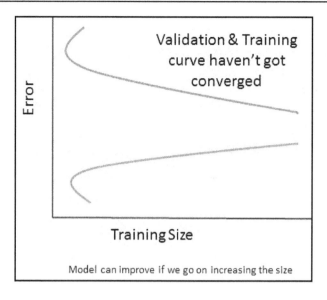

So far, we have learned about the learning curve and its significance. However, it only comes into the picture once we tried fitting a curve on the available data and features. But what does curve fitting mean? Let's try to understand this.

Curve fitting

So far, we have learned about the learning curve and its significance. However, it only comes into the picture once we tried fitting a curve on the available data and features. But what does curve fitting mean? Let's try to understand this.

Curve fitting is nothing but establishing a relationship between a number of features and a target. It helps in finding out what kind of association the features have with respect to the target.

Establishing a relationship (curve fitting) is nothing but coming up with a mathematical function that should be able to explain the behavioral pattern in such a way that it comes across as a best fit for the dataset.

There are multiple reasons behind why we do curve fitting:

- To carry out system simulation and optimization
- To determine the values of intermediate points (interpolation)
- To do trend analysis (extrapolation)
- To carry out hypothesis testing

There are two types of curve fitting:

1. **Exact fit**: In this scenario, the curve would pass through all the points. There is no residual error (we'll discuss shortly what's classed as an error) in this case. For now, you can understand an error as the difference between the actual error and the predicted error. It can be used for interpolation and is majorly involved with a distribution fit.

   The following diagram shows the polynomial but exact fit:

   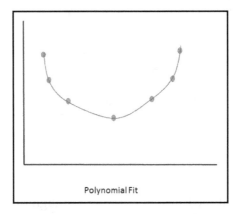

   Polynomial Fit

   The following diagram shows the line but exact fit:

   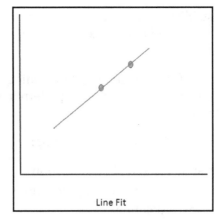

   Line Fit

2. **Best fit**: The curve doesn't pass through all the points. There will be a residual associated with this.

Let's look at some different scenarios and study them to understand these differences.

Here, we will fit a curve for two numbers:

```
# importing libraries
import numpy as np
import matplotlib.pyplot as plt
from scipy.optimize import curve_fit

# writing a function of Line
def func(x, a, b):
return a + b * x
x_d = np.linspace(0, 5, 2) # generating 2 numbers between 0 & 5
y = func(x_d,1.5, 0.7)
y_noise = 0.3 * np.random.normal(size=x_d.size)
y_d = y + y_noise
plt.plot(x_d, y_d, 'b-', label='data')

popt, pcov = curve_fit(func, x_d, y_d) # fitting the curve
plt.plot(x_d, func(x_d, *popt), 'r-', label='fit')
```

From this, we will get the following output:

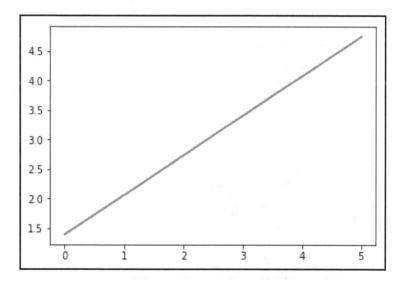

Here, we have used two points to fit the line and we can very well see that it becomes an **exact fit**. When introducing three points, we will get the following:

```
x_d = np.linspace(0, 5, 3) # generating 3 numbers between 0 & 5
```

Run the entire code and focus on the output:

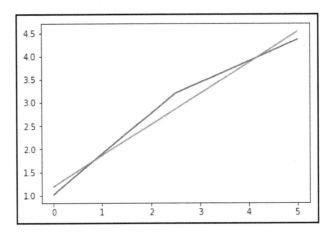

Now, you can see the drift and effect of noise. It has started to take the shape of a curve. A line might not be a good fit here (however, it's too early to say). It's no longer an exact fit.

What if we try to introduce 100 points and study the effect of that? By now, we know how to introduce the number of points.

By doing this, we get the following output:

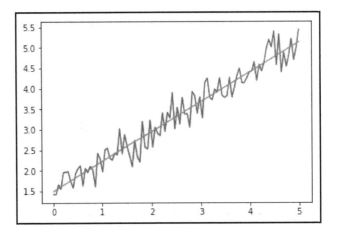

This is not an exact fit, but rather a best fit that tries to generalize the whole dataset.

Residual

Residuals are the difference between an observed or true value and a predicted (fitted) value. For example, in the following diagram, one of the residuals is **(A-B)**, where **A** is the observed value and **B** is the fitted value:

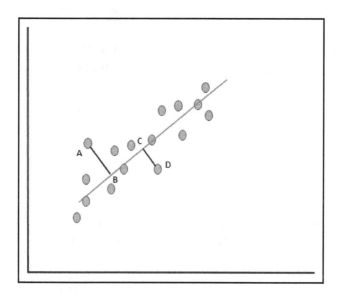

The preceding scatter plot depicts that we are fitting a line that could represent the behavior of all the data points. However, one thing that's noticeable is that the line doesn't pass through all of the points. Most of the points are off the line.

The sum and mean of residuals will always be 0. $\sum e = 0$ and mean of $e = 0$.

Statistical modeling – the two cultures of Leo Breiman

Whenever we try to analyze data and finally make a prediction, there are two approaches that we consider, both of which were discovered by Leo Breiman, a Berkeley professor, in his paper titled *Statistical Modeling: Two Cultures* in 2001.

Any analysis needs data. An analysis can be as follows:

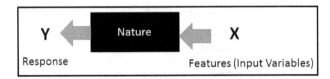

A vector of **X** (**Features**) undergoes a nature box, which translates into a response. A nature box tries to establish a relationship between **X** and **Y**. Typically, there are goals pertaining to this analysis, as follows:

- **Prediction**: To predict the response with the future input features
- **Information**: To find out and understand the association between the response and driving input variables

Breiman states that, when it comes to solving business problems, there are two distinct approaches:

- **The data modeling culture**: In this kind of model, nature takes the shape of a stochastic model that estimates the necessary parameters. Linear regression, logistic regression, and the Cox model usually act under the nature box. This model talks about observing the pattern of the data and looks to design an approximation of what is being observed. Based on their experience, the scientist or a statistician would decide which model to be used. It is the case of a model coming before the problem and the data, the solutions from this model is more towards the model's architecture. Breiman says that over-reliance on this kind of approach doesn't help the statisticians cater to a diverse set of problems. When it comes to finding out solutions pertaining to earthquake prediction, rain prediction, and global warming causes, it doesn't give accurate results, since this approach doesn't focus on accuracy, and instead focuses on the two goals.
- **The algorithm modeling culture**: In this approach, pre-designed algorithms are used to make a better approximation. Here, the algorithms use complex mathematics to reach out to the conclusion and acts inside the nature box. With better computing power and using these models, it's easy to replicate the driving factors as the model keeps on running until it learns and understands the pattern that drives the outcome. It enables us to address more complex problems, and emphasizes more on accuracy. With more data coming through, it can give a much better result than the data modeling culture.

Training data development data – test data

This is one of the most important steps of building a model and it can lead to lots of debate regarding whether we really need all three sets (train, dev, and test), and if so, what should be the breakup of those datasets. Let's understand these concepts.

After we have sufficient data to start modelling, the first thing we need to do is partition the data into three segments, that is, **Training Set**, **Development Set**, and **Test Set**:

Let's examine the goal of having these three sets:

1. **Training Set**: The training set is used to train the model. When we apply any algorithm, we are fitting the parameter in the training set. In the case of a neural network, finding out about the weights takes place.

   Let's say in one scenario that we are trying to fit polynomials of various degrees:

   - $f(x) = a + bx \rightarrow 1^{st}$ degree polynomial
   - $f(x) = a + bx + cx^2 \rightarrow 2^{nd}$ degree polynomial
   - $f(x) = a + bx + cx^2 + dx^3 \rightarrow 3^{rd}$ degree polynomial

   After fitting the model, we calculate the training error for all the fitted models:

   $$TrainingError = ActualValue - FittedValue = y(hat) - f(x)$$

   We cannot assess how good the model is based on the training error. If we do that, it will lead us to a biased model that might not be able to perform well on unseen data. To counter that, we need to head into the development set.

2. **Development set**: This is also called the **holdout set** or **validation set**. The goal of this set is to tune the parameters that we have got from the training set. It is also part of an assessment of how well the model is performing. Based on its performance, we have to take steps to tune the parameters. For example, controlling the learning rate, minimizing the overfitting, and electing the best model of the lot all take place in the development set. Here, again, the development set error gets calculated and tuning of the model takes place after seeing which model is giving the least error. The model giving the least error at this stage still needs tuning to minimize overfitting. Once we are convinced about the best model, it is chosen and we head toward the test set.

3. **Test set**: The test set is primarily used to assess the best selected model. At this stage, the accuracy of the model is calculated, and if the model's accuracy is not too deviated from the training accuracy and development accuracy, we send this model for deployment.

Size of the training, development, and test set

Typically, machine learning practitioners choose the size of the three sets in the ratio of 60:20:20 or 70:15:15. However, there is no hard and fast rule that states that the development and test sets should be of equal size. The following diagram shows the different sizes of the training, development, and test sets:

Training Set	Development Set	Test Set
60%	20%	20%

Another example of the three different sets is as follows:

Training Set	Development Set	Test Set
70%	15%	15%

But what about the scenarios where we have big data to deal with? For example, if we have 10,000,000 records or observations, how would we partition the data? In such a scenario, ML practitioners take most of the data for the training set—as much as 98-99%—and the rest gets divided up for the development and test sets. This is done so that the practitioner can take different kinds of scenarios into account. So, even if we have 1% of data for development and the same for the test test, we will end up with 100,000 records each, and that is a good number.

Bias-variance trade off

Before we get into modelling and try to figure out what the trade-off is, let's understand what bias and variance are from the following diagram:

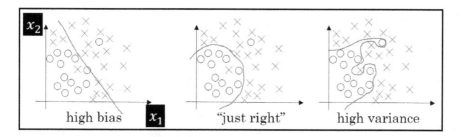

There are two types of errors that are developed in the bias-variance trade off, as follows:

- **Training error**: This is a measure of deviation of the fitted value from the actual value while predicting the output by using the training inputs. This error depends majorly on the model's complexity. As the model's complexity increases, the error appears to plummet.
- **Development error**: This is a measure of deviation of the predicted value, and is used by the development set as input (while using the same model trained on training data) from the actual values. Here, the prediction is being done on unseen data. We need to minimize this error. Minimizing this error will determine how good this model will be in the actual scenario.

As the complexity of the algorithm keeps on increasing, the training error goes down. However, the development error or validation error keeps going down until a certain point, and then rises, as shown in the following diagram:

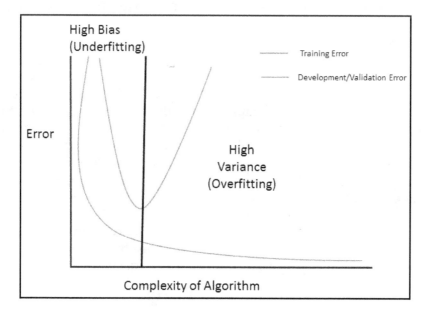

The preceding diagram can be explained as follows:

- **Underfitting**: Every dataset has a specific pattern and properties due to the existing variables in the dataset. Along with that, it also has a random and latent pattern which is caused by the variables that are not part of the dataset. Whenever we come up with a model, the model should ideally be learning patterns from the existing variables. However, the learning of these patterns also depends on how good and robust your algorithm is. Let's say we have picked up a model that is not able to derive even the essential patterns out of the dataset—this is called **underfitting**. In the preceding plots, it is a scenario of classification and we are trying to classify x and o. In plot 1, we are trying to use a linear classification algorithm to classify the data, but we can see that it is resulting in lots of misclassification errors. This is a case of underfitting.

- **Overfitting**: Going further afield from plot 1, we are trying to use complex algorithms to find out the patterns and classify them. It is noticeable that the misclassification errors have gone down in the second plot, since the complex model being used here is able to detect the patterns. The development error (as shown in the preceding diagram) goes down too. We will increase the complexity of the model and see what happens. Plot 3 suggests that there is no misclassification error in the model now. However, if we look at the plot below it, we can see that the development error is way too high now. This happens because the model is learning from the misleading and random patterns that were exhibited due to the non-existent variables in the dataset. This means that it has started to learn the noise that's present in the set. This phenomenon is called **overfitting**.

- **Bias**: How often have we seen this? This occurs in a situation wherein we have used an algorithm and it doesn't fit properly. This means that the function that's being used here has been of little relevance to this scenario and it's not able to extract the correct patterns. This causes an error called **bias**. It crops up majorly due to making a certain assumption about the data and using a model that might be correct but isn't. For example, if we had to use a second degree polynomial for a situation, we would use simple linear regression, which doesn't establish a correct relationship between the response and explanatory variables.

- **Variance**: When we have a dataset that is being used for training the model, the model should remain immune, even if we change the training set to a set that's coming from the same population. If variation in the dataset brings in a change in the performance of the model, it is termed a **variance error**. This takes place due to noise (an unexplained variation) being learned by the model and, due to that, this model doesn't give a good result on unseen data:

Training Error	1%	16%	16%	0.8%
Development Error	10%	17%	30%	1%
	High Variance	High Bias	High Bias High Variance	Low Bias Low Variance

We will explain the preceding diagram as follows:

- If the **Training Error** goes down and (**Development Error-Training Error**) rises, it implies a **High Variance** situation (scenario 1 in the preceding table)
- If the **Training Error** and **Development Error** rises and (**Development Error-Training Error**) goes down, it implies a **High Bias** situation (scenario 2 in the preceding table)
- If the **Training Error** and **Development Error** rises and (**Development Error-Training Error**) goes up as well, it implies **High Bias** and **High Variance** (scenario 3 in the preceding table)
- If the **Training Error** goes up and the **Development Error** declines, that is, (**Development Error-Training Error**) goes down, it implies **Low Bias** and **Low Variance** (scenario 4 in the preceding table)

We should always strive for the fourth scenario, which depicts the training error being low, as well as a low development set error. In the preceding table, this is where we have to find out a bias variance trade-off, which is depicted by a vertical line.

Now, the following question arises: how we can counter overfitting? Let's find out the answer to this by moving on to the next section.

Regularization

We have now got a fair understanding of what overfitting means when it comes to machine learning modeling. Just to reiterate, when the model learns the noise that has crept into the data, it is trying to learn the patterns that take place due to random chance, and so overfitting occurs. Due to this phenomenon, the model's generalization runs into jeopardy and it performs poorly on unseen data. As a result of that, the accuracy of the model takes a nosedive.

Can we combat this kind of phenomenon? The answer is yes. Regularization comes to the rescue. Let's figure out what it can offer and how it works.

Regularization is a technique that enables the model to not become complex to avoid overfitting.

Let's take a look at the following regression equation:

$$y = \beta o + \beta_1 x_1 + \beta_2 x_2$$

The loss function for this is as follows:

$$\sum_{i=1}^{n}(y_i - \beta_o - \sum_{j=1}^{p}\beta_j x_{ij})^2$$

The loss function would help in getting the coefficients adjusted and retrieving the optimal one. In the case of noise in the training data, the coefficients wouldn't generalize well and would run into overfitting. Regularization helps get rid of this by making these estimates or coefficients drop toward 0.

Now, we will cover two types of regularization. In later chapters, the other types will be covered.

Ridge regression (L2)

Due to ridge regression, we need to make some changes to the loss function. The original loss function gets added by a shrinkage component:

$$\sum_{i=1}^{n}(y_i - \beta_0 - \sum_{j=1}^{p}\beta_j x_{ij})^2 + \lambda\sum_{j=1}^{p}\beta_j^2$$

Now, this modified loss function needs to be minimized to adjust the estimates or coefficients. Here, the lambda is tuning the parameter that regularizes the loss function. That is, it decides how much it should penalize the flexibility of the model. The flexibility of the model is dependent on the coefficients. If the coefficients of the model go up, the flexibility also goes up, which isn't a good sign for our model. Likewise, as the coefficients go down, the flexibility is restricted and the model starts to perform better. The shrinkage of each estimated parameter makes the model better here, and this is what ridge regression does. When lambda keeps going higher and higher, that is, $\lambda \to \infty$, the penalty component rises, and the estimates start shrinking. However, when $\lambda \to 0$, the penalty component decreases and starts to become an **ordinary least square (OLS)** for estimating unknown parameters in a linear regression.

Least absolute shrinkage and selection operator

The **least absolute shrinkage and selection operator** (**LASSO**) is also called *L1*. In this case, the preceding penalty parameter is replaced by $|\beta j|$:

$$\sum_{i=1}^{n}(y_i - \beta_0 - \sum_{j=1}^{p} \beta_j x_{ij})^2 + \lambda \sum_{j=1}^{p} |\beta_j|$$

By minimizing the preceding function, the coefficients are found and adjusted. In this scenario, as lambda becomes larger, $\lambda \to \infty$, the penalty component rises, and so estimates start shrinking and become 0 (it doesn't happen in the case of ridge regression; rather, it would just be close to 0).

Cross-validation and model selection

We have already spoken about overfitting. It is something to do with the stability of a model since the real test of a model occurs when it works on unseen and new data. One of the most important aspects of a model is that it shouldn't pick up on noise, apart from regular patterns.

Validation is nothing but an assurance of the model being a relationship between the response and predictors as the outcome of input features and not noise. A good indicator of the model is not through training data and error. That's why we need cross-validation.

Here, we will stick with k-fold cross-validation and understand how it can be used.

K-fold cross-validation

Let's walk through the steps of k-fold cross-validation:

1. The data is divided into k-subsets.
2. One set is kept for testing/development and the model is built on the rest of the data (*k-1*). That is, the rest of the data forms the training data.

3. *Step 2* is repeated k-times. That is, once the preceding step has been performed, we move on to the second set and it forms a test set. The rest of the (*k-1*) data is then available for building the model:

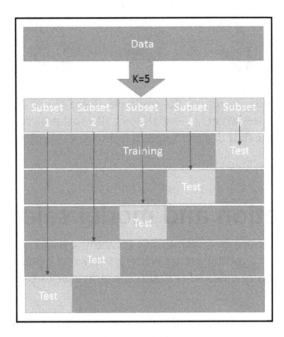

4. An error is calculated and an average is taken over all k-trials.

Every subset gets one chance to be a validation/test set since most of the data is used as a training set. This helps in reducing bias. At the same time, almost all the data is being used as validation set, which reduces variance.

As shown in the preceding diagram, $k = 5$ has been selected. This means that we have to divide the whole dataset into five subsets. In the first iteration, subset 5 becomes the test data and the rest becomes the training data. Likewise, in the second iteration, subset 4 turns into the test data and the rest becomes the training data. This goes on for five iterations.

Now, let's try to do this in Python by splitting the train and test data using the K neighbors classifier:

```
from sklearn.datasets import load_breast_cancer # importing the dataset
from sklearn.cross_validation import train_test_split,cross_val_score # it
will help in splitting train & test
from sklearn.neighbors import KNeighborsClassifier
from sklearn import metrics
```

```
BC =load_breast_cancer()
X = BC.data
y = BC.target

X_train, X_test, y_train, y_test = train_test_split(X, y, random_state=4)

knn = KNeighborsClassifier(n_neighbors=5)
knn.fit(X_train, y_train)
y_pred = knn.predict(X_test)
print(metrics.accuracy_score(y_test, y_pred))

knn = KNeighborsClassifier(n_neighbors=5)
scores = cross_val_score(knn, X, y, cv=10, scoring='accuracy')
print(scores)
print(scores.mean())
```

Model selection using cross-validation

We can make use of cross-validation to find out which model is performing better by using the following code:

```
knn = KNeighborsClassifier(n_neighbors=20)
print(cross_val_score(knn, X, y, cv=10, scoring='accuracy').mean())
```

The 10-fold cross-validation is as follows:

```
# 10-fold cross-validation with logistic regression
from sklearn.linear_model import LogisticRegression
logreg = LogisticRegression()
print(cross_val_score(logreg, X, y, cv=10, scoring='accuracy').mean())
```

0.632 rule in bootstrapping

Before we get into the 0.632 rule of bootstrapping, we need to understand what bootstrapping is. Bootstrapping is the process wherein random sampling is performed with a replacement from a population that's comprised of *n* observations. In this scenario, a sample can have duplicate observations. For example, if the population is (2,3,4,5,6) and we are trying to draw two random samples of size 4 with replacement, then sample 1 will be (2,3,3,6) and sample 2 will be (4,4,6,2).

Now, let's delve into the 0.632 rule.

We have already seen that the estimate of the training error while using a prediction is *1/n* $\sum L(y_i, y\text{-}hat)$. This is nothing but the loss function:

$$Training\_ Err = 1/n \sum L(yi, y - hat)$$

Cross-validation is a way to estimate the expected output of a sample error:

$$Err = E[L(Y, f(X))]$$

However, in the case of k-fold cross-validation, it is as follows:

$$Error\ of\ CV = \sum L(y_i, f(x_i))$$

Here, the training data is *X=(x1,x2.....,xn)* and we take bootstrap samples from this set *(z1,.....,zb)* where each *zi* is a set of *n* samples.

In this scenario, the following is our out-of-sample error:

$$OOSE = L(y_i, fb(x_i))$$

Here, *fb(xi)* is the predicted value at *xi* from the model that's been fit to the bootstrap dataset.

Unfortunately, this is not a particularly good estimator because bootstrap samples that have been used to produce *fb(xi)* may have contained *xi*. OOSE solves the overfitting problem, but is still biased. This bias is due to non-distinct observations in the bootstrap samples that result from sampling with replacement. The average number of distinct observations in each sample is about *0.632n*. To solve the bias problem, Efron and Tibshirani proposed the *0.632* estimator:

$$Err = 0.368 * Training\_ Err + 0.632 * OOSE$$

Model evaluation

Let's look at some of the model evaluation techniques that are currently being used.

Confusion matrix

A confusion matrix is a table that helps in assessing how good the classification model is. It is used when true values/labels are known. Most beginners in the field of data science feel intimidated by the confusion matrix and think it looks more difficult to comprehend than it really is; let me tell you—it's pretty simple and easy.

Let's understand this by going through an example. Let's say that we have built a classification model that predicts whether a customer would like to buy a certain product or not. To do this, we need to assess the model on unseen data.

There are two classes:

- **Yes**: The customer will buy the product
- **No**: The customer will not buy the product

From this, we have put the matrix together:

N=80	Actual:Yes	Actual:No
Predicted: Yes	50	6
Predicted: No	4	20

What are the inferences we can draw from the preceding matrix at first glance?

- The classifier has made a total of 80 predictions. What this means is that 80 customers were tested in total to find out whether he/she will buy the product or not.
- **54** customers bought the product and **26** didn't.

- The classifier predicts that **56** customers will buy the product and that **24** won't:

N=80	Actual:Yes	Actual:No	
Predicted: Yes	TP= 50	FP=6	56
Predicted: No	FN=4	TN= 20	24
	54	26	

The different terms pertaining to the confusion matrix are as follows:

- **True Positive (TP)**: These are the cases in which we predicted that the customer will buy the product and they did.
- **True Negative (TN)**: These are the cases in which we predicted that the customer won't buy the product and they didn't.
- **False Positive (FP)**: We predicted *Yes the customer will buy the product,* but they didn't. This is known as a *Type 1* error.
- **False Negative (FN)**: We predicted *No,* but the customer bought the product. This is known as a *Type 2* error.

Now, let's talk about a few metrics that are required for the assessment of a classification model:

- **Accuracy**: This measures the overall accuracy of the classifier. To calculate this, we will use the following formula: *(TP+TN)/Total cases*. In the preceding scenario, the accuracy is (50+20)/80, which turns out to be 0.875. So, we can say that this classifier will predict correctly in 87.5% of scenarios.
- **Misclassification rate**: This measures how often the classifier has got the results wrong. The formula *(FP+FN)/Total cases* will give the result. In the preceding scenario, the misclassification rate is *(6+4)/80*, which is 0.125. So, in 12.5% of cases, it won't produce correct results. It can also be calculated as (1- Accuracy).
- **TP rate**: This is a measure of what the chances are that it would predict *yes* as the answer, and the answer actually is *yes*. The formula to calculate this is **TP/(Actual:Yes)**. In this scenario, *TPR = (50/54)= 0.92*. It's also called **Sensitivity** or **Recall**.
- **FP rate**: This is a measure of what the chances are that it would predict *yes*, when the actual answer is *no*. The formula to calculate this rate is **FP/(Actual:No)**. For the preceding example, *FPR = (6/26)= 0.23*.

- **TN rate**: This is a measure of what the chances are that it would predict *no*, when the answer is actually *no*. The formula to calculate this is *TN/(Actual:No)*. In this scenario, *TNR= (20/26)= 0.76*. It can also be calculated using (1-FPR). It's also called **Specificity**.

- **Precision**: This is a measure of correctness of the prediction of *yes* out of all the *yes* predictions. It finds out how many times a prediction of *yes* was made correctly out of total *yes* predictions. The formula to calculate this is *TP/(Predicted:Yes)*. Here, *Precision = (50/56)=0.89*.

- **Prevalence**: This is a measure of how many *yes* were given out of the total sample. The formula is *(Actual:Yes/ Total Sample)*. Here, this is 54/80 = 0.67.

- **Null error rate**: This is a measure of how wrong the classifier would be if it predicted just the majority class. The formula is *(Actual:No/Total Sample)*. Here, this is *26/80=0.325*.

- **Cohen's Kappa value**: This is a measure of how well the classifier performed compared to how well it would have performed simply by chance.

- **F-Score**: This is a harmonic mean of recall and precision, that is, *(2*Recall*Precision)/(Recall+Precision)*. It considers both Recall and Precision as important measures of a model's evaluation. The best value of the F-score is 1, wherein Recall and Precision are at their maximum. The worst value of the F-score is 0. The higher the score, the better the model is:

		True condition			
Total population		Condition positive	Condition negative	Prevalence $= \frac{\Sigma \text{ Condition positive}}{\Sigma \text{ Total population}}$	Accuracy (ACC) = $\frac{\Sigma \text{ True positive} + \Sigma \text{ True negative}}{\Sigma \text{ Total population}}$
Predicted condition	Predicted condition positive	True positive, Power	False positive, Type I error	Positive predictive value (PPV), Precision = $\frac{\Sigma \text{ True positive}}{\Sigma \text{ Predicted condition positive}}$	False discovery rate (FDR) = $\frac{\Sigma \text{ False positive}}{\Sigma \text{ Predicted condition positive}}$
	Predicted condition negative	False negative Type II error	True negative	False omission rate (FOR) = $\frac{\Sigma \text{ False negative}}{\Sigma \text{ Predicted condition negative}}$	Negative predictive value (NPV) $= \frac{\Sigma \text{ True negative}}{\Sigma \text{ Predicted condition negative}}$
		True positive rate (TPR), Recall, Sensitivity, probability of detection $= \frac{\Sigma \text{ True positive}}{\Sigma \text{ Condition positive}}$	False positive rate (FPR), Fall-out, probability of false alarm $= \frac{\Sigma \text{ False positive}}{\Sigma \text{ Condition negative}}$	Positive likelihood ratio (LR+) $= \frac{TPR}{FPR}$	Diagnostic odds ratio $(DOR) = \frac{LR+}{LR-}$ $\quad F_1 \text{ score} = \frac{2}{\frac{1}{Recall} + \frac{1}{Precision}}$
		False negative rate (FNR), Miss rate $= \frac{\Sigma \text{ False negative}}{\Sigma \text{ Condition positive}}$	True negative rate (TNR), Specificity (SPC) $= \frac{\Sigma \text{ True negative}}{\Sigma \text{ Condition negative}}$	Negative likelihood ratio (LR-) $= \frac{FNR}{TNR}$	

Receiver operating characteristic curve

We have come across many budding data scientists who would build a model and, in the name of evaluation, are just content with the **overall accuracy**. However, that's not the correct way to go about evaluating a model. For example, let's say there's a dataset that has got a response variable that has two categories: customers willing to buy the product and customers not willing to buy the product. Let's say that the dataset has 95% of customers not willing to buy the product and 5% of customers willing to buy it. Let's say that the classifier is able to correctly predict the majority class and not the minority class. So, if there are 100 observations, *TP=0, TN= 95*, and the rest misclassified, this will still result in 95% accuracy. However, it won't be right to conclude that this is a good model as it's not able to classify the minority class at all.

Hence, we need to look beyond accuracy so that we have a better judgement about the model. In this situation, Recall, Specificity, Precision, and the **receiver operating characteristic (ROC)** curve come to rescue. We learned about Recall, specificity, and precision in the previous section. Now, let's understand what the ROC curve is.

Most of the classifiers produce a score between 0 and 1. The next step occurs when we're setting up the threshold, and, based on this threshold, the classification is decided. Typically, 0.5 is the threshold—if it's more than 0.5, it creates a class, 1, and if the threshold is less than 0.5 it falls into another class, 2:

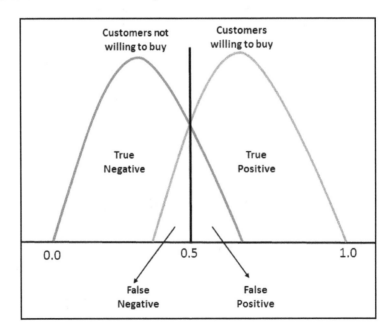

For ROC, every point between **0.0** and **1.0** is treated as a threshold, so the line of threshold keeps on moving from **0.0** to **1.0**. The threshold will result in us having a TP, TN, FP, and FN. At every threshold, the following metrics are calculated:

- *True Positive Rate = TP/(TP+FN)*

- *True Negative Rate = TN/(TN + FP)*

- *False Positive Rate = 1- True Negative Rate*

The calculation of (TPR and FPR) starts from 0. When the threshold line is at 0, we will be able to classify all of the customers who are willing to buy (positive cases), whereas those who are not willing to buy will be misclassified as there will be too many false positives. This means that the threshold line will start moving toward the right from zero. As this happens, the false positive starts to decline and the true positive will continue increasing.

Finally, we will need to plot a graph of the TPR versus FPR after calculating them at every point of the threshold:

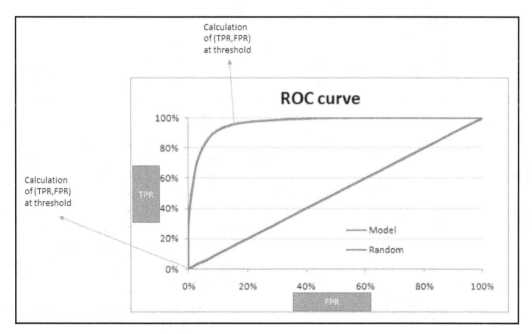

The red diagonal line represents the classification at random, that is, classification without the model. The perfect ROC curve will go along the y axis and will take the shape of an absolute triangle, which will pass through the top of the y axis.

Area under ROC

To assess the model/classifier, we need to determine the **area under ROC (AUROC)**. The whole area of this plot is 1 as the maximum value of FPR and TPR – both are 1 here. Hence, it takes the shape of a square. The random line is positioned perfectly at 45 degrees, which partitions the whole area into two symmetrical and equilateral triangles. This means that the areas under and above the red line are 0.5. The best and perfect classifier will be the one that tries to attain the AUROC as 1. The higher the AUROC, the better the model is.

In a situation where you have got multiple classifiers, you can use AUROC to determine which is the best one among the lot.

H-measure

Binary classification has to apply techniques so that it can map independent variables to different labels. For example, a number of variables exist such as gender, income, number of existing loans, and payment on time/not, that get mapped to yield a score that helps us classify the customers into good customers (more propensity to pay) and bad customers.

Typically, everyone seems to be caught up with the misclassification rate or derived form since the **area under curve (AUC)** is known to be the best evaluator of our classification model. You get this rate by dividing the total number of misclassified examples by the total number of examples. But does this give us a fair assessment? Let's see. Here, we have a misclassification rate that keeps something important under wraps. More often than not, classifiers come up with a tuning parameter, the side effect of which tends to be favoring false positives over false negatives, or vice versa. Also, picking the AUC as sole model evaluator can act as a double whammy for us. AUC has got different misclassification costs for different classifiers, which is not desirable. This means that using this is equivalent to using different metrics to evaluate different classification rules.

As we have already discussed, the real test of any classifier takes place on the unseen data, and this takes a toll on the model by some decimal points. Adversely, if we have got scenarios like the preceding one, the decision support system will not be able to perform well. It will start producing misleading results.

H-measure overcomes the situation of incurring different misclassification costs for different classifiers. It needs a severity ratio as input, which examines how much more severe misclassifying a class 0 instance is than misclassifying a class 1 instance:

Severity Ratio = cost_0/cost_1

Here, *cost_0 > 0* is the cost of misclassifying a class 0 datapoint as class 1.

It is sometimes more convenient to consider the normalized cost *c = cost_0/(cost_0 + cost_1)* instead. For example, *severity.ratio = 2* implies that a false positive costs twice as much as a false negative.

Dimensionality reduction

Let's talk about a scenario wherein we have been given a dataset from a bank and it has got features pertaining to bank customers. These features comprise customer's income, age, gender, payment behavior, and so on. Once you take a look at the data dimension, you realize that there are 850 features. You are supposed to build a model to predict the customer who is going to default if a loan is given. Would you take all of these features and build the model?

The answer should be a clear **no**. The more features in a dataset, the more likely it is that the model will overfit. Although having fewer features doesn't guarantee that overfitting won't take place, it reduces the chance of that. Not a bad deal, right?

Dimensionality reduction is one of the ways to deal with this. It implies a reduction of dimensions in the feature space.

There are two ways this can be achieved:

- **Feature elimination**: This is a process in which features that are not adding value to the model are rejected. Doing this makes the model quite simple. We know from Occam's Razor that we should strive for simplicity when it comes to building models. However, doing this step may result in the loss of information as a combination of such variables may have an impact on the model.
- **Feature extraction**: This is a process in which we create new independent variables that are a combination of existing variables. Based on the impact of these variables, we either keep or drop them.

Principal component analysis is a feature extraction technique that takes all of the variables into account and forms a linear combination of the variables. Later, the least important variable can be dropped while the most important part of that variable is retained.

Newly formed variables (components) are independent of each other, which can be a boon for a model-building process wherein data distribution is linearly separable. Linear models have the underlying assumption that variables are independent of each other.

To understand the functionality of PCA, we have to become familiar with a few terms:

- **Variance**: This is the average squared deviation from the mean. It is also called a **spread**, which measures the variability of the data:

$$var(x) = \frac{\sum (x_i - \bar{x})^2}{N}$$

Here, x is the mean.

- **Covariance**: This is a measure of the degree to which two variables move in the same direction:

$$cov(x, y) = \frac{\sum (x_i - \bar{x})(y_i - \bar{y})}{N}$$

In PCA, we find out the pattern of the data as follows: in the case of the dataset having high covariance when represented in n of dimensions, we represent those dimensions with a linear combination of the same n dimensions. These combinations are orthogonal to each other, which is the reason why they are independent of each other. Besides, dimension follows an order by variance. The top combination comes first.

Let's go over how PCA works by talking about the following steps:

1. Let's split our dataset into Y and X sets, and just focus on X.
2. A matrix of X is taken and standardized with a mean of 0 and a standard deviation of 1. Let's call the new matrix Z.
3. Let's work on Z now. We have to transpose it and multiply the transposed matrix by Z. By doing this, we have got our covariance matrix:

Covariance Matrix = $Z^T Z$

4. Now, we need to calculate the eigenvalues and their corresponding eigenvectors of Z^TZ. Typically, the eigen decomposition of the covariance matrix into PDP^{-1} is done, where P is the matrix of eigenvectors and D is the diagonal matrix with eigenvalues on the diagonal and values of 0 everywhere else.

5. Take the eigenvalues $\lambda_1, \lambda_2, ..., \lambda p$ and sort them from largest to smallest. In doing so, sort the eigenvectors in P accordingly. Call this sorted matrix of eigenvectors P^*.

6. Calculate $Z^* = ZP^*$. This new matrix, Z^*, is a centered/standardized version of X, but now each observation is a combination of the original variables, where the weights are determined by the eigenvector. As a bonus, because our eigenvectors in P^* are independent of one another, the columns of Z^* are independent of one another.

Summary

In this chapter, we studied the statistical model, the learning curve, and curve fitting. We also studied two cultures that Leo Breiman introduced, which describe that any analysis needs data. We went through the different types of training, development, and test data, including their sizes. We studied regularization, which explains what overfitting means in machine learning modeling.

This chapter also explained cross validation and model selection, the 0.632 rule in bootstrapping, and also ROC and AUC in depth.

In the next chapter, we will study evaluating kernel learning, which is the most widely used approach in machine learning.

Evaluating Kernel Learning 2

In machine learning, pattern finding is an area that is being explored to the hilt. There are many methods and algorithms that can drive this kind of work and analysis. However, in this chapter, we will try to focus on how kernels are making a significant difference to the whole machine learning outlook. The application of kernel learning doesn't have any boundaries: starting from a simple regression problem to a computer vision classification, it has made its presence felt everywhere. **Support vector machine** (**SVM**) is one of those algorithms that happens to make use of kernel learning.

In this chapter, we will be focusing on the following concepts:

- Concepts of vectors, linear separability, and hyperplanes
- SVM
- Kernel tricks
- Gaussian process
- Parameter optimization

Introduction to vectors

Before moving on to the core topic, we would like to build a foundation for getting there. Hence, this segment of the chapter is very important. It might look familiar to you and many of you will be cognizant about this. However, going through this channel will set the flow.

A vector is an object that has both a direction and magnitude. It is represented by an arrow and with a coordinate (x, y) in space, as shown in the following plot:

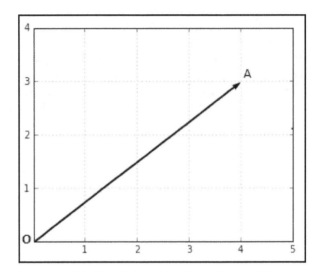

As shown in the preceding diagram, the vector OA has the coordinates *(4,3)*:

$$Vector\ OA= (4,3)$$

However, it is not sufficient to define a vector just by coordinates—we also need a direction. That means the direction from the x axis.

Magnitude of the vector

The magnitude of the vector is also called the **norm**. It is represented by $||OA||$:

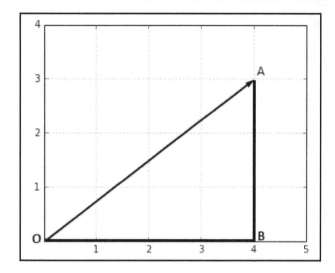

To find out magnitude of this vector, we can follow the Pythagorean theorem:

$$OA^2 = OB^2 + AB^2$$

$$= 4^2 + 3^2$$

$$= 16 + 9$$

$$= 25$$

Hence:

$$OA = \sqrt{25} = 5$$

$$||OA|| = 5$$

So, if there is a vector $x = (x_1, x_2, ..., x_n)$:

$$||x|| = x_1^2 + x_2^2 + ... + x_n^2$$

And direction of this vector as:

$$x = \left(\frac{x_1}{||x||}, \frac{x_2}{||x||}, ..., \frac{x_n}{||x||} \right)$$

Dot product

The dot product of two vectors returns a number that happens to be scalar. It is a representation of how two vectors are associated with each other.

Geometrically, the dot product of two vectors x and y would be as follows:

$$x.y= ||x|| \; ||y|| \; cos\theta$$

θ is the angle between the vector x and y.

However, algebraically, we get the following:

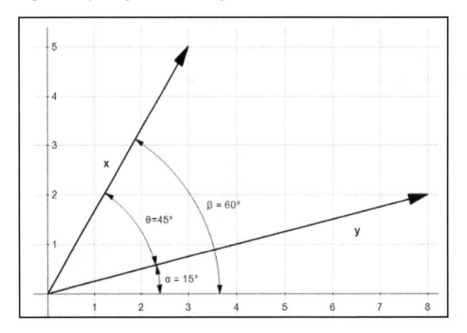

Geometrically, we get the following:

$$\theta=\beta-\alpha$$

$$cos\theta=cos(\beta-\alpha)$$

$$cos\theta = cos\beta \; cos\alpha + sin\beta \; sin\alpha$$

$$cos\theta = (x_1/||x||) \, (y_1/||y||) + (x2/||x||) \, (y2/||y||)$$

$$||x||\,||y||\,cos\theta = x_1\,y_1 + x_2 y_2$$

$$x \cdot y = x_1\,y_1 + x_2 y_2$$

Linear separability

Linear separability implies that if there are two classes then there will be a point, line, plane, or hyperplane that splits the input features in such a way that all points of one class are in one-half space and the second class is in the other half-space.

For example, here is a case of selling a house based on area and price. We have got a number of data points for that along with the class, which is house **Sold/Not Sold**:

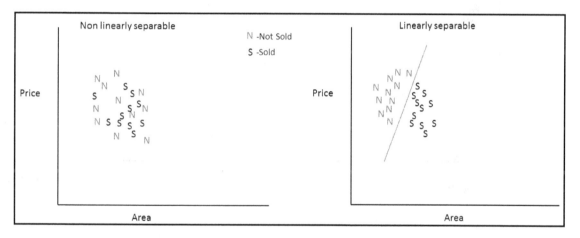

In the preceding figure, all the **N**, are the class (event) of **Not Sold**, which has been derived based on the **Price** and **Area** of the house and all the instances of **S** represent the class of the house getting sold. The number of **N** and **S** represent the data points on which the class has been determined.

In the first diagram, **N** and **S** are quite close and happen to be more random, hence, it's difficult to have linear separability achieved as no matter how you try to separate two classes, at least one of them would be in the misclassified region. It implies that there won't be a correct possible line to separate the two. But the second diagram depicts datasets that can easily be separated based on given conditions.

Separation methodology changes based on the number of dimensions. If there is just one dimensional situation, we can have a point separating classes. Adding more dimensions will require a different arrangement to split the class. Once we have got a 2D situation, a line (as seen previously) will be required to separate it. Similarly, more than 2D will need a plane (a set of points) in order to separate the classes, as shown:

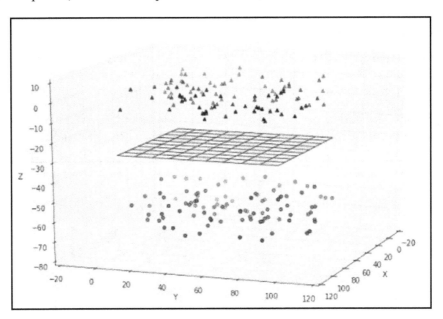

Separation method:

Number of dimensions	Separation method
1	Point
2	Line
3	Plane

What if we have more than 3D? What do we do? What's the solution? Any guesses?

Hyperplanes

Many of you will have guessed it right. We use hyperplanes when it comes to more than 3D. We will define it using a bit of mathematics.

A linear equation looks like this: $y = ax + b$ has got two variables, x and y, and a y-intercept, which is b. If we rename y as x_2 and x as x_1, the equation comes out as $x_2 = ax_1 + b$ which implies $ax_1 - x_2 + b = 0$. If we define 2D vectors as $x = (x_1, x_2)$ and $w = (a, -1)$ and if we make use of the dot product, then the equation becomes $w.x + b = 0$.

 Remember, $x.y = x_1 y_1 + x_2 y_2$.

So, a hyperplane is a set of points that satisfies the preceding equation. But how do we classify with the help of hyperplane?

We define a hypothesis function h:

$$h(x_i) = +1 \ \text{if} \ w.x_i + b \geq 0$$

$$-1 \ \text{if} \ w.x_i + b < 0$$

This could be equivalent to the following:

$$h(x_i) = sign(w.x_i + b)$$

It could also be equivalent to the following:

$$sign(w.x_i) \ \text{if} \ (x_0 = 1 \ \text{and} \ w_0 = b)$$

What it means is that it will use the position of x with respect to the hyperplane to predict a value for y. A data point on one side of the hyperplane gets a classification and a data point on other side of hyperplane gets another class.

Because it uses the equation of a hyperplane that happens to be the linear combination of the values, it is called a **linear classifier**. The shape of hyperplane is by w as it has elements as b and a responsible for the shape.

SVM

Now we are ready to understand SVMs. SVM is an algorithm that enables us to make use of it for both classification and regression. Given a set of examples, it builds a model to assign a group of observations into one category and others into a second category. It is a non-probabilistic linear classifier. Training data being linearly separable is the key here. All the observations or training data are a representation of vectors that are mapped into a space and SVM tries to classify them by using a margin that has to be as wide as possible:

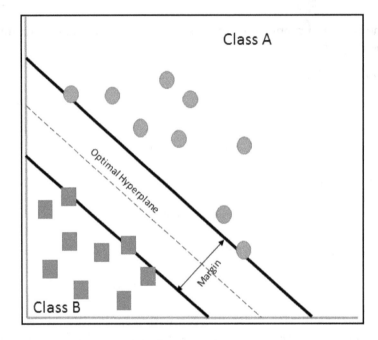

Let's say there are two classes **A** and **B** as in the preceding screenshot.

And from the preceding section, we have learned the following:

$$g(x) = w. x + b$$

Where:

- w: Weight vector that decides the orientation of the hyperplane
- b: Bias term that decides the position of the hyperplane in n-dimensional space by biasing it

The preceding equation is also called a **linear discriminant function**. If there is a vector x_1 that lies on the positive side of the hyperplane, the equation becomes the following:

$$g(x_1) = w.x_1 + b > 0$$

The equation will become the following:

$$g(x_1) < 0$$

If x_1 lies on the positive side of the hyperplane.

What if $g(x_1) = 0$? Can you guess where x_1 would be? Well, yes, it would be on the hyperplane, since our goal is to find out the class of the vector.

So, if $g(x_1) > 0 \Rightarrow x_1$ belongs to **Class A**, $g(x_1) < 0 \Rightarrow x_1$ belongs to **Class B**.

Here, it's evident that we can find out the classification by using the previous equation. But can you see the issue in it? Let's say the boundary line is like the following plot:

Even in the preceding scenario, we are able to classify those feature vectors here. But is it desirable? What can be seen here is that the boundary line or the classifier is close to the **Class B**. It implies that it brings in a large bias in the favor of **Class A** but penalizes **Class B**. As a result of that, due to any disturbances in the vectors close to the boundary, they might cross over and become part of **Class A**, which might not be correct. Hence, our goal is to find an optimal classifier that has got the widest margin, like what is shown in the following plot:

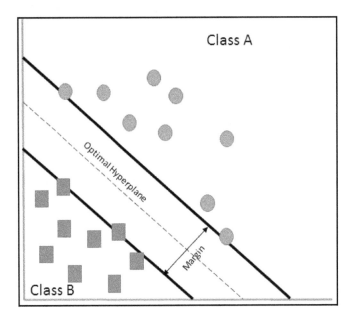

Through SVM, we are attempting to create a boundary or hyperplane such that the distance from each of the feature vectors to the boundary is maximized so that any slight noise or disturbance won't cause the change in classification. So, in this scenario, if we try to bring in certain y_i which happens to be the class belonging to xi, we get the following:

$$y_i = \pm 1$$

$y_i\,(w.x_i + b)$ will always be greater than 0. $y_i(w.x_i + b) > 0$ because when $x_i \in class\ A$, $w.x_i + b > 0$ then $y_i > 0$, so the whole term will be positive. Also, if $x_i \in class\ B$, $w.x_i + b < 0$ then $y_i < 0$, and it will make the term positive.

So, now if we have to redesign it, we say the following:

$w.x_i + b > \gamma$ where γ is the measure of the distance of hyperplane from xi.

And if there is a hyperplane $w.x + b = 0$, then the distance of point x from the preceding hyperplane is as follows:

$$w.x + b/ ||w||$$

Hence, as mentioned previously:

$$w.x + b/ ||w|| \geq \gamma$$

$$w.x + b \geq \gamma. ||w||$$

On performing proper scaling, we can say the following:

$$w.x + b \geq 1 \text{ (since } \gamma. ||w|| = 1)$$

It implies that if there is a classification to be arrived at based on the previous result, it follows this:

$$w.x + b \geq 1 \text{ if } x \in class\ A\ and$$

$$w.x + b \leq -1 \text{ if } x \in class\ B$$

And now, again, if we bring in a class belonging to y_i here, the equation becomes the following:

$$yi\ (w.xi + b) \geq 1$$

But, if $y_i\ (w.x_i + b) = 1$, x_i is a support vector. Next, we will learn what a support vector is.

Support vector

We draw two boundary lines passing through feature vectors of one class closest to the feature vectors of another class. The center line of these boundary lines is the hyperplane we have been talking about. For example, for **Class B**, a boundary line is passing through **p** and **q** along the way and another boundary line through **r** and **s** because **p** and **q** are the closest to the feature vectors of **Class B** and so are **r** and **s**. These are called **support vectors**. We will understand now why these are called **support vectors**:

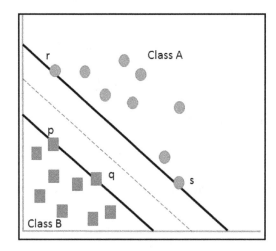

Let's say that if we try to remove one of the feature vectors that is not so close to the boundary line, we will not have an impact on the position or orientation of the hyperplane because the hyperplane's position is decided by boundary lines crossing through vectors **p**, **q**, **r**, and **s**. And, since these are the points holding (supporting) the hyperplane together, they have been named support vectors.

So, this equation $y_i (w.x_i + b) = 1$ holds true when x_i is **p**, **q**, **r**, or **s**.

We will go back to the equation $w.x + b/ ||w|| \geq \gamma$; here, we are trying to maximize γ, and in order to do so either we need to maximize b or minimize $||w||$.

Or we can say we have to minimize $w.w$. If we convert that into a function, $\Phi(w) = w.w$ has to be minimized. $\Phi(w) = 1/2(\ w.w)$ (here 1/2 has been added for mathematical convenience).

So, the objective function of SVM becomes $\Phi(w) = 1/2(\ w.w)$, which has to be minimized subject to constraints, as follows:

$$y_i\ (w.x_i + b) = 1$$

Since it is a constrained optimization problem, it can be converted into an unconstrained optimization problem using the Lagrangian multiplier.

Hence, $L(w,b) = 1/2(w.w) - \sum \alpha i\ [yi(w.xi+b) - 1]$ where αi is the Lagrangian multiplier, $L(w,b) = 1/2(w.w) - \sum \alpha_i\ y_i\ (w.x_i) - \sum \alpha_i\ y_i\ b + \sum \alpha_i$.

Let's find out w and b by using maxima and minima calculus:

$$\delta L/\delta b = 0$$

It results in $\sum \alpha_i\ y_i = 0$, $\delta L/\delta w = 0$ would result in $\sum \alpha i\ yi\ xi = w$. Now, putting these results back into the Lagrangian function yields the following:

$$L = \sum \alpha_i - 1/2\ \sum \alpha_i\ \alpha_j\ y_i\ y_j\ (x_j.x_i)$$

It means that if the value of α_i is very high then the corresponding x. There will be a lot of influence on the position of the hyperplane. Hence, for classification and for unknown feature vector z, the required equation would be the following:

$$D(z) = Sign(\ \sum \alpha i\ xi\ yi\ z + b)$$

If $D(z) > 0$, then z would belong to class A and if $D(z) < 0$, $z \in class\ B$. Let's try to perform a case study in Python:

Loading Libraries

```
In [1]: from sklearn.svm import SVC
        from sklearn import datasets
        from sklearn.preprocessing import StandardScaler
        import numpy as np
```

Loading the data set

```
In [2]: data= datasets.load_iris()
```

```
In [3]: X=data.data
        y= data.target
```

Standardization

```
In [4]: scaler = StandardScaler()
        X_std = scaler.fit_transform(X)
```

Model Building

```
In [6]: sv= SVC(kernel="linear",probability= True,random_state=0)

        #training

        model = sv.fit(X_std, y)
```

Probability for a new data

```
In [8]: new_observation = [[.3, .4, .5, .6]]
```

```
In [9]: model.predict_proba(new_observation)
```

```
Out[9]: array([[ 0.00832731,  0.85200651,  0.13966618]])
```

Kernel trick

We have already seen that SVM works smoothly when it comes to having linear separable data. Just have a look at the following figure; it depicts that vectors are not linearly separable, but the noticeable part is that it is not being separable in 2D space:

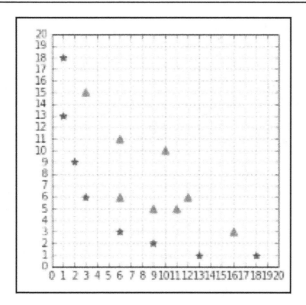

With a few adjustments, we can still make use of SVM here.

Transformation of a two-dimensional vector into a 3D vector or any other higher dimensional vector can set things right for us. The next step would be to train the SVM using a higher dimensional vector. But the question arises of how high in dimension we should go to transform the vector. What this means is if the transformation has to be a two-dimensional vector, or 3D or 4D or more. It actually depends on the which brings separability into the dataset.

Kernel

A non-separable dataset like the one used previously is always a tough thing to deal with, however, there are ways to deal with it. One way is to set the vectors into higher dimensions through transformation. But, can we really do it when we have millions of data or vector in reckoning? It will take lots of computation and, also, time. That's where kernel to saves our day.

We have seen the following equation. In this, only the dot product of the training examples are responsible for making the model learn. Let's try to do a small exercise here:

$$W(\alpha) = \sum_{i=1}^{m} \alpha_i - \frac{1}{2} \sum_{i=1}^{m} \sum_{j=1}^{m} \alpha_i \alpha_j y_i y_j x_i . x_j$$

Let's take two vectors here:

```
x1=[4,8]
x2= [20,30]
```

Now, build a transformation function that will help in transforming these 2D vectors into 3D.

The function to be used in order to transform is the following:

$$t(x1,x2) = (x1^2, x1\ x2\ \sqrt{2}, x2^2)$$

```
#transformation from 2-D to 3-D vector
def t(x):
    return [x[0]**2, np.sqrt(2)*x[0]*x[1], x[1]**2]
```

Now let's use this function:

```
x1_3D= t(x1)
x2_3D= t(x2)

print(np.dot(x1_3D,x2_3D))# the result is 102400
```

But can't we do this without transforming the values. Kernel can help us in doing it:

```
def kernel(a, b):
    return a[0]**2 * b[0]**2 + 2*a[0]*b[0]*a[1]*b[1] + a[1]**2 * b[1]**2
```

It's the time to use this `kernel` now:

```
kernel(x1,x2) #the result is 102400
```

Isn't it quite thrilling to see such an amazing result that is the same as before, without using transformation? So, kernel is a function that leads to the dot-product-like result in another space.

Back to Kernel trick

So, now we have got a fair understanding of kernel and its importance. And, as discussed in the last section, the `kernel` function is:

$$K(x_i, x_j) = x_i . \ x_j$$

So, now the margin problem becomes the following:

$$maximize_\alpha = \sum_{i=1}^{m} \alpha_i - \frac{1}{2} \sum_{i=1}^{m} \sum_{j=1}^{m} \alpha_i \alpha_j y_i y_j K(x_i . x_j x1_{x2})$$

This is subject to $0 \leq \alpha_i \leq C$, for any $i = 1, ..., m$:

$$\sum_{i=1}^{m} \alpha_i y_i = 0$$

Applying the kernel trick simply means replacing the dot product of two examples with a `kernel` function.

Now even the hypothesis function will change as well:

$$h(x_i) = sign(\sum_{j=1}^{S} \alpha_j y_j K(x_j, x_i) + b)$$

This function will be able to decide on and classify the categories. Also, since S denotes the set of support vectors, it implies that we need to compute the `kernel` function only on support vectors.

Kernel types

We're going to explain the types of in this section.

Linear kernel

Let's say there are two vectors, x_1 and x_2, so the linear kernel can be defined by the following:

$$K(x_1, x_2) = x_1 . x_2$$

Polynomial kernel

If there are two vectors, x_1 and x_2, the linear kernel can be defined by the following:

$$K(x_1, x_2) = (x_1 . x_2 + c)^d$$

Where:

- c: Constant
- d: Degree of polynomial:

```
def polynomial_kernel(x1, x2, degree, constant=0):
    result = sum([x1[i] * x2[i] for i in range(len(x1))]) +
constant
    return pow(result, degree)
```

If we use the same x1 and x2 as used previously, we get the following:

```
x1= [4,8]
x2=[20,30]
polynomial_kernel(x1,x2,2,0)
# result would be 102400
```

If we increase the degree of polynomial, we will try to get influenced by other vectors as the decision boundary becomes too complex and it will result in overfitting:

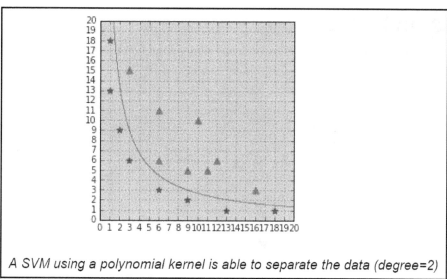

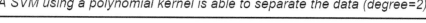

A SVM using a polynomial kernel is able to separate the data (degree=2)

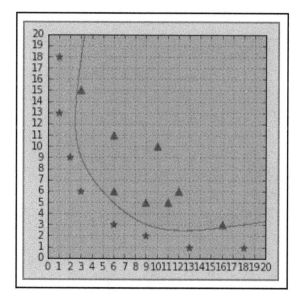

Polynomial kernel using degree as 6.

Gaussian kernel

The polynomial kernel has given us a good boundary line. But can we work with polynomial kernels all the time? Not in the following scenario:

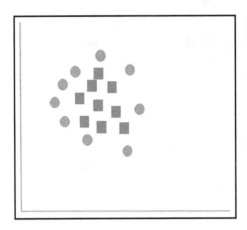

The solution is a radial basis function or Gaussian kernel. It's nothing but the similarity function of the vectors to translate them into a high dimensional space or infinite dimensional space. Its value depends on the distance from the Gaussian kernel function, as follows:

$$K(x,x') = exp(-\gamma \ ||x-x'||^2)$$

Without loss of generality, let $\gamma = \frac{1}{2}$:

$$
\begin{aligned}
K_{RBF}(x, x') &= exp[-\tfrac{1}{2}||x - x'||^2] \\
&= exp[-\tfrac{1}{2}(x - x', x - x')] \\
&= exp[-\tfrac{1}{2}((x, x - x') - (x', x - x'))] \\
&= exp[-\tfrac{1}{2}((x, x) - (x, x') - (x', x) + (x', x'))] \\
&= exp[-\tfrac{1}{2}(||x||^2 + ||x'||^2 - 2(x, x'))] \\
&= exp[-\tfrac{1}{2}||x||^2 - \tfrac{1}{2}||x'||^2]exp\left[-\tfrac{1}{2} - 2(x, x')\right] \\
&= Ce^{(x,x')}
\end{aligned}
$$
$$whereas, \ C := exp[-\tfrac{1}{2}||x||^2 - \tfrac{1}{2}||x'||^2] \ is \ a \ constant$$

With the help of this RBF as a similarity function, all the feature vectors get calculated.

SVM example and parameter optimization through grid search

Here, we are taking a breast cancer dataset wherein we have classified according to whether the cancer is benign/malignant.

The following is for importing all the required libraries:

```
import pandas as pd
import numpy as np
from sklearn import svm, datasets
from sklearn.svm import SVC
import matplotlib.pyplot as plt
from sklearn.model_selection import train_test_split
from sklearn.model_selection import GridSearchCV
from sklearn.metrics import classification_report
from sklearn.utils import shuffle
%matplotlib inline
```

Now, let's load the breast cancer dataset:

```
BC_Data = datasets.load_breast_cancer()
```

The following allows us to check the details of the dataset:

```
print(BC_Data.DESCR)
```

This if for splitting the dataset into train and test:

```
X_train, X_test, y_train, y_test = train_test_split(BC_Data.data,
BC_Data.target, random_state=0)
```

This is for setting the model with the linear kernel and finding out the accuracy:

```
C= 1.0
svm= SVC(kernel="linear",C=C)
svm.fit(X_train, y_train)
print('Accuracy-train dataset: {:.3f}'.format(svm.score(X_train,y_train)))
print('Accuracy- test dataset: {:.3f}'.format(svm.score(X_test,y_test)))
```

We get the accuracy output as shown:

```
Accuracy-train dataset: 0.967

Accuracy- test dataset: 0.958
```

Setting the model with the Gaussian/RBF kernel and accuracy is done like this:

```
svm= SVC(kernel="rbf",C=C)
svm.fit(X_train, y_train)
print('Accuracy-train dataset: {:.3f}'.format(svm.score(X_train,y_train)))
print('Accuracy- test dataset: {:.3f}'.format(svm.score(X_test,y_test)))
```

The output can be seen as follows:

```
Accuracy-train dataset: 1.000

Accuracy- test dataset: 0.629
```

It's quite apparent that the model is overfitted. So, we will go for normalization:

```
min_train = X_train.min(axis=0)
range_train = (X_train - min_train).max(axis=0)
X_train_scaled = (X_train - min_train)/range_train
X_test_scaled = (X_test - min_train)/range_train
```

This code is for setting up the model again:

```
svm= SVC(kernel="rbf",C=C)
svm.fit(X_train_scaled, y_train)
print('Accuracy-train dataset:
{:.3f}'.format(svm.score(X_train_scaled,y_train)))
print('Accuracy test dataset:
{:.3f}'.format(svm.score(X_test_scaled,y_test)))
```

The following shows the output:

```
Accuracy-train dataset: 0.948

Accuracy test dataset: 0.951
```

Now, the overfitting issue cannot be seen any more. Let's move on to having an optimal result:

```
parameters = [{'kernel': ['rbf'],
  'gamma': [1e-4, 1e-3, 0.01, 0.1, 0.2, 0.5],
  'C': [1, 10, 100, 1000]},
  {'kernel': ['linear'], 'C': [1, 10, 100, 1000]}]
clf = GridSearchCV(SVC(decision_function_shape='ovr'), parameters, cv=5)
```

```
clf.fit(X_train, y_train)
print("Best parameters set found on development set:")
print()
print(clf.best_params_)
print()
print("Grid scores on training set:")
print()
means = clf.cv_results_['mean_test_score']
stds = clf.cv_results_['std_test_score']
for mean, std, params in zip(means, stds, clf.cv_results_['params']):
 print("%0.3f (+/-%0.03f) for %r"
 % (mean, std * 2, params))
print()
```

With the help of grid search, we get the optimal combination for gamma, kernel, and C as shown:

```
Best parameters set found on development set:

{'kernel': 'linear', 'C': 1}

Grid scores on training set:

0.937 (+/-0.057) for {'gamma': 0.0001, 'kernel': 'rbf', 'C': 1}
0.923 (+/-0.071) for {'gamma': 0.001, 'kernel': 'rbf', 'C': 1}
0.627 (+/-0.006) for {'gamma': 0.01, 'kernel': 'rbf', 'C': 1}
0.627 (+/-0.006) for {'gamma': 0.1, 'kernel': 'rbf', 'C': 1}
0.627 (+/-0.006) for {'gamma': 0.2, 'kernel': 'rbf', 'C': 1}
0.627 (+/-0.006) for {'gamma': 0.5, 'kernel': 'rbf', 'C': 1}
0.937 (+/-0.044) for {'gamma': 0.0001, 'kernel': 'rbf', 'C': 10}
0.918 (+/-0.047) for {'gamma': 0.001, 'kernel': 'rbf', 'C': 10}
0.629 (+/-0.015) for {'gamma': 0.01, 'kernel': 'rbf', 'C': 10}
0.627 (+/-0.006) for {'gamma': 0.1, 'kernel': 'rbf', 'C': 10}
0.627 (+/-0.006) for {'gamma': 0.2, 'kernel': 'rbf', 'C': 10}
0.627 (+/-0.006) for {'gamma': 0.5, 'kernel': 'rbf', 'C': 10}
0.934 (+/-0.031) for {'gamma': 0.0001, 'kernel': 'rbf', 'C': 100}
0.918 (+/-0.047) for {'gamma': 0.001, 'kernel': 'rbf', 'C': 100}
0.629 (+/-0.015) for {'gamma': 0.01, 'kernel': 'rbf', 'C': 100}
0.627 (+/-0.006) for {'gamma': 0.1, 'kernel': 'rbf', 'C': 100}
0.627 (+/-0.006) for {'gamma': 0.2, 'kernel': 'rbf', 'C': 100}
0.627 (+/-0.006) for {'gamma': 0.5, 'kernel': 'rbf', 'C': 100}
0.930 (+/-0.040) for {'gamma': 0.0001, 'kernel': 'rbf', 'C': 1000}
0.918 (+/-0.047) for {'gamma': 0.001, 'kernel': 'rbf', 'C': 1000}
0.629 (+/-0.015) for {'gamma': 0.01, 'kernel': 'rbf', 'C': 1000}
0.627 (+/-0.006) for {'gamma': 0.1, 'kernel': 'rbf', 'C': 1000}
0.627 (+/-0.006) for {'gamma': 0.2, 'kernel': 'rbf', 'C': 1000}
0.627 (+/-0.006) for {'gamma': 0.5, 'kernel': 'rbf', 'C': 1000}
0.960 (+/-0.048) for {'kernel': 'linear', 'C': 1}
0.946 (+/-0.048) for {'kernel': 'linear', 'C': 10}
0.953 (+/-0.039) for {'kernel': 'linear', 'C': 100}
0.953 (+/-0.039) for {'kernel': 'linear', 'C': 1000}
```

With the help of this, we can see and find out which combination of parameters is giving us the better result.

Here, the best combination turns out to be a linear kernel with a C value of 1.

Summary

In this chapter, we were introduced to vectors, magnitude of vector, and the dot product. We learned about SVMs that can be used for both classification and regression. We studied support vectors and kernels and the different types of kernels. Lastly, we studied the SVM example and parameter optimization through grid search.

In the next chapter, we will learn about performance in ensemble learning.

3
Performance in Ensemble Learning

So far, we have learned that no two models will give the same result. In other words, different combinations of data or algorithms will result in a different outcome. This outcome can be good for a particular combination and not so good for another combination. What if we have a model that tries to take these combinations into account and comes up with a generalized and better result? This is called an **ensemble model**.

In this chapter, we will be learning about a number of concepts in regard to ensemble modeling, which are as follows:

- Bagging
- Random forest
- Boosting
- Gradient boosting
- Optimization of parameters

What is ensemble learning?

Sometimes, one machine learning model is not good enough for a certain scenario or use case as it might not give you the desired accuracy, recall, and precision. Hence, multiple learning models—or an ensemble of models captures the pattern of the data and gives better output.

As an example, let's say we are trying to decide on a place where we would like to go in the summer. Typically, if we are planning for a trip, the suggestions for the place pours in from all corners. That is, these suggestions might come from our family, websites, friends, and travel agencies, and then we have to decide on the basis of a good experience that we had in the past:

- **Family**: Let's say that whenever we have consulted a family member and listened to them, there has been a 60% chance that they were proven right and we ended up having a good experience on the trip.
- **Friends**: Similarly, if we listen to our friends, they suggest places where we might have a good experience. In these instances, a good experience occurred in 50% of cases.
- **Travel websites**: Travel websites are another source where we can get loads of information regarding where to visit. If we choose to take their advice, there's a 35% chance that they were right and we had a good experience.
- **Travel agencies**: Another piece of advice and information might flow from travel agencies if we go and check with them first. Based on our past experiences, we saw that they were right in 45% of cases.

However, we have to accumulate all of the preceding inputs and make a decision since no source has been 100% correct so far. If we combine these results, the accuracy scenario will be as follows:

```
1 - (60% * 50% * 35% * 45%)
1- 0.04725 = 0.95275

# Accuracy is close to 95%.
```

From this, we are able to see the impact of ensemble modeling.

Ensemble methods

Primarily, there are three methods of building an ensemble model, that is, **Bagging**, **Boosting**, and **Stacking**:

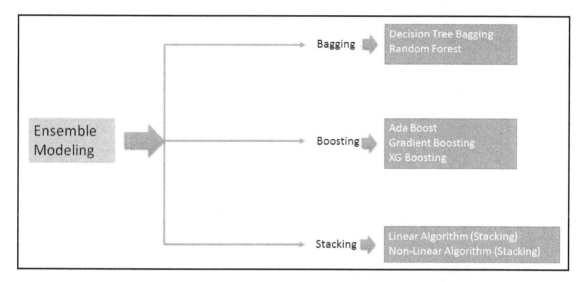

We will discuss each method one by one. However, before we get into this, we need to understand what bootstrapping is, which sets the basis for **Bagging** and **Boosting**.

Bootstrapping

Bootstrapping is a statistical technique that's used to draw an inference about the parameters of population based on the samples drawn from it with replacement and averaging these results out. In the event of sampling with replacement, samples are drawn one after another, and once one sample is drawn from the population, the population is replenished with the sampled data:

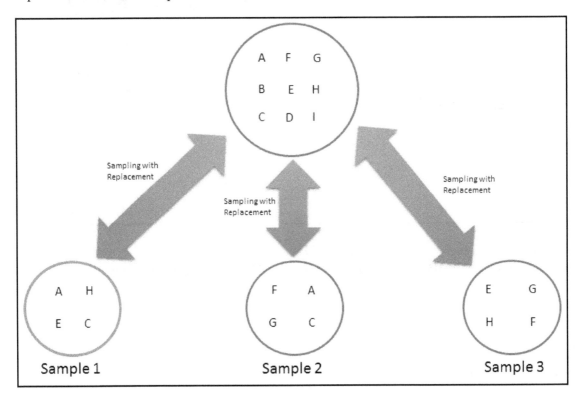

In the preceding diagram, there is a dataset that has got multiples components (**A, B, C, D, E, F, G, H**, and **I**). To start, we need to draw three samples of the same size. Let's draw **Sample 1** randomly and say that the first element turned out to be **A**. However, before we draw the second element of **Sample 1**, **A** is returned to the dataset. A similar process takes place for the entire draw. This is called **Sampling with Replacement**. Hence, we have a chance of selecting the same item multiple times in a set. By following this process, we have drawn three samples, that is, **Sample 1**, **Sample 2**, and **Sample 3**.

When we take a step further down, which is determining the statistics (various metrics) on **Sample 1**, **Sample 2**, and **Sample 3**, we find out a mean or an average of all the statistics to infer something about the dataset (population). This entire process is called **bootstrapping** and the drawn samples are termed bootstrapped samples. This can be defined with the following equation:

Inference about the Dataset(Population) = Average(sample 1,sample 2,............,sample N)

If you look at the preceding diagram carefully, there might be a scenario wherein a few elements of the dataset haven't been picked or are not part of those three samples:

- **Sample 1**: (A, E, H, C)
- **Sample 2**: (F, G, A, C)
- **Sample 3**: (E, H, G, F)

Therefore, the elements that haven't been picked are **B**, **D**, and **I**. The samples that were not part of the drawn samples are called **out-of-bag** (**OOB**) samples.

Let's do a simple coding exercise to see how this can be done in Python:

1. Here, we will be using the `sklearn` and `resample` functions. Let's import the necessary libraries:

```
#importing Libraries
from sklearn.utils import resample
```

2. Next, create a dataset that we will need to sample:

```
dataset=[10,2
```

3. Now, we will extract a bootstrap sample with the help of the `resample` function:

```
0,30,40,50,60,70,80,90,100]

#using "resample" function generate a bootstrap sample
boot_samp = resample(dataset, replace=True, n_samples=5,
random_state=1)
```

4. We will use list comprehension to extract an OOB sample:

```
#extracting OOB sample
OOB=[x for x in dataset if x not in boot_samp]
```

5. Now, let's print it:

```
print(boot_samp)
```

We get the following output:

```
[60, 90, 100, 60, 10]
```

We can see that there is a repetition of 60 in the sampling. This is due to sampling with replacement.

6. Next, we need to print the following code:

```
print(OOB)
```

We get the following output:

```
[20, 30, 40, 50, 70, 80]
```

By this end of this, we want to have a result that's as follows:

$$OOB = Dataset - Boot\_Sample$$

$$=[10,20,30,40,50,60,70,80,90,100] - [60,90,100,60,10]$$

$$=[20,30,40,50,70,80]$$

This is the same result we have got from the code.

Bagging

Bagging stands for bootstrap **aggregation**. Hence, it's clear that the bagging concept stems from bootstrapping. It implies that bagging has got the elements of bootstrapping. It is a bootstrap ensemble method wherein multiple classifiers (typically from the same algorithm) are trained on the samples that are drawn randomly with replacements (bootstrap samples) from the training set/population. Aggregation of all the classifiers takes place in the form of average or by voting. It tries to reduce the affect of the overfitting issue in the model as shown in the following diagram:

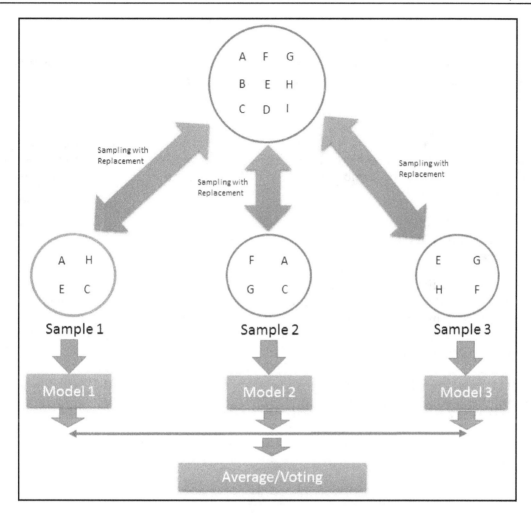

There are three stages of bagging:

- **Bootstrapping**: This is a statistical technique that's used to generate random samples or bootstrap samples with replacement.
- **Model fitting**: In this stage, we build models on bootstrap samples. Typically, the same algorithm is used for building the models. However, there is no restriction on using different algorithms.
- **Combining models**: This step involves combining all the models and taking an average. For example, if we have applied a decision tree classifier, then the probability that's coming out of every classifier is averaged.

Decision tree

A decision tree is a supervised learning technique that works on the divide-and-conquer approach. It can be used to address both classification and regression. The population undergoes a split into two or more homogeneous samples based on the most significant feature.

For example, let's say we have got a sample of people who applied for a loan from the bank. For this example, we will take the count as 50. Here, we have got three attributes, that is, gender, income, and the number of other loans held by the person, to predict whether to give them a loan or not.

We need to segment the people based on gender, income, and the number of other loans they hold and find out the most significant factor. This tends to create the most homogeneous set.

Let's take income first and try to create the segment based on it. The total number of people who applied for the loan is 50. Out of 50, the loan was awarded to 20 people. However, if we break this up by income, we can see that the breakup has been done by income <100,000 and >=100,000. This doesn't generate a homogeneous group. We can see that 40% of applicants (20) have been given a loan. Of the people whose income was less than 100,000, 30% of them managed to get the loan. Similarly, 46.67 % of people whose income was greater than or equal to 100,000 managed to get the loan. The following diagram shows the tree splitting on the basis of income:

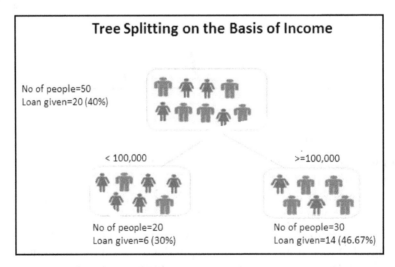

Let's take up the number of loans now. Even this time around, we are not able to see the creation of a homogeneous group. The following diagram shows the tree splitting on the basis of the number of loans:

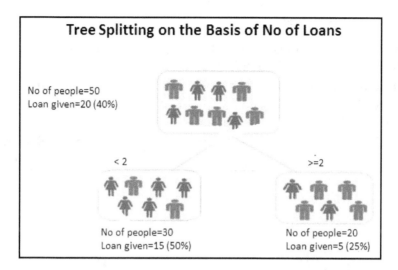

Let's get on with gender and see how it fares in terms of creating a homogeneous group. This turns out to be the homogeneous group. There were 15 who were female, out of which 53.3% got the loan. 34.3% of male also ended up getting the loan. The following diagram shows the tree splitting based on gender:

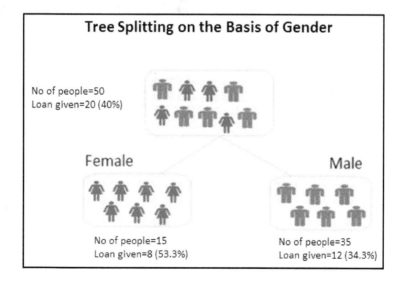

With the help of this, the most significant variable has been found. Now, we will dwell on how significant the variables are.

Before we do that, it's imperative for us to understand the terminology and nomenclature associated with the decision tree:

- **Root Node**: This stands for the whole population or dataset that undergoes a split into two or more homogeneous groups
- **Decision Node**: This is created when a node is divided into further subnodes
- **Leaf Node**: When there is no possibility of nodes splitting any further, that node is termed a leaf node or terminal node
- **Branch**: A subsection of the entire tree is called a **branch** or a **Sub-tree**:

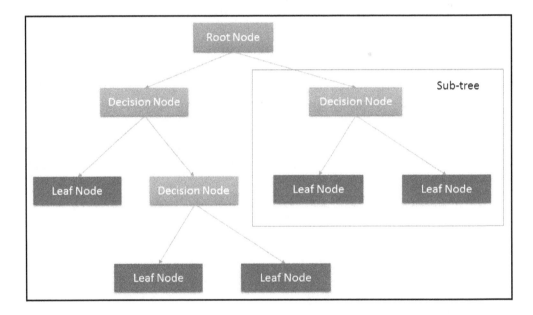

Tree splitting

There are various algorithms that help when it comes to tree splitting, all of which take us to the leaf node. The decision tree takes all of the features (variables) that are available into account and selects the feature that would result in the most pure or most homogeneous split. The algorithm that's used to split the tree also depends on the target variable. Let's go through this, step by step:

1. **Gini index**: This says that if we select two items at random from a population, they must be from the same class. The probability for this event would turn out to be 1 if the population is totally pure. It only performs binary splits. **Classification and regression trees (CARTs)** make use of this kind of split.

    The following formula is how you calculate the Gini index:

    $$1 - \sum_{t=0}^{t=k} p_t^2$$

    Here, *p(t)* is the proportion of observations with a target variable with a value of *t*.

    For the binary target variable, *t=1*, the max Gini index value is as follows:

    $$= 1 - (1/2)^\wedge 2 - (1/2)^\wedge 2$$
    $$= 1 - 2*(1/2)^\wedge 2$$
    $$= 1 - 2*(1/4)$$
    $$= 1 - 0.5$$
    $$= 0.5$$

    A Gini score gives an idea of how good a split is by how mixed the classes are in the two groups that were created the by the split. A perfect separation results in a Gini score of 0, whereas the worst case split results in 50/50 classes.

    For a nominal variable with *k* level, the maximum value of the Gini index is *(1-1/k)*.

2. **Information gain**: Let's delve into this and find out what it is. If we happened to have three scenarios, as shown in the following diagram, which can be described easily?

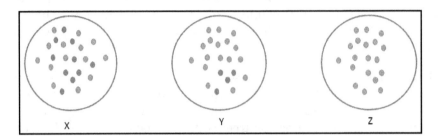

Since **Z** seem to be quite homogeneous and all of the values of it are similar, it is called a **pure set**. Hence, it requires less effort to explain it. However, **Y** would need more information to explain as it's not pure. **X** turns out to be the impurest of them all. What it tries to convey is that randomness and disorganization adds to complexity and so it needs more information to explain. This degree of randomness is known as **entropy**. If the sample is completely homogeneous, then the entropy is *0*. If the sample is equally divided, its entropy will be *1*:

$$Entropy = -p \ log_2p - q \ log_2q$$

Here, *p* means the probability of success and *q* means the probability of failure.

Entropy is also used with a categorical target variable. It picks the split that has the lowest entropy compared to the parent node.

Here, we must calculate the entropy of parent node first. Then, we need to calculate entropy of each individual node that's been split and post that, including the weighted average of all subnodes.

3. **Reduction in variance**: When it comes to the continuous target variable, reduction in variance is used. Here, we are using variance to decide the best split. The split with the lowest variance is picked as the criteria to split:

$$Variance = \sum(X - \bar{X})^2/n$$

Here, $\bar{X}$ is the mean of all the values, *X*, is the real values, and *n* is the number of values.

The calculation of variance for each node is done first and then the weighted average of each node's variance makes us select the best node.

Parameters of tree splitting

There are a number of parameters that we need to tune or be aware of:

- `Max_depth`: One of the most important parameters is `max_depth`. It captures the essence of how deep the tree can get. More depth in the tree means that it is able to extract more information from the features. However, sometimes, excessive depth might be a cause of worry as it tends to bring along overfitting as well.
- `min_samples_split`: This represents the minimum number of samples required to split an internal node. This can vary between considering at least one sample at each node to considering all of the samples at each node. When we increase this parameter, the tree becomes more constrained as it has to consider more samples at each node. An increase in the value of `min_samples_split` tends to be underfitted.
- `min_samples_leaf`: This is the minimum number of samples required to be at a leaf node. Increasing this value to the maximum might cause underfitting.
- `max_features`: This is maximum number of features to be considered for the best split. It might cause overfitting when there is an increase in the max number of features.

Now, we are well equipped to understand the random forest algorithm. We're going to talk about that next.

Random forest algorithm

The random forest algorithm works with the bagging technique. The number of trees are planted and grown in the following manner:

- There are N observations in the training set. Samples out of N observations are taken at random and with replacement. These samples will act as a training set for different trees.
- If there are M input features (variables), m features are drawn as a subset out of M and of course $m < M$. What this does is select m features at random at each node of the tree.
- Every tree is grown to the largest extent possible.

- Prediction takes place based on the aggregation of the results coming out of all the trees. In the case of classification, the method of aggregation is voting, whereas it is an average of all the results in the case of regression:

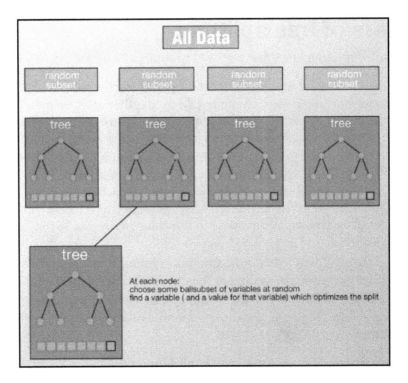

Let's work on a case study, since that will help us understand this concept more in detail. Let's work on breast cancer data.

Case study

The data that is given in this case study is about patients who were detected with two kinds of breast cancer:

- Malignant
- Benign

A number of features are given here that have characteristics in regard to the cell nuclei that have been computed from the **fine-needle aspiration** (**FNA**) of a breast mass. Based on these features, we need to predict whether the cancer is malignant or benign. Follow these steps to get started:

1. Import all the required libraries:

```
import numpy as np
import pandas as pd
import seaborn as sns
import matplotlib.pyplot as plt
%matplotlib inline
from sklearn import preprocessing
from sklearn.model_selection import train_test_split
from sklearn.metrics import confusion_matrix
#importing our parameter tuning dependencies
from sklearn.model_selection import (cross_val_score,
GridSearchCV,StratifiedKFold, ShuffleSplit )
#importing our dependencies for Feature Selection
from sklearn.feature_selection import (SelectKBest, RFE, RFECV)
from sklearn.ensemble import ExtraTreesClassifier
from sklearn.cross_validation import ShuffleSplit
from sklearn.ensemble import RandomForestClassifier
from sklearn.metrics import f1_score
from collections import defaultdict
# Importing our sklearn dependencies for the modeling
from sklearn.ensemble import RandomForestClassifier
from sklearn.preprocessing import StandardScaler
from sklearn.cross_validation import KFold
from sklearn import metrics
from sklearn.metrics import (accuracy_score, confusion_matrix,
 classification_report, roc_curve, auc)
```

2. Load the breast cancer data:

```
data= pd.read_csv("breastcancer.csv")
```

3. Let's understand the data:

```
data.info()
```

We get the following output:

```
<class 'pandas.core.frame.DataFrame'>
RangeIndex: 569 entries, 0 to 568
Data columns (total 32 columns):
id                        569 non-null int64
diagnosis                 569 non-null object
radius_mean               569 non-null float64
texture_mean              569 non-null float64
perimeter_mean            569 non-null float64
area_mean                 569 non-null float64
smoothness_mean           569 non-null float64
compactness_mean          569 non-null float64
concavity_mean            569 non-null float64
concave points_mean       569 non-null float64
symmetry_mean             569 non-null float64
fractal_dimension_mean    569 non-null float64
radius_se                 569 non-null float64
texture_se                569 non-null float64
perimeter_se              569 non-null float64
area_se                   569 non-null float64
smoothness_se             569 non-null float64
compactness_se            569 non-null float64
concavity_se              569 non-null float64
concave points_se         569 non-null float64
symmetry_se               569 non-null float64
fractal_dimension_se      569 non-null float64
radius_worst              569 non-null float64
texture_worst             569 non-null float64
perimeter_worst           569 non-null float64
area_worst                569 non-null float64
smoothness_worst          569 non-null float64
compactness_worst         569 non-null float64
concavity_worst           569 non-null float64
concave points_worst      569 non-null float64
symmetry_worst            569 non-null float64
fractal_dimension_worst   569 non-null float64
dtypes: float64(30), int64(1), object(1)
memory usage: 142.3+ KB
```

4. Let's consider `data.head()` here:

```
data.head()
```

From this, we get the following output:

	id	diagnosis	radius_mean	texture_mean	perimeter_mean	area_mean	smoothness_mean	compactness_mean	concavity_mean	concave points_mean	...	ra
0	842302	M	17.99	10.38	122.80	1001.0	0.11840	0.27760	0.3001	0.14710	...	
1	842517	M	20.57	17.77	132.90	1326.0	0.08474	0.07864	0.0869	0.07017	...	
2	84300903	M	19.69	21.25	130.00	1203.0	0.10960	0.15990	0.1974	0.12790	...	
3	84348301	M	11.42	20.38	77.58	386.1	0.14250	0.28390	0.2414	0.10520	...	
4	84358402	M	20.29	14.34	135.10	1297.0	0.10030	0.13280	0.1980	0.10430	...	

5 rows × 32 columns

5. We get the data diagnosis from the following code:

```
data.diagnosis.unique()
```

The following is the output for the preceding code:

```
array(['M', 'B'], dtype=object)
```

6. The data is described as follows:

```
data.describe()
```

We get this output from the preceding code:

	id	radius_mean	texture_mean	perimeter_mean	area_mean	smoothness_mean	compactness_mean	concavity_mean	concave points_mean
count	5.690000e+02	569.000000	569.000000	569.000000	569.000000	569.000000	569.000000	569.000000	569.000000
mean	3.037183e+07	14.127292	19.289649	91.969033	654.889104	0.096360	0.104341	0.088799	0.048919
std	1.250206e+08	3.524049	4.301036	24.298981	351.914129	0.014064	0.052813	0.079720	0.038803
min	8.670000e+03	6.981000	9.710000	43.790000	143.500000	0.052630	0.019380	0.000000	0.000000
25%	8.692180e+05	11.700000	16.170000	75.170000	420.300000	0.086370	0.064920	0.029560	0.020310
50%	9.060240e+05	13.370000	18.840000	86.240000	551.100000	0.095870	0.092630	0.061540	0.033500
75%	8.813129e+06	15.780000	21.800000	104.100000	782.700000	0.105300	0.130400	0.130700	0.074000
max	9.113205e+08	28.110000	39.280000	188.500000	2501.000000	0.163400	0.345400	0.426800	0.201200

8 rows × 31 columns

```
data['diagnosis'] = data['diagnosis'].map({'M':1,'B':0})

datas = pd.DataFrame(preprocessing.scale(data.iloc[:,1:32]))
datas.columns = list(data.iloc[:,1:32].columns)
datas['diagnosis'] = data['diagnosis']

datas.diagnosis.value_counts().plot(kind='bar', alpha = 0.5, facecolor =
'b', figsize=(12,6))
plt.title("Diagnosis (M=1, B=0)", fontsize = '18')
plt.ylabel("Total Number of Patients")
plt.grid(b=True)
```

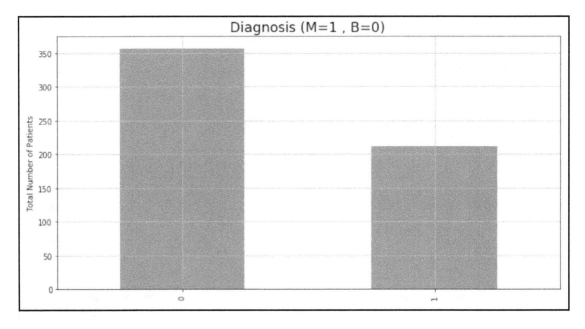

```
data_mean =
data[['diagnosis','radius_mean','texture_mean','perimeter_mean','area_mean'
,'smoothness_mean', 'compactness_mean', 'concavity_mean','concave
points_mean', 'symmetry_mean', 'fractal_dimension_mean']]

plt.figure(figsize=(10,10))
foo = sns.heatmap(data_mean.corr(), vmax=1, square=True, annot=True)
```

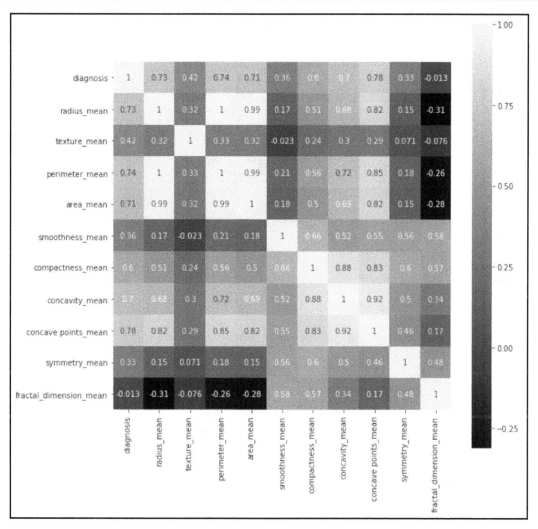

```
from sklearn.model_selection import train_test_split, cross_val_score,
cross_val_predict
from sklearn import metrics
predictors = data_mean.columns[2:11]
target = "diagnosis"
X = data_mean.loc[:,predictors]
y = np.ravel(data.loc[:,[target]])
# Split the dataset in train and test:
X_train, X_test, y_train, y_test = train_test_split(X, y, test_size=0.2,
random_state=0)
print ('Shape of training set : %i & Shape of test set : %i' %
(X_train.shape[0],X_test.shape[0]) )
```

```
print ('There are very few data points so 10-fold cross validation should
give us a better estimate')
```

The preceding input gives us the following output:

```
Shape of training set : 455 & Shape of test set : 114
There are very few data points so 10-fold cross validation should give us a better estimate
```

```
param_grid = {
  'n_estimators': [ 25, 50, 100, 150, 300, 500],
  "max_depth": [ 5, 8, 15, 25],
  "max_features": ['auto', 'sqrt', 'log2']
  }
#use OOB samples ("oob_score= True") to estimate the generalization
accuracy.
rfc = RandomForestClassifier(bootstrap= True, n_jobs= 1, oob_score= True)
#let's use cv=10 in the GridSearchCV call
#performance estimation
#initiate the grid
grid = GridSearchCV(rfc, param_grid = param_grid, cv=10, scoring
='accuracy')
#fit your data before you can get the best parameter combination.
grid.fit(X,y)
grid.cv_results_
```

```
{'mean_fit_time': array([ 0.03339021, 0.06928167, 0.12723982, 0.18830116, 0.37480223,
        0.62295649, 0.03198514, 0.06366966, 0.13215754, 0.19233065,
        0.37359273, 0.6272675 , 0.03098235, 0.06176491, 0.12673779,
        0.18218436, 0.37519989, 0.62526178, 0.03318925, 0.06437261,
        0.13265123, 0.19200687, 0.37980766, 0.64130707, 0.03298304,
        0.06457033, 0.1324533 , 0.19311185, 0.37760334, 0.64290974,
        0.03268728, 0.06437161, 0.13275001, 0.19471939, 0.38081119,
        0.62576702, 0.03238645, 0.06457105, 0.13024404, 0.19472077,
        0.38281748, 0.63689423, 0.03278713, 0.06437168, 0.12603452,
        0.19481535, 0.38311908, 0.63247719, 0.03178444, 0.06337047,
        0.12833807, 0.19582243, 0.37660072, 0.63127663, 0.03188739,
        0.06417322, 0.12814078, 0.19571686, 0.381515  , 0.62877288,
        0.03278725, 0.06447268, 0.12914252, 0.19521923, 0.3822166 ,
        0.62776752, 0.03258617, 0.06427264, 0.12723784, 0.19631989,
        0.38231587, 0.63749213]),
```

```
# Let's find out the best scores, parameter and the estimator from the
gridsearchCV
print("GridSearhCV best model:\n ")
print('The best score: ', grid.best_score_)
print('The best parameter:', grid.best_params_)
print('The best model estimator:', grid.best_estimator_)
```

```
GridSearhCV best model:

The best score:  0.949033391916
The best parameter: {'max_depth': 8, 'max_features': 'sqrt', 'n_estimators': 150}
The best model estimator: RandomForestClassifier(bootstrap=True, class_weight=None, criterion='gini',
        max_depth=8, max_features='sqrt', max_leaf_nodes=None,
        min_impurity_decrease=0.0, min_impurity_split=None,
        min_samples_leaf=1, min_samples_split=2,
        min_weight_fraction_leaf=0.0, n_estimators=150, n_jobs=1,
        oob_score=True, random_state=None, verbose=0, warm_start=False)
```

```
# model = RandomForestClassifier() with optimal values
model = RandomForestClassifier(bootstrap=True, class_weight=None,
criterion='gini',
 max_depth=8, max_features='sqrt', max_leaf_nodes=None,
 min_impurity_decrease=0.0, min_impurity_split=None,
 min_samples_leaf=1, min_samples_split=2,
 min_weight_fraction_leaf=0.0, n_estimators=150, n_jobs=1,
 oob_score=True, random_state=None, verbose=0, warm_start=False)
model.fit(X_train, y_train)
```

```
RandomForestClassifier(bootstrap=True, class_weight=None, criterion='gini',
        max_depth=8, max_features='sqrt', max_leaf_nodes=None,
        min_impurity_decrease=0.0, min_impurity_split=None,
        min_samples_leaf=1, min_samples_split=2,
        min_weight_fraction_leaf=0.0, n_estimators=150, n_jobs=1,
        oob_score=True, random_state=None, verbose=0, warm_start=False)
```

```
print("Performance Accuracy on the Testing data:",
round(model.score(X_test, y_test) *100))
```

From this, we can see that the performance accuracy on the testing data is 95.0:

```
#Getting the predictions for X
y_pred = model.predict(X_test)
print('Total Predictions {}'.format(len(y_pred)))
```

Here, the total predictions is 114:

```
truth = pd.DataFrame(y_test, columns= ['Truth'])
predictions = pd.DataFrame(y_pred, columns= ['Predictions'])
frames = [truth, predictions]
_result = pd.concat(frames, axis=1)
print(_result.shape)
_result.head()
```

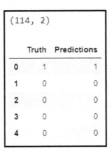

10 fold cross-validation with a Tree classifier on the training dataset#
10 fold
#splitting the data, fitting a model and computing the score 10 consecutive
times
cv_scores = []
scores = cross_val_score(rfc, X_train, y_train, cv=10, scoring='accuracy')
cv_scores.append(scores.mean())
cv_scores.append(scores.std())

#cross validation mean score
print("10 k-fold cross validation mean score: ", scores.mean() *100)

From this, we can see that the 10 k-fold cross validation mean score is 94.9661835749:

```
# printing classification accuracy score rounded
print("Classification accuracy: ", round(accuracy_score(y_test, y_pred,
normalize=True) * 100))
```

Here, we can see that the classification accuracy is 95.0:

```
# Making the Confusion Matrix
cm = confusion_matrix(y_test, y_pred)
plt.figure(figsize=(12,6))
ax = plt.axes()
ax.set_title('Confusion Matrix for both classes\n', size=21)
sns.heatmap(cm, cmap= 'plasma',annot=True, fmt='g') # cmap
plt.show()
```

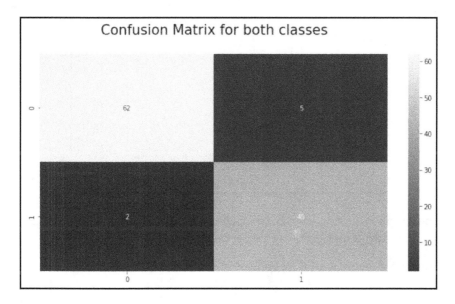

```
# The classification Report
target_names = ['Benign [Class 0]', 'Malignant[Class 1]']
print(classification_report(y_test, y_pred, target_names=target_names))
```

	precision	recall	f1-score	support
Benign [Class 0]	0.97	0.93	0.95	67
Malignant[Class 1]	0.90	0.96	0.93	47
avg / total	0.94	0.94	0.94	114

```
y_pred_proba = model.predict_proba(X_test)[::,1]
fpr, tpr, _ = metrics.roc_curve(y_test, y_pred_proba)
auc = metrics.roc_auc_score(y_test, y_pred_proba)
plt.plot(fpr,tpr,label="curve, auc="+str(auc))
plt.legend(loc=4)
plt.show()
```

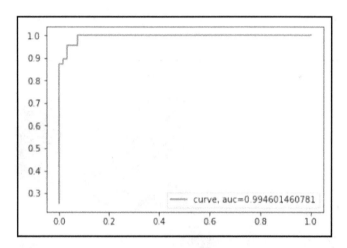

The preceding graph is a **receiver operating characteristic (ROC)** metric, which is used to evaluate classifier output quality using cross-validation.

The preceding plot shows the ROC response to our chosen features (`['compactness_mean', 'perimeter_mean', 'radius_mean', 'texture_mean', 'concavity_mean', 'smoothness_mean']`) and the diagnosis-dependent variable that was created from k-fold cross-validation.

A ROC area of `0.99` is quite good.

Boosting

When it comes to bagging, it can be applied to both classification and regression. However, there is another technique that is also part of the ensemble family: boosting. However, the underlying principle of these two are quite different. In bagging, each of the models runs independently and then the results are aggregated at the end. This is a parallel operation. Boosting acts in a different way, since it flows sequentially. Each model here runs and passes on the significant features to another model:

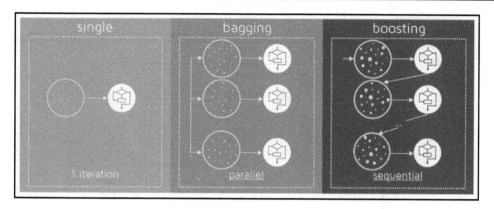

Gradient boosting

To explain gradient boosting, we will take the route of Ben Gorman, a great data scientist. He has been able to explain it in a mathematical yet simple way. Let's say that we have got nine training examples wherein we are required to predict the age of a person based on three features, such as whether they like gardening, playing video games, or surfing the internet. The data for this is as follows:

Person ID	Age	LikesGardening	PlaysVideoGames	LikesSurfingNet
1	13	FALSE	TRUE	TRUE
2	14	FALSE	TRUE	FALSE
3	15	FALSE	TRUE	FALSE
4	25	TRUE	TRUE	TRUE
5	35	FALSE	TRUE	TRUE
6	49	TRUE	FALSE	FALSE
7	68	TRUE	TRUE	TRUE
8	71	TRUE	FALSE	FALSE
9	73	TRUE	FALSE	TRUE

To build this model, the objective is to minimize the mean squared error.

Now, we will build the model with a regression tree. To start with, if we want to have at least three samples at the training nodes, the first split of the tree might look like this:

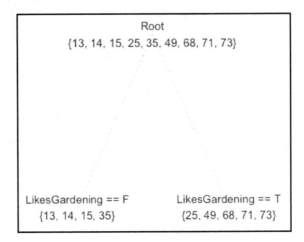

This seems to be fine, but it's not including information such as whether they play video games or browse the internet. What if we plan to have two samples at the training nodes?

Root
{13, 14, 15, 25, 35, 49, 68, 71, 73}

LikesGardening == F
{13, 14, 15, 35}

LikesGardening == T
{25, 49, 68, 71, 73}

SurfInternet == F
{14, 15}

SurfInternet== T
{13, 35}

PlaysVideoGames == F
{49, 71, 73}

PlaysVideoGames == T
{25, 68}

Through the preceding tree, we are able to get certain information from features, such as **SurfInternet** and **PlaysVideoGames**. Let's figure out how residuals/errors come along:

Person ID	Age	Prediction	Residual
1	13	19.25	-6.25
2	14	19.25	-5.25
3	15	19.25	-4.25
4	25	57.2	-32.2
5	35	19.25	15.75
6	49	57.2	-8.2
7	68	57.2	10.8
8	71	57.2	13.8
9	73	57.2	15.8

Now, we will work on the residuals of the first model:

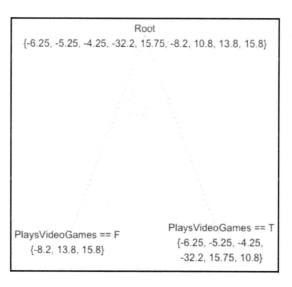

Once we have built the model on residuals, we have to combine the previous model with the current one, as shown in the following table:

Person ID	Age	Prediction	Residual	Prediction on residuals	Combined Prediction	Final Residuals
1	13	19.25	-6.25	-3.567	15.683	2.683
2	14	19.25	-5.25	-3.567	15.683	1.683
3	15	19.25	-4.25	-3.567	15.683	0.683
4	25	57.2	-32.2	-3.567	53.633	28.633
5	35	19.25	15.75	-3.567	15.683	-19.317
6	49	57.2	-8.2	7.133	64.333	15.333
7	68	57.2	10.8	-3.567	53.633	-14.367
8	71	57.2	13.8	7.133	64.333	-6.667
9	73	57.2	15.8	7.133	64.333	-8.667

We can see that the residuals have come down and that the model is getting better.

Let's try to formulate what we have done up until this point:

1. First, we built a model on the data $f_1(x) = y$.
2. The next thing we did was calculate the residuals and build the model on residuals:

$$h_1(x)=y- f_1(x)$$

3. The next step is to combine the model, that is, $f_2(x)= f_1(x) + h_1(x)$.

   Adding more models can correct the errors of the previous models. The preceding equation will turn out to be as follows:

$$f3(x)= f2(x) + h2(x)$$

The equation will finally look as follows:

$$f_m(x)= f_{m-1}(x) + h_{m-1}(x)$$

Alternatively, we can write the following:

$$h_m(x)= y- f_m(x)$$

4. Since our task is to minimize the squared error, f will be initialized with the mean of the training target values:

$$f_o(x) = min \sum_{i=1}^{n} L(y_i, \gamma) = min \sum_{i=1}^{n} L(\gamma - y_i)^2 = \frac{1}{n} \sum_{i=1}^{n} y_i$$

5. Then, we can find out f_{m+1}, just like before:

$$f_m(x) = f_{m-1}(x) + h_{m-1}(x)$$

Now, we can use gradient descent for our gradient boosting model. The objective function we want to minimize is L. Our starting point is $f_o(x)$. For iteration $m=1$, we compute the gradient of L with respect to $f_o(x)$. Then, we fit a weak learner to the gradient components. In the case of a regression tree, leaf nodes produce an **average gradient** among samples with similar features. For each leaf, we step in the direction of the average gradient. The result is f_1 and this can be repeated until we have f_m.

We modified our gradient boosting algorithm so that it works with any differentiable loss function. Let's clean up the preceding ideas and reformulate our gradient boosting model once again.

Parameters of gradient boosting

There are different parameters to consider before applying gradient boosting for the breast cancer use case:

- `Min_samples_split`: The minimum number of samples required in a node to be considered for splitting is termed `min_samples_split`.
- `Min_samples_leaf`: The minimum number of samples required at the terminal or leaf node is termed `min_samples_leaf`.
- `Max_depth`: This is the maximum number of nodes allowed from the root to the farthest leaf of a tree. Deeper trees can model more complex relationships, however, causing the model to overfit.
- `Max_leaf_nodes`: The maximum number of nodes at the leaves in a tree. Since binary trees are created, a depth of n would produce a maximum of 2^n leaves. Hence, either `max_depth` or `max_leaf_nodes` can be defined.

Now, we will apply gradient boosting for the breast cancer use case. Here, we are loading the libraries that are required to build the model:

```
from sklearn.ensemble import GradientBoostingClassifier
from sklearn.metrics import classification_report, confusion_matrix,
roc_curve, auc
```

We are now done with the various steps of data cleaning and exploration while performing random forest. Now, we will jump right into building the model.

Here, we will perform a grid search to find out the optimal parameters for the gradient boosting algorithm:

```
param_grid = {
  'n_estimators': [ 25, 50, 100, 150, 300, 500], # the more parameters, the
more computational expensive
  "max_depth": [ 5, 8, 15, 25],
  "max_features": ['auto', 'sqrt', 'log2']
  }
gbm =
GradientBoostingClassifier(learning_rate=0.1,random_state=10,subsample=0.8)
#performance estimation
#initiate the grid
grid = GridSearchCV(gbm, param_grid = param_grid, cv=10, scoring
='accuracy')
#fit your data before you can get the best parameter combination.
grid.fit(X,y)
grid.cv_results_
```

We get the following output:

```
{'mean_fit_time': array([ 0.03494983,  0.06627471,  0.12813728,  0.18599195,  0.24799919,
         0.33799727,  0.02897744,  0.06652975,  0.12413988,  0.1881336 ,
         0.23819361,  0.29800813,  0.03043046,  0.05891035,  0.11034069,
         0.18427889,  0.221032  ,  0.30923851,  0.06096241,  0.12604637,
         0.20514412,  0.2363739 ,  0.28559666,  0.33619659,  0.06156273,
         0.11972167,  0.2156975 ,  0.21138661,  0.26119628,  0.31739309,
         0.05794506,  0.12085245,  0.19251099,  0.20506291,  0.2632467 ,
         0.31910994,  0.06727653,  0.15261815,  0.25119522,  0.26912684,
         0.30465198,  0.38809872,  0.07574708,  0.15285401,  0.2602922 ,
         0.27513788,  0.29188688,  0.35694766,  0.06843309,  0.14909971,
         0.22379372,  0.23729031,  0.28556411,  0.34478147,  0.06652713,
         0.14558716,  0.23933291,  0.25528142,  0.29443026,  0.35715394,
         0.06782725,  0.1500011 ,  0.22931345,  0.24915528,  0.28485856,
         0.35234025,  0.06879389,  0.1524158 ,  0.23522427,  0.24537499,
         0.28084641,  0.34170115]),
 'mean_score_time': array([ 0.00045459,  0.00025072,  0.00040183,  0.00055137,  0.00049999,
         0.0014482 ,  0.0003505 ,  0.00030062,  0.00044746,  0.00094807,
```

Now, let's find out the optimal parameters:

```
#Let's find out the best scores, parameter and the estimator from the
gridsearchCV
print("GridSearhCV best model:\n ")
print('The best score: ', grid.best_score_)
print('The best parameter:', grid.best_params_)
print('The best model estimator:', grid.best_estimator_)
```

The output can be seen as follows:

```
GridSearhCV best model:

The best score:  0.952548330404
The best parameter: {'n_estimators': 150, 'max_depth': 5, 'max_features': 'sqrt'}
The best model estimator: GradientBoostingClassifier(criterion='friedman_mse', init=None,
            learning_rate=0.1, loss='deviance', max_depth=5,
            max_features='sqrt', max_leaf_nodes=None,
            min_impurity_decrease=0.0, min_impurity_split=None,
            min_samples_leaf=1, min_samples_split=2,
            min_weight_fraction_leaf=0.0, n_estimators=150,
            presort='auto', random_state=10, subsample=0.8, verbose=0,
            warm_start=False)
```

Now, we will build the model:

```
model2 = GradientBoostingClassifier(criterion='friedman_mse', init=None,
  learning_rate=0.1, loss='deviance', max_depth=5,
  max_features='sqrt', max_leaf_nodes=None,
  min_impurity_decrease=0.0, min_impurity_split=None,
  min_samples_leaf=1, min_samples_split=2,
  min_weight_fraction_leaf=0.0, n_estimators=150,
  presort='auto', random_state=10, subsample=0.8, verbose=0,
  warm_start=False)
model2.fit(X_train, y_train)

print("Performance Accuracy on the Testing data:",
  round(model2.score(X_test, y_test) *100))
```

The performance accuracy on the testing data is `96.0`:

```
#getting the predictions for X
y_pred2 = model2.predict(X_test)
print('Total Predictions {}'.format(len(y_pred2)))
```

The total number of predictions is `114`:

```
truth = pd.DataFrame(y_test, columns= ['Truth'])
predictions = pd.DataFrame(y_pred, columns= ['Predictions'])
frames = [truth, predictions]
_result = pd.concat(frames, axis=1)
print(_result.shape)
_result.head()
```

(114, 2)

	Truth	Predictions
0	1	1
1	0	0
2	0	0
3	0	0
4	0	0

Let's perform cross-validation:

```
cv_scores = []

scores2 = cross_val_score(gbm, X_train, y_train, cv=10, scoring='accuracy')
cv_scores.append(scores2.mean())
cv_scores.append(scores2.std())

#cross validation mean score
print("10 k-fold cross validation mean score: ", scores2.mean() *100)
```

The 10 k-fold cross-validation mean score is `94.9420289855`:

```
#printing classification accuracy score rounded
print("Classification accuracy: ", round(accuracy_score(y_test, y_pred2,
normalize=True) * 100))
```

The classification accuracy is `96.0`:

```
# Making the Confusion Matrix
cm = confusion_matrix(y_test, y_pred2)
plt.figure(figsize=(12,6))
ax = plt.axes()
ax.set_title('Confusion Matrix for both classes\n', size=21)
sns.heatmap(cm, cmap= 'plasma',annot=True, fmt='g') # cmap
plt.show()
```

By looking at the confusion matrix, we can see that this model is better than the previous one:

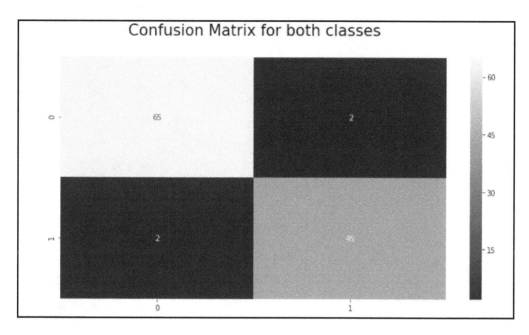

Summary

In this chapter, we studied ensemble learning and its different methods, namely bagging, boosting, and stacking. We even saw what is bootstrapping which is the root for ensemble learning methods such as bagging and boosting. We also learned about decision trees and its approach of divide and rule with example of people applying for loan. Then we covered tree splitting and the parameters to split a decision tree, moving on to the random forest algorithm. We worked on a case study of breast cancer using the concepts covered. We also discovered the difference between bagging and boosting and gradient boosting. We also discussed on parameters of gradient boosting to use it our example of breast cancer.

In the next chapter, we will learn about training neural networks.

4
Training Neural Networks

When you hear the term **neural networks**, it gives you a sense that its a form of biological terminology pertaining to brains. And I have to tell you candidly that it's a no brainer to guess that and, in fact, we are treading along the right path by doing so. We will see how it is connected to that.

Neural networks have brought in a revolution in the data science world. Until 2011, due to not having enough computation power, the people rooting for neural networks were not able to propagate it to the extent that they wanted. But, with the advent of cheaper computation solutions and more research in the area of neural networks, they have taken the data science and artificial world by storm. Neural networks are an algorithm that can be applied in both supervised and unsupervised learning. With deeper networks, they are able to provide solutions to unstructured data, such as images and text.

In this chapter, we will cover the following topics:

- Neural networks
- Network initialization
- Overfitting
- Dropouts
- Stochastic gradient descent
- Recurrent neural networks

Neural networks

Let me explain first of all what neurons are and how they are structured. The following labelled diagram shows a typical neuron:

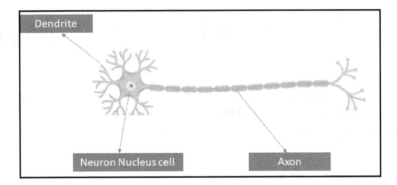

We define neuron as an electrically excitable cell that receives, processes, and transmits information through electric and chemical signals. A dendrite is a part of it that receives signals from other neurons. One thing that we need to pay attention to is that just a single neuron can't do anything and there are billions of neurons connected to each other, which enables the electro-chemical signal flow and, in turn, the information to flow through it. The information passes through an axon and a synapse, before being transmitted.

When it comes to a neural network, the structure doesn't change much. Let's have a look at it. In the middle, we have a neuron and this neuron gets signals from three other neurons, X1, X2, and X3. All three neurons are connected by arrows that act like a synapse. These neurons, X1, X2, and X3, are called **input layer neurons**. After passing through the neuron, we get the output value. It's interesting to see that the human brain gets an input signal through all the sensors such as eyes, ear, touch, and nose and that all the synapses let these electro-chemical signals go, and output comes as vision, voice, sense of touch, and smell. A similar process is followed in the case of a neural network.

How a neural network works

Let's say we have one set of input and output as follows:

Input (X)	Output (Y)
2	4
3	6
4	8

5	10
6	12

In the preceding table, input and output might look to have a linear relationship; however, that is not always the case. In addition, every time the model needs to initialize. Let's understand the meaning of initialization.

Model initialization

Going by the preceding table, the network is trying to find a relationship between input and output. For example, let's assume the relationship that comes through is the following:

$$Y = W. X$$

In the preceding equation, Y and X are known, and based on that W has to be found out. But, finding out the value of W in one iteration is rare. It has to be initialized first. Let's say W is initialized with the value of 3. And the equation turns out to be as follows:

$$Y = 3X$$

Input (X)	Actual Output (Y)
2	6
3	9
4	12
5	15
6	18

Now we have to assess the output and whether it is close to the desired output.

Loss function

So far, the model has been randomly initialized and with this we have been able to get an output. In order to assess if the actual output is close to the desired output, **loss function** is introduced. It enables the generalization of the model, and figures out how well the model is able to reach the desired output.

We can have a look at the new table, which has got actual output as well as desired output:

Input (X)	Actual Output (Y_a)	Desired Output (Y)
2	6	4
3	9	6
4	12	8
5	15	10
6	18	12

If we have to put the loss function down, it has to be as follows:

Loss Function = Desired Output-Actual Output

However, putting loss function this way would invite both kinds of values: negative and positive. In the case of a negative value for the loss function, it would mean that the network is overshooting as *Desired Output < Actual Output* and in the reverse scenario (*Desired Output > Actual Output*), the network would undershoot. In order to get rid of this kind of thing, we will go for having an absolute loss:

Input(X)	Actual Output (Y_a)	Desired Output (Y)	Loss=Y-Y_a	Absolute Loss
2	6	4	-2	2
3	9	6	-3	3
4	12	8	-4	4
5	15	10	-5	5
6	18	12	-6	6

Total Absolute Loss = 20

Having this approach of absolute loss will do no good to the model, as if we try to see the preceding table gingerly, the smallest loss is of 2 units and the maximum coming through is 6 units. One might get a feeling that the difference between maximum and minimum loss is not much (here, 4 units), but it can be huge for the model. Hence, a different route is taken altogether. Rather than taking absolute loss, we would go for the square of losses:

Input(X)	Actual output (Y_a)	Desired output (Y)	Loss=Y-Y_a	Square of Loss
2	6	4	-2	4
3	9	6	-3	9
4	12	8	-4	16
5	15	10	-5	25
6	18	12	-6	36

Now, the more the loss, the more the penalization. It can easily make things evident where we have more losses.

Optimization

We have to figure out a way to minimize the total loss function and it can be achieved by changing the weight. It can be done by using a crude method like modifying the parameter W over a range of -500 to 500 with a step 0.001. It will help us to find a point where the sum of squares of error becomes 0 or minimum.

But this approach will work out in this scenario because we don't have too many parameters here and computation won't be too challenging. However, when we have a number of parameters, the computation would take a hit.

Here, mathematics comes to our rescue in the form of differentiation (maxima and minima approach) in order to optimize the weights. The derivative of a function at a certain point gives the rate at which this function is changing its values. Here, we would take the derivative of loss function. What it will do is to assess an impact on total error by making a slight adjustment or change in weight. For example, if we try to make a change in weight which is δW, $W = W + \delta W$, we can find out how it is influencing loss function. Our end goal is to minimize the loss function through this.

We know that the minima will be arrived at $w=2$; hence, we are exploring different scenarios here:

- $w<2$ implies a positive loss function, negative derivative, meaning that an increase of weight will decrease the loss function
- $w>2$ implies positive loss function, but the derivative is positive, meaning that any more increase in the weight will increase the losses
- At $w=2$, loss=0 and the derivative is 0; minima is achieved:

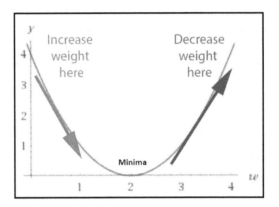

Computation in neural networks

Now, let's look at a simple and shallow network:

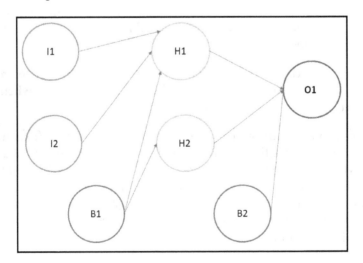

Where:

- **I1**: Input neuron 1
- **I2**: Input neuron 2
- **B1**: Bias 1
- **H1**: Neuron 1 in hidden layer
- **H2**: Neuron 2 in hidden layer
- **B2**: Bias 2
- **O1**: Neuron at output layer

The final value comes at the output neuron **O1**. **O1** gets the input from **H1**, **H2**, and **B2**. Since **B2** is a bias neuron, the activation for it is always 1. However, we need to calculate the activation for **H1** and **H2**. In order to calculate activation of **H1** and **H2**, activation for **I1**, **I2**, and **B1** would be required. It may look like **H1** and **H2** will have the same activation, since they have got the same input. But this is not the case here as weights of **H1** and **H2** are different. The connectors between two neurons represent weights.

Calculation of activation for H1

Let's have a look at the part of network involving just **H1**:

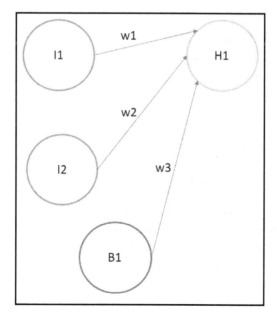

The hidden layer comes out as in the following formula:

$$H1 = A \sum_{i=1}^{n} x_i * w_i$$

Where:

- *A*: Activation function
- x_i: Input values
- w_i: Weight values

In our scenario, there are three input values, *n=3*:

- x_1 = *I1* = Input value 1 from first neuron
- x_2 = *I2*= Input value 2 from second neuron
- x_3= *B1* = 1
- *w1* = Weight from *I1* to *H1*
- *w2* = Weight from *I2* to *H1*
- *w3* = Weight from *B1* to *H1*

Backward propagation

In this step, we calculate the gradients of the loss function *f(y, y_hat)* with respect to *A, W,* and *b* called *dA, dW,* and *db*. Using these gradients, we update the values of the parameters from the last layer to the first.

Activation function

Activation function is typically introduced in the neural network in order to induce non-linearity. Without non-linearity, a neural network will have little chance to learn non-linearity. But you might question as to why why we need non-linearity in the first place. If we deem every relationship as a linear one, then the model won't be able to do justice to the actual relationship because having a linear relationship is a rarity. If applied linearity, the model's output won't be a generalized one.

Also, the main purpose of an activation function is to convert an input signal into an output. Let's say if we try to do away with an activation function, it will output a linear result. Linear function is a polynomial of the first degree and it's easy to solve but, again, it's not able to capture complex mapping between various features, which is very much required in the case of unstructured data.

Non-linear functions are those that have a degree more than one. Now we need a neural network model to learn and represent almost anything and any arbitrary complex function that maps inputs to outputs. Neural networks are also called **universal function approximators**. It means that they can compute and learn any function. Hence, activation function is an integral part of a neural network to make it learn complex functions.

Types of activation functions

1. **Sigmoid**: This type of activation function comes along as follows:

$$f(x) = 1/(1 + e^{-x})$$

   The value of this function ranges between *0* and *1*. It comes with a lot of issues:

   - Vanishing gradient
   - Its output is not zero-centered
   - It has slow convergence

2. **Hyperbolic tangent function (tanh)**: The mathematical formula to represent it is this:

$$f(x) = (1 - e^{-2x})/(1 + e^{-2x})$$

The value of this function ranges between -1 and +1. However, it still faces the vanishing gradient problem:

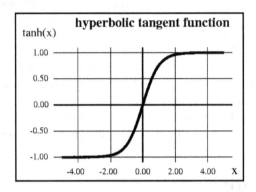

3. **Rectified Linear Units (ReLU)**: Mathematically, we represent it in the following manner:

$$f(x) = max(0, x)$$

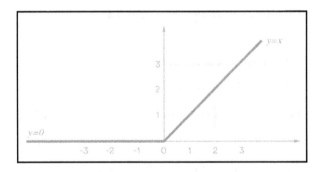

Going by the preceding diagram, ReLU is linear for all positive values, and zero for all negative values. This means that the following are true:

- It's cheap to compute as there is no complicated math. The model can therefore take less time to train.
- It converges faster. Linearity means that the slope doesn't hit the plateau when x gets large. It doesn't have the vanishing gradient problem suffered by other activation functions such as sigmoid or tanh.

Network initialization

So far, we have seen that there are a number of stages in a neural network model. We already know that weight exists between two nodes (of two different layers). The weights undergo a linear transformation and, along with values from input nodes, it crosses through nonlinear activation function in order to yield the value of the next layer. It gets repeated for the next and subsequent layers and later on, with the help of backpropagation, optimal values of weights are found out.

For a long time, weights used to get randomly initialized. Later on, it was realized that the way we initialize the network has a massive impact on the model. Let's see how we initialize the model:

- **Zero initialization**: In this kind of initialization, all the initial weights are set to zero. Due to this, all the neurons of all the layers perform the same calculation, which results in producing the same output. It will make the whole deep network futile. Predictions coming out of this network would be as good as random. Intuitively speaking, it doesn't perform symmetry breaking. Normally, during forward propagation of a neural network, each hidden node gets a signal and this signal is nothing but the following:

$$S = \sum_i^n w_i x_i$$

  If a network is initialized with zero, then all the hidden nodes will get zero signal because all the inputs will be multiplied by zero. Hence, no matter what the input value is, if all weights are the same, all units in the hidden layer will be the same too. This is called **symmetry**, and it has to be broken in order to have more information capturing a good model. Hence, the weights are supposed to be randomly initialized or with different values:

$$w = np.\,zeros((layersize[l], layersize[l-1]))$$

- **Random initialization**: This kind of initialization helps in symmetry breaking. In this method, the weights are randomly initialized very close to zero. Every neuron doesn't perform the same computation as the weight is not equal to zero:

$$w = np.\,random.\,randn(layersize[l], layersize[l-1]) * 0.01$$

- **He-et-al initialization**: This initialization depends on the size of the previous layer. It helps in attaining a global minimum of the cost function. The weights are random but differ in range depending on the size of the previous layer of neurons:

$$w = np.\,random.\,randn(layersize[l], layersize[l-1]) * np.\,sqrt(2/layersize[l-1])$$

Backpropagation

Backpropagation takes place once feed forward is completed. It stands for **backward propagation of errors**. In the case of neural networks, this step begins to compute the gradient of error function (loss function) with respect to the weights. One can wonder why the term **back** is associated with it. It's due to gradient computation that starts backwards through the network. In this, the gradient of the final layer of weights gets calculated first and the the weights of the first layer are calculated last.

Backpropagation needs three elements:

- **Dataset**: A dataset that consists of pairs of input-output $(\vec{x_i}, \vec{y_i})$ where $\vec{x_i}$ is the input and $\vec{y_i}$ is the output that we are expecting. Hence, a set of such input-outputs of size N is taken and denoted as $X = [(\vec{x_1}, \vec{y_1}), \ldots\ldots, (\vec{x_N}, \vec{y_N})]$.
- **Feed-forward network**: In this, the parameters are denoted as θ. The parameters, w_{ij}^k, the weight between node j in layer l_k and node i in layer l_{k-1}, and the b_i^k bias for node i in layer l_{k-1}. There are no connections between nodes in the same layer and layers are fully connected.
- **Loss function**: $L(X,\theta)$.

Training a neural network with gradient descent requires the calculation of the gradient of the loss/error function $E(X,\theta)$ with respect to the weights w_{ij}^k and biases b_i^k. Then, according to the learning rate α, each iteration of gradient descent updates the weights and biases collectively, denoted according to the following:

$$\theta^{t+1} = \theta^t - \alpha(\delta L(X, \theta^t)/\delta\theta)$$

Here θ denotes the parameters of the neural network at iteration in gradient descent.

Overfitting

We have already discussed overfitting in detail. However, let's have a recap of what we learned and what overfitting is in a neural network scenario.

By now, we are cognizant of the fact that, when a large number of parameters (in deep learning) are available at our disposal to map and explain an event, more often than not, the model built using these parameters will tend to have a good fit and try to showcase that it has the ability to describe the event properly. However, the real test of any model is always on unseen data, and we were able to assess how the model fares on such unseen data points. We expect our model to have an attribute of generalization and it will enable the model to score on test data (unseen) in alignment with the trained one. But, a number of times our model fails to generalize when it comes to the unseen data, as the model has not learned the insights and causal relationship of the event. In this scenario, one might be able to see the huge gulf of variance in training accuracy and test accuracy and, needless to say, it is not what we are seeking out of the model. This phenomenon is called **overfitting**.

In deep learning, there are millions of parameters you may encounter and in all likelihood, you might fall into the trap of overfitting. As we had defined overfitting in the first chapter, it happens when a model learns the detail and noise in the training data to the extent that it negatively impacts the performance of the model on new data.

Prevention of overfitting in NNs

As we already discussed in the earlier chapters, overfitting is a major issue that needs to be considered while building models as our work doesn't get over only at training phase. The litmus test for any model takes place on unseen data. Let's explore the techniques of handling overfitting issues in neural networks.

Vanishing gradient

Neural networks have been a revelation in extracting complex features out of the data. Be it images or texts, they are able to find the combinations that result in better predictions. The deeper the network, the higher the chances of picking those complex features. If we keep on adding more hidden layers, the learning speed of the added hidden layers get faster.

However, when we get down to backpropagation, which is moving backwards in the network to find out gradients of the loss with respect to weights, the gradient tends to get smaller and smaller as we head towards the first layer. It that initial layers of the deep network become slower learners and later layers tend to learn faster. This is called the **vanishing gradient problem**.

Initial layers in the network are important because they are responsible to *learn and detect the simple patterns* and are actually the **building blocks** of our network. Obviously, if they give improper and **inaccurate** results, then how can we expect the next layers and the complete network to perform effectively and produce accurate results? The following diagram shows the figure of a ball that rolls on a steeper slope:

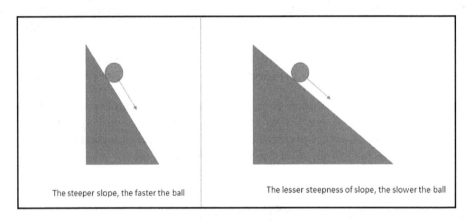

The steeper slope, the faster the ball   The lesser steepness of slope, the slower the ball

Just to make it a little simpler for us all, let's say that there are two slopes: one being steeper and the other being less steep. Both slopes have got balls rolling down them and it is a no brainer that the ball will roll down the steeper slope faster than the one that is not as steep. Similar to that, if the gradient is large, the learning and training gets faster; otherwise, training gets too slow if the gradient is less steep.

From backpropagation intuition, we are aware of the fact that the optimization algorithms such as gradient descent slowly seeko attain the local optima by regulating weights such that the cost function's output is decreased. The gradient descent algorithm updates the weights by the negative of the gradient multiplied by the learning rate (α) (which is small):

$$repeat\ until\ \frac{\partial J}{\partial W^{layer}_{ij}} \to 0:$$

$$\{\ \ W^{layer}_{ij} := W^{layer}_{ij} - \alpha \frac{\partial J}{\partial W^{layer}_{ij}}$$

It says that we have to repeat until it attains convergence. However, there are two scenarios here. The first is that, if there are fewer iterations, then the accuracy of the result will take a hit; the second is that more iterations result in training taking too much time. This happens because weight does not change enough at each iteration as the gradient is small (and we know α is already very small). Hence, weight does not move to the lowest point in the assigned iterations.

Let's talk about that activation function, which might have an impact on the vanishing gradient problem. Here, we talk about the sigmoid function, which is typically used as an activation function:

$$S(x) = \frac{1}{1 + e^{-x}}$$

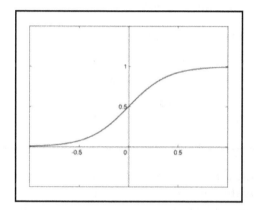

It translates all input values into a range of values between *(0,1)*. If we have to find out the derivative of the sigmoid function then:

$$\frac{1}{1 + e^{-x}}[1 - \frac{1}{1 + e^{-x}}]$$

Let's plot it now:

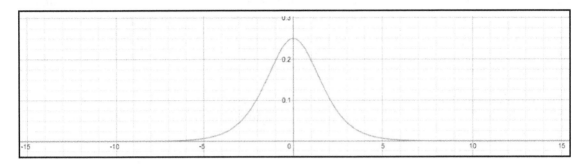

It is quite evident that the derivative has got the maximum value as 0.25. Hence, the range of values under which it would lie is *(0,1/4)*.

A typical neural network looks like the following diagram:

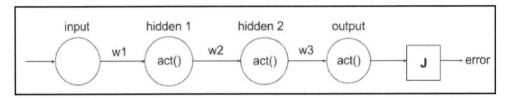

Once the weight parameters are initialized, the input gets multiplied by weights and gets passed on through an activation function and, finally, we get a cost function (**J**). Subsequently, backpropagation takes place to modify the weights through gradient descent in order to minimize **J**.

In order to calculate the derivative with respect to first weight, we are using the chain rule. It will turn out to be like the following:

$$\frac{\partial error}{\partial w1} = \frac{\partial error}{\partial output} * \frac{\partial output}{\partial hidden2} * \frac{\partial hidden2}{\partial hidden1} * \frac{\partial hidden1}{\partial w1}$$

If we just try to study the derivatives in the middle of the preceding expression, we get the following:

$$\frac{\partial output}{\partial hidden2} * \frac{\partial hidden2}{\partial hidden1}$$

Part 1—from the output to hidden2.

Since the output is the activation of the 2nd hidden unit, the expression turns out to be like the following:

$$z_1 = hidden2 * w3$$

$$\frac{\partial output}{\partial hidden2} = \frac{\partial Sigmoid(z_1)}{\partial z_1} w3$$

Similarly for part 2, from hidden 2 to hidden 1, the expression turns out to be like the following:

$$z_2 = hidden2 * w3$$

$$\frac{\partial output}{\partial hidden2} = \frac{\partial Sigmoid(z_1)}{\partial z_1} w3$$

On putting everything together, we get the following:

$$\frac{\partial output}{\partial hidden2} \frac{\partial hidden2}{\partial hidden1} = \frac{\partial Sigmoid(z_1)}{\partial z_1} w3 * \frac{\partial Sigmoid(z_2)}{\partial z_2} w2$$

We know that the maximum value of the derivative of the sigmoid function is 1/4 and the weights can typically take the values between -1 and 1 if weights have been initialized with standard deviation 1 and mean 0. It will lead to the whole expression being smaller. If there is a deep network to be trained, then this expression will keep on getting even smaller and, as a result of that, the training time will become slow-paced.

Overcoming vanishing gradient

From the preceding explanation of vanishing gradient, it comes out that the root cause of this problem is the sigmoid function being picked as an activation function. The similar problem has been detected when *tanh* is chosen as an activation function.

In order to counter such a scenario, the ReLU function comes to the rescue:

$$ReLU(x) = max(0,x)$$

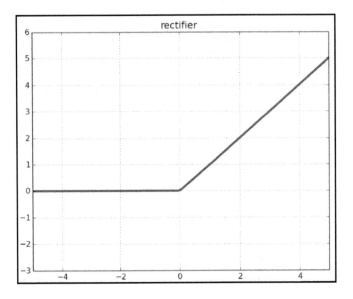

If the input is negative or less than zero, the function outputs as zero. In the second scenario, if the input is greater than zero, then the output will be equal to input.

Let's take the derivative of this function and see what happens:

Case 1: $x<0$:

$$\frac{\partial 0}{\partial x} = 0$$

Case 2: $x>0$:

$$\frac{\partial x}{\partial x} = 1$$

If we have to plot it, we get the following:

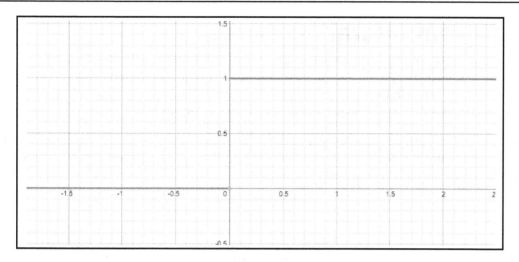

So, the derivative of ReLU is either 0 or 1. The plot comes out to be like a step function. Now, we can see that we won't face the vanishing gradient problem as the value of the derivative doesn't lie between 0 and 1.

However, it's still not true. We might still face this problem when the input value happens to be negative and we know that derivative turns out to be zero in this scenario. Typically, it doesn't happen that the weighted sum ends up negative, and we can indeed initialize weights to be only positive and/or normalize input between 0 and 1, if we are concerned about the chance of an issue like this occurring.

There is still a workaround for this kind of scenario. We have got another function called **Leaky ReLU**, which appears as the following formula:

$$RELU\ (x) = max\ (\varepsilon x,\ x)$$

Here, the value of ε is typically 0.2–0.3. We could plot it, as follows:

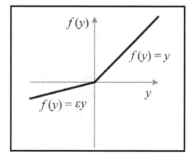

Recurrent neural networks

Our thought process always has a sequence. We always understand things in an order. For example, if we watch a movie, we understand the next sequence by connecting it with the previous one. We retain the memory of the last sequence and get an understanding of the whole movie. We don't always go back to the first sequence in order to get it.

Can a neural network act like this? Traditional ones typically cannot operate in this manner and that is a major shortcoming. This is where recurrent neural networks make a difference. It comes with a loop that allows information to flow:

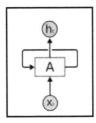

Here, a neural network takes an input as X_t and throws an output in the form of h_t. A recurrent neural network is made up of multiple copies of the same network that pass on the message to the successor.

If we were to go and unroll the preceding network, it would look like the following:

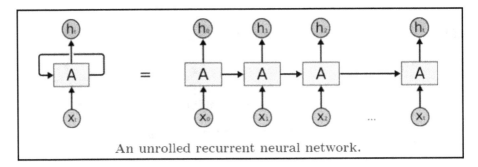

An unrolled recurrent neural network.

This chain-like nature reveals that recurrent neural networks are intimately related to sequences and lists. They are the natural architecture of neural networks to use for such data. Since the network has got an internal memory, RNNs are able to remember the input they received which, in turn, enables them to come up with accurate and precise results and predictions.

So far, we have been talking about sequential data. But we need to have a proper understanding of this term, sequential data. This form of data is an order data where there exists a relationship between data at time *t* and the data at time *t-1*. An example of that kind of data can be financial data, time-series data, video, and so on. RNNs allow us to operate over sequences of vectors. For example, look at the following image:

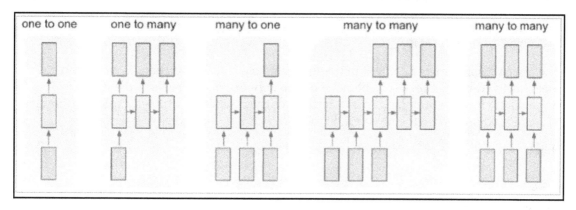

Each rectangle is represented as a vector, and arrows stand for functions. Input vectors are in red, output vectors are in blue, and green vectors hold the RNN's state:

- Vanilla mode of processing can be done without including RNN, from a fixed-sized input to output
- Sequencing the output in a proper format
- Sequencing the input
- Sequencing the input and output (for example, machine translation: an RNN which reads a sentence in English and then outputs a sentence in some other language, like German).
- Syncing the sequenced input and output (for example, video classification where label each frame of the video)

Limitations of RNNs

Recurrent neural networks function just right when it comes to short-term dependencies. What this means is that, if there is just a single statement to be dealt with, a neural network operates fine. For example, if there is a sentence, *India's capital is __*, in this scenario we would invariably get the correct result as this is a universal statement and there is nothing like a context here. This statement has no dependency on the previous sentence and here, there is no previous sentence either.

Hence, the prediction would be *India's capital is New Delhi.*

Afterall, the vanilla RNN's does not understand the context behind an input. We will understand with an example:

Staying in India meant that I gravitated towards cricket. But, after 10 years, I moved to the US for work.

The popular game in India is ___.

One can see that there is a context in the first sentence and then it changes in the second one. However, prediction has to be done by the network on the basis of the first one. It is highly likely that the popular game in India is cricket, but context plays a role here and it has to be understood by the network. Simple RNN is a failure here.

That is where **Long Short-Term Memory (LSTM)** comes into the picture.

Use case

Let's work on a use case that will help us in understanding the network.

We will work on a time series problem. We have got the Google stock price dataset. One being training and the other being test. We will now look at a use case to forecast the stock prices of Google:

1. Let's start by importing the libraries:

```
import numpy as np
import matplotlib.pyplot as plt
import pandas as pd
```

2. Next, import the training set:

```
dataset_train = pd.read_csv('Google_Stock_Price_Train.csv')
training_set = dataset_train.iloc[:, 1:2].values
```

3. Feature scaling is done in the next step:

```
from sklearn.preprocessing import MinMaxScaler
sc = MinMaxScaler(feature_range = (0, 1))
training_set_scaled = sc.fit_transform(training_set)
```

4. Let's create a data structure with 60 time steps and 1 output:

```
X_train = []
y_train = []
for i in range(60, 1258):
  X_train.append(training_set_scaled[i-60:i, 0])
  y_train.append(training_set_scaled[i, 0])
X_train, y_train = np.array(X_train), np.array(y_train)
```

5. Next, reshape the data:

```
X_train = np.reshape(X_train, (X_train.shape[0], X_train.shape[1],
1))
```

6. Now, import the Keras libraries and packages:

```
from keras.models import Sequential
from keras.layers import Dense
from keras.layers import LSTM
from keras.layers import Dropout
```

7. We will initialize the RNN with the regressor function:

```
regressor = Sequential()
```

8. Now, add the first LSTM layer and some dropout regularization:

```
regressor.add(LSTM(units = 50, return_sequences = True, input_shape
= (X_train.shape[1], 1)))
regressor.add(Dropout(0.2))
```

9. Now, add the second LSTM layer and some dropout regularization:

```
regressor.add(LSTM(units = 50, return_sequences = True))
regressor.add(Dropout(0.2))
```

10. Add the third LSTM layer and some dropout regularization:

```
regressor.add(LSTM(units = 50, return_sequences = True))
regressor.add(Dropout(0.2))
```

11. Add a fourth LSTM layer and some dropout regularization:

```
regressor.add(LSTM(units = 50))
regressor.add(Dropout(0.2))
```

12. Finally, add the output layer:

```
regressor.add(Dense(units = 1))
```

13. Next, we will compile the RNN:

```
regressor.compile(optimizer = 'adam', loss = 'mean_squared_error')
```

14. We will fit the RNN to the training set:

```
regressor.fit(X_train, y_train, epochs = 100, batch_size = 32)
```

15. We get the real stock price of 2017 as shown:

```
dataset_test = pd.read_csv('Google_Stock_Price_Test.csv')
real_stock_price = dataset_test.iloc[:, 1:2].values
```

16. We get the predicted stock price of 2017 as shown:

```
dataset_total = pd.concat((dataset_train['Open'],
dataset_test['Open']), axis = 0)
inputs = dataset_total[len(dataset_total) - len(dataset_test) -
60:].values
inputs = inputs.reshape(-1,1)
inputs = sc.transform(inputs)
X_test = []
for i in range(60, 80):
 X_test.append(inputs[i-60:i, 0])
X_test = np.array(X_test)
X_test = np.reshape(X_test, (X_test.shape[0], X_test.shape[1], 1))
predicted_stock_price = regressor.predict(X_test)
predicted_stock_price = sc.inverse_transform(predicted_stock_price)
```

17. Finally, we will visualize the results as shown:

```
plt.plot(real_stock_price, color = 'red', label = 'Real Google
Stock Price')
plt.plot(predicted_stock_price, color = 'blue', label = 'Predicted
Google Stock Price')
plt.title('Google Stock Price Prediction')
plt.xlabel('Time')
plt.ylabel('Google Stock Price')
plt.legend()
plt.show()
```

Summary

In this chapter, we have learned about neural networks along with their working, and were introduced to backward propagation and the activation function. We studied network initialization and how can we initialize the different types of models. We learned about overfitting and dropouts in the neural network scenario.

We introduced the concept of RNN, and studied a use case regarding the Google stock price dataset. In the next chapter, we will study time series analysis.

Time Series Analysis 5

In this chapter, we will take a look at time series analysis and learn several ways of observing and capturing an event at different points in time. We will introduce the concept of white noise and learn about its detection in a series.

We will take the time series data and compute the differences between the consecutive observations, which will lead to the formation of a new series. These concepts will help us deep dive into time series analysis and help us build a deeper understanding around it.

In this chapter, we will cover the following topics:

- Introduction to time series analysis
- White noise
- Random walk
- Autoregression
- Autocorrelation
- Stationarity
- Differencing
- AR model
- Moving average model
- Autoregressive integrated moving average
- Optimization of parameters
- Anomaly detection

Introduction to time series analysis

There are several occasions when we might try to observe and capture an event at different points in time. Often, we would end up drawing a correlation or association between adjacent observations that cannot be handled by an approach that deals with data that is independent and identically distributed. The approach that takes all of this into consideration in a mathematical and statistical manner is called **time series analysis**.

Time series analysis has been used in a number of fields, such as the automotive, banking, and retail industries, product development, and so on. There is no boundary for its use, and so analysts and data scientists are exploring this area to the hilt in order to derive the maximum benefit for organizations.

In this section, we will go through a few of the concepts around time series analysis that will lay the foundation for a deeper understanding in the future. Once we have established this foundation, we will jump into modeling.

White noise

A simple series with a collection of uncorrelated random variables with a mean of zero and a standard deviation of σ^2 is called **white noise**. In this, variables are independent and identically distributed. All values have the same variance of σ^2. In this case, the series is drawn from Gaussian distribution, and is called **Gaussian white noise**.

When the series turns out to be white noise, it implies that the nature of the series is totally random and there is no association within the series. As a result, the model can't be developed, and prediction is not possible in this scenario.

However, when we typically build a time series model with a nonwhite noise series, we try to attain a white noise phenomenon within the residuals or errors. In simple terms, whenever we try to build a model, the motive is to extract the maximum amount of information from the series so that no more information exists in the variable. Once we build a model, noise will always be part of it. The equation is as follows:

$$Y_t = X_t + Error$$

So the error series should be totally random in nature, which implies that it is white noise. If we have got these errors as white noise, then we can go ahead and say that we have extracted all the information possible from the series.

Detection of white noise in a series

We can detect white noise by using the following tools:

- **Line plot**: Once we have a line plot, we can have an idea of whether the series has a constant mean and variance
- **Autocorrelation plot**: Having a correlation plot can give us an inkling as to whether there is an association among lagged variables
- **Summary**: Checking the mean and variance of the series against the mean and variance of meaningful contiguous blocks of values in the series

Let's do this in Python:

1. First, we will import all the required libraries as follows:

```
from random import gauss
from random import seed
from pandas import Series
from pandas.tools.plotting import autocorrelation_plot
from matplotlib import pyplot
```

2. Next, we will set up the white noise series for us to analyze, as follows:

```
seed(1000)
#creating white noise series
series = [gauss(0.0, 1.0) for i in range(500)]
series = Series(series)
```

3. Let's take the summary or statistic of it using the following code:

```
print(series.describe())
```

We will get the following output:

```
count    500.000000
mean       0.026039
std        1.050492
min       -3.102231
25%       -0.622977
50%        0.047703
75%        0.694352
max        3.192393
dtype: float64
```

Here, we can see that the mean is approaching zero and the standard deviation is close to 1.

4. Let's make a line plot now to check out the trend, using the following code:

```
series.plot()
pyplot.show()
```

We will get the following output:

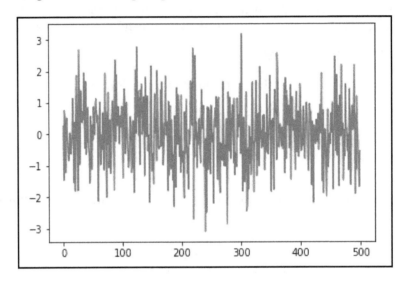

The line plot looks totally random, and no trend can be observed here.

5. It's time to make an autocorrelation plot. Let's set one up using the following code:

```
autocorrelation_plot(series)
pyplot.show()
```

We will get the following output:

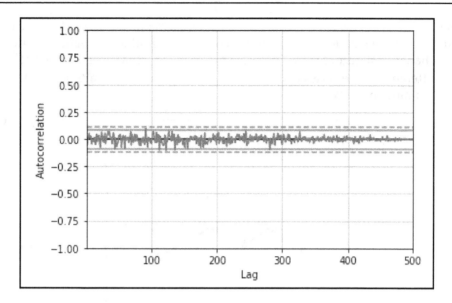

Even in an **autocorrelation** function plot, the correlation breaches the band of our confidence level. This tells us that it is a white noise series.

Random walk

Random walk is a time series model where the current observation is equal to the previous observations with a random modification. It can be described in the following manner:

$$x_t = x_{t-1} + w_t$$

In the preceding formula, w_t is a white noise series.

Sometimes, we might come across a series that reflects irregular growth. In these cases, the strategy to predict the next level won't be the correct one. Rather, it might be better to try to predict the change that occurs from one period to the next—that is, it may be better to look at the first difference of the series in order to find out a significant pattern. The following figure shows a random walk pattern:

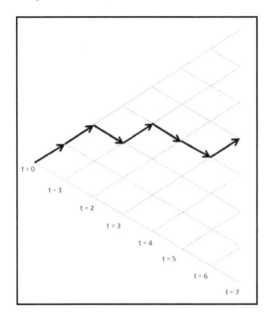

In each time period, going from left to right, the value of the variable takes an independent random step up or down, which is called a **random walk**.

It can also be described in the following way:

$$y(t) = b_0 + b_1 {}^* x_{t-1} + w_t$$

The following list explains the preceding formula:

- $y(t)$: Next value in the series
- b_0: Coefficient, which, if set to a number other than zero, means that the random walk comes along with a drift
- b_1: Coefficient, which is set to 1
- w_t: White noise

Autoregression

An autoregression is a time series model that typically uses the previous values of the same series as an explanatory factor for the regression in order to predict the next value. Let's say that we have measured and kept track of a metric over time, called y_t, which is measured at time t when this value is regressed on previous values from that same time series. For example, y_t on y_{t-1}:

$$y_t = \beta_0 + \beta_1 y_{t-1} + \epsilon_t$$

As shown in the preceding equation, the previous value y_{t-1} has become the predictor here and y_t is the response value that is to be predicted. Also, ε_t is normally distributed with a mean of zero and variance of 1. The order of the autoregression model is defined by the number of previous values that are being used by the model to determine the next value. Therefore, the preceding equation is a first-order autoregression, or **AR(1)**. If we have to generalize it, a kth order autoregression, written as **AR(k)**, is a multiple linear regression in which the value of the series at any time (t) is a (linear) function of the values at times $t-1, t-2, ..., t-k$.

The following list shows what the following values means for an AR(1) model:

- When $\beta_1 = 0$, yt, it is equivalent to white noise
- When $\beta_1 = 1$ and $\beta_0 = 0$, y_t, it is equivalent to a random walk
- When $\beta_1 = 1$ and $\beta_0 \neq 0$, y_t, it is equivalent to a random walk with drift
- When $\beta_1 < 1$, y_t, it tends to oscillate between positive and negative values

Autocorrelation

Autocorrelation is a measure of the correlation between the lagged values of a time series. For example, r_1 is the autocorrelation between y_t and y_{t-1}; similarly, r_2 is the autocorrelation between y_t and y_{t-2}. This can be summarized in the following formula:

$$r_k = \frac{\sum_{t=k+1}^{T}(y_t - \bar{y})(y_{t-k} - \bar{y})}{\sum_{t=1}^{T}(y_t - \bar{y})^2}$$

In the preceding formula, T is the length of the time series.

For example, say that we have the correlation coefficients, as shown in the following diagram:

r_1	r_2	r_3	r_4	r_5	r_6	r_7	r_8	r_9
-0.102	-0.657	-0.060	0.869	-0.089	-0.635	-0.054	0.832	-0.108

To plot it, we get the following:

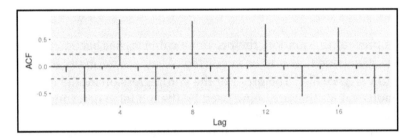

The following are some observations from this autocorrelation function plot:

- r_4 is higher than other lags, which is mostly because of a seasonal pattern
- The blue lines are the indicators of whether correlations are significantly different from zero
- Autocorrelation at lag 0 is always 1

Stationarity

A common assumption for a few of the time series models is that data has to be stationary. Let's look at what stationarity means regarding time series.

A stationary process is one for which the mean, variance, and autocorrelation structure doesn't change over time. What this means is that the data doesn't have a trend (increasing or decreasing).

We can describe this by using the following formulas:

$$E(x_t) = \mu, \text{ for all } t$$

$$E(x_t^2) = \sigma^2, \text{ for all } t$$

$$cov(x_t, x_k) = cov(x_{t+s}, x_{k+s}), \text{ for all } t, k, \text{ and } s$$

Detection of stationarity

There are multiple methods that can help us in figuring out whether the data is stationary, listed as follows:

- **Plotting the data**: Having a plot of the data with respect to the time variable can help us to see whether it has got a trend. We know from the definition of stationarity that a trend in the data means that there is no constant mean and variance. Let's do this in Python. For this example, we are using international airline passenger data.

  First, let's load all the required libraries, as follows:

  ```
  from pandas import Series
  from matplotlib import pyplot
  %matplotlib inline

  data = Series.from_csv('AirPassengers.csv', header=0)
    series.plot()
    pyplot.show()
  ```

  We will get the following output:

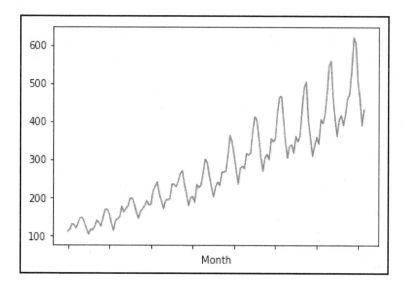

It is quite clear from the plot that there is an increasing trend here and that it would vindicate our hypothesis that it is a non-stationary series.

- **Dividing the data set and computing the summary**: The next method would be to divide the data series into two parts and compute the mean and variance. By doing this, we will be able to figure out whether the mean and variance are constant. Let's do this by using the following code:

```
X = data.values
partition =int(len(X) / 2)
X1, X2 = X[0:partition], X[partition:]
mean1, mean2 =np.nanmean(X1),np.nanmean(X2)
var1, var2 = np.nanvar(X1), np.nanvar(X2)
print('mean1=%f, mean2=%f' % (mean1, mean2))
print('variance1=%f, variance2=%f' % (var1, var2))
```

The output is as follows:

```
mean1=182.902778, mean2=377.694444 variance1=2244.087770,
variance2=7367.962191
```

We can see that the mean and variance of series 1 and series 2 are not equal, and so we can conclude that the series is not stationary.

- **Augmented Dickey-Fuller test**: The augmented Dickey-Fuller test is a statistical test that tends to give an indication with a certain level of confidence as to whether the series is stationary. A statistical test takes the data and tests our hypothesis about the data using its assumption and process. Eventually, it yields the result with a certain degree of confidence, which helps us in taking the decision.

This test is nothing but the unit root test, which tries to find out whether the time series is influenced by the trend. It makes use of the **autoregressive (AR)** model and optimizes the information criterion at different lag values.

Here, the null hypothesis is as follows:

- H_o: The time series has got the unit root, which implies that the series is nonstationary

The alternate hypothesis is as follows:

- H_1: The time series doesn't have a unit root and, as such, it is stationary

As we know from the rules of hypothesis testing, if we have chosen a significance level of 5% for the test, then the result would be interpreted as follows:

If *p-value* >0.05 =>, then we fail to reject the null hypothesis. That is, the series is nonstationary.

If *p-value* <0.05 =>, then the null hypothesis is rejected which means that the series is stationary.

Let's perform this in Python:

1. First, we will load the libraries, as follows:

```
import pandas as pd
import numpy as np
import matplotlib.pylab as plt
%matplotlib inline
from matplotlib.pylab import rcParams
rcParams['figure.figsize'] = 25, 6
```

2. Next, we load the data and time plot as follows:

```
data = pd.read_csv('AirPassengers.csv')
print(data.head())
print('\n Data Types:')
print(data.dtypes)
```

The output can be seen in the following diagram:

```
        Month  #Passengers
0     1949-01          112
1     1949-02          118
2     1949-03          132
3     1949-04          129
4     1949-05          121

 Data Types:
Month              object
#Passengers         int64
dtype: object
```

3. We then parse the data as follows:

```
dateparse = lambda dates: pd.datetime.strptime(dates, '%Y-%m')
data = pd.read_csv('./data/AirPassengers.csv',
parse_dates=['Month'], index_col='Month',date_parser=dateparse)
print(data.head())
```

We then get the following output:

```
                    #Passengers
Month
1949-01-01              112
1949-02-01              118
1949-03-01              132
1949-04-01              129
1949-05-01              121
```

```
ts= data["#Passengers"]
ts.head()
```

From this, we get the following output:

```
Month
1949-01-01     112
1949-02-01     118
1949-03-01     132
1949-04-01     129
1949-05-01     121
Name: #Passengers, dtype: int64
```

4. Then we plot the graph, as follows:

```
plt.plot(ts)
```

The output can be seen as follows:

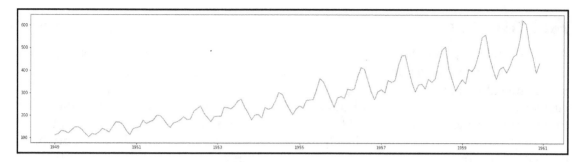

5. Let's create a function to perform a stationarity test using the following code:

```
from statsmodels.tsa.stattools import adfuller
def stationarity_test(timeseries):
 dftest = adfuller(timeseries, autolag='AIC')
 dfoutput = pd.Series(dftest[0:4], index=['Test Statistic','p-
value','#Lags Used','Number of Observations Used'])
 for key,value in dftest[4].items():
             dfoutput['Critical Value (%s)'%key] = value
 print(dfoutput)

stationarity_test(ts)
```

The output can be seen as follows:

```
Test Statistic                      0.815369
p-value                             0.991880
#Lags Used                         13.000000
Number of Observations Used       130.000000
Critical Value (10%)               -2.578770
Critical Value (5%)                -2.884042
Critical Value (1%)                -3.481682
dtype: float64
```

Since *p-value* > *0.05* and the *t*-statistic is greater than all the critical values (1%,5%,10%), *tt* implies that the series is nonstationary as we failed to reject the null hypothesis.

So what can be done if the data is nonstationary? We use differencing to make the nonstationary data into stationary data.

AR model

An AR model is a part of the stochastic process, wherein specific lagged values of y_t are used as predictor variables and regressed on y_t in order to estimate its values. Lagged values are values of the series of the previous period that tend to have an impact on the current value of the series. Let's look at an example. Say we have to assess and predict tomorrow's weather. We would start by thinking of what today's weather is and what yesterday's weather was, as this will help us in predicting whether it will be rainy, bright and sunny, or cloudy. Subconsciously, we are also cognizant of the fact that the weather of the previous day might have an association with today's weather. This is what we call an **AR model**.

This has a degree of uncertainty that results in less accuracy in the prediction of future values. The formula is the same as the formula for a series with p lag, as follows:

$$y_t = \alpha_1 y_{t-1} + \ldots + \alpha_p y_{t-p} + \omega_t$$

In the previous equation, ω is the white noise term and α is the coefficient, which can't be zero. The aggregated equation appears as follows:

$$y_t = \sum_{i=1}^{p} \alpha_i y_{t-i} + \omega_t$$

Occasionally, we might talk about the order of a model. For example, we might describe an AR model as being of order p. In this case, the p represents the number of lagged variables used within the model. For example, an AR(2) model or second-order AR model looks like the following:

$$y_t = \alpha_1 y_{t-1} + \alpha_2 y_{t-2} + \omega_t$$

Moving average model

A **moving average model** (**MA**) is a linear combination of historic white noise error terms. Let's have a look at the equation of the model:

$$y_t = \omega_t + \beta_1 \omega_{t-1} + \ldots + \beta_p \omega_{t-p}$$

$$=> y_t = \omega_t + \sum_{i=1}^{p} \beta_i \omega_{t-i}$$

Here, ω is the white noise with $E(\omega_t)=0$ and variance $= \sigma^2$.

In order to find out the order of the AR model, we need to plot a partial autocorrelation function plot, and then look for the lag where the upper confidence level has been crossed for the first time.

Autoregressive integrated moving average

An **autoregressive integrated moving average** (**ARIMA**) model is a combination of the following elements:

- **Autoregressive operator**: We have already learned what this means; just to reiterate, it is the lags of the stationarized series. It is denoted by p, which is nothing but the number of autoregressive terms. The PACF plot yields this component.
- **Integration operator**: A series that needs to be differenced to be made stationary is said to be an integrated version of a stationary series. It is denoted by d, which is the amount of differencing that is needed to transform the nonstationary time series into a stationary one. This is done by subtracting the observation from the current period from the previous one. If this has been done only once to the series, it is called **first differenced**. This process eliminates the trend out of the series that is growing at a constant rate. In this case, the series is growing at an increasing rate, and the differenced series needs another round of differencing, which is called **second differencing**.
- **Moving average operator**: The lags of the forecasted errors, which is denoted by q. It is the number of lagged forecast errors in the equation. The ACF plot would yield this component.

The ARIMA model can only be applied on stationary series. Therefore, before applying it, the stationarity condition has to be checked in the series. The ADF test can be performed to establish this.

The equation of ARIMA turns looks like the following:

$$y_t = \alpha_1 y_{t-1} + \ldots + \alpha_p y_{t-p} - (\beta_1 \omega_{t-1} + \ldots + \beta_p \omega_{t-p}) + \omega_t$$

The first part of the equation (before the - sign) is the autoregressive section, and the second part (after the - sign)is the MA section.

We can go ahead and add a seasonal component in ARIMA as well, which would be ARIMA $(p,d,q)(p,d,q)_s$. While adding it, we need to perform seasonal differencing, which means subtracting the current observation from the seasonal lag.

Let's plot ACF and PACF in order to find out the p and q parameters.

Here, we take the number of lags as 20 and use the `statsmodel.tsa.stattools` library to import the `acf` and `pacf` functions, as follows:

```
from statsmodels.tsa.stattools import acf,pacf
lag_acf= acf(ts_log_dif,nlags=20)
lag_pacf = pacf(ts_log_dif, nlags=20,method="ols")
```

Now we will plot with the help of `matplotlib` using the following code:

```
plt.subplot(121)
plt.plot(lag_acf)
plt.axhline(y=0,linestyle='--',color='gray')
plt.axhline(y=-1.96/np.sqrt(len(ts_log_diff)),linestyle='--',color='gray')
plt.axhline(y=1.96/np.sqrt(len(ts_log_diff)),linestyle='--',color='gray')
plt.title('Autocorrelation Function')
```

The output is as follows:

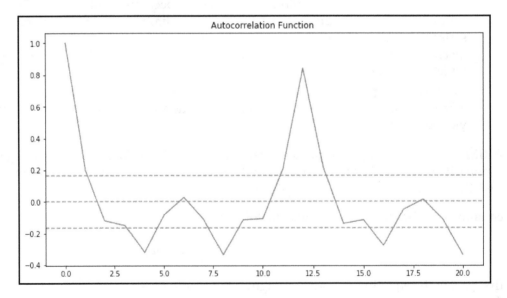

Here, we are measuring the correlation between the time series with a lagged version of itself. For instance, at lag 5, ACF would compare the series at time instant *t1*, *t2* with the series at instant t_{1-5}, ..., t_{2-5}. It is a plot of the coefficients of the correlation with its lagged values.

If we look at the preceding plot carefully, we will see that the upper confidence level line has been crossed at lag 2. Therefore, the order of MA would be 2 and *q=2*.

A partial correlation between the series and lagged values is plotted, and it gives us a **partial auto correlation functional (PACF)** plot. It's a very interesting term. If we go on and compute the correlation between a *Y* variable and *X3* while we know that *Y* has a separation association with *X1* and *X2*, the partial correlation addresses that portion of the correlation that is not explained by their correlations with *X1* and *X2*.

Here, the partial correlation is the square root (reduction in variance by adding a variable (here, *X3*) while regressing *Y* on the other variables (here *X1*, *X2*)).

In the case of a time series, partial autocorrelation between Y & lagged value Y_{t-3} will be the value that is not explained by a correlation between *Y* and Y_{t-1} and Y_{t-2}, as shown in the following code:

```
#Plot PACF:
plt.subplot(122)
plt.plot(lag_pacf)
plt.axhline(y=0,linestyle='--',color='gray')
plt.axhline(y=-1.96/np.sqrt(len(ts_log_diff)),linestyle='--',color='gray')
plt.axhline(y=1.96/np.sqrt(len(ts_log_diff)),linestyle='--',color='gray')
plt.title('Partial Autocorrelation Function')
plt.tight_layout()
```

We will get the following output:

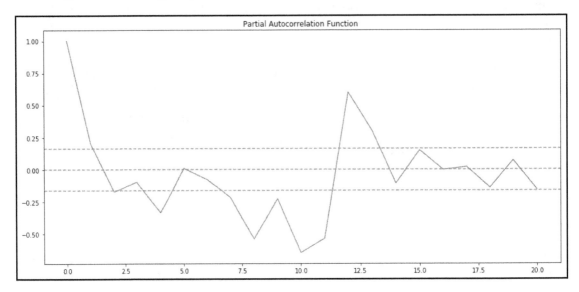

If we look at the preceding plot carefully, we will see that the upper confidence level line has been crossed at lag 2. Therefore, the order of AR would be 2 and *p=2*.

Let's try out an AR model that is of the order *(p=2, d=1, q=0)*. The *d* value has been taken as 1, since it is a case of single differencing. The residual sum of the square has been calculated as well to judge how good the model is and compare it with others, as shown in the following code:

```
from statsmodels.tsa.arima_model import ARIMA
model1 = ARIMA(ts_log, order=(2, 1, 0))
results_AR = model1.fit(disp=-1)
plt.plot(ts_log_dif)
plt.plot(results_AR.fittedvalues, color='red')
plt.title('RSS: %.4f'% sum((results_AR.fittedvalues-ts_log_dif)**2))
```

The output can be seen as follows:

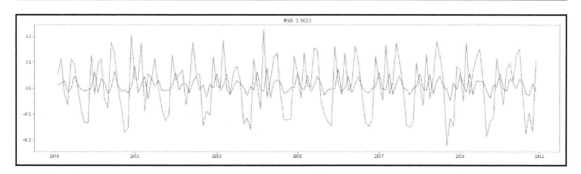

Now, we can have a look at the model summary that depicts the coefficients of AR1 and AR2 using the following code:

```
results_AR.summary()
```

ARIMA Model Results

Dep. Variable:	D.#Passengers	No. Observations:	143
Model:	ARIMA(2, 1, 0)	Log Likelihood	122.802
Method:	css-mle	S.D. of innovations	0.102
Date:	Fri, 12 Oct 2018	AIC	-237.605
Time:	11:17:16	BIC	-225.753
Sample:	02-01-1949	HQIC	-232.789
	- 12-01-1960		

	coef	std err	z	P>|z|	[0.025	0.975]
const	0.0096	0.009	1.048	0.296	-0.008	0.028
ar.L1.D.#Passengers	0.2359	0.083	2.855	0.005	0.074	0.398
ar.L2.D.#Passengers	-0.1725	0.083	-2.070	0.040	-0.336	-0.009

0.6838 -2.3088j 2.4079 -0.2042 0.6838 +2.3088j 2.4079 0.2042

Now, let's build an MA model of the order *(p=0,d=1,q=2)* using the following code:

```
model2 = ARIMA(ts_log, order=(0, 1, 2))
results_MA = model2.fit(disp=-1)
plt.plot(ts_log_dif)
plt.plot(results_MA.fittedvalues, color='red')
plt.title('RSS: %.4f'% sum((results_MA.fittedvalues-ts_log_dif)**2))
```

The output can be seen as follows:

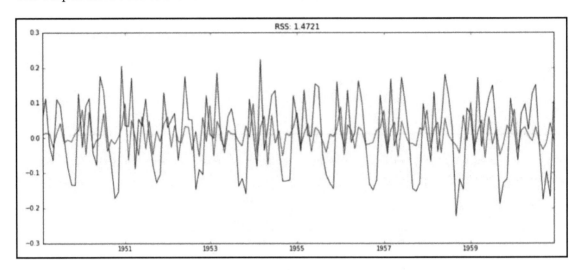

Now, let's combine these two models and build an ARIMA model using the following code:

```
model3 = ARIMA(ts_log, order=(2, 1, 2))
results_ARIMA = model.fit(disp=-1)
plt.plot(ts_log_dif)
plt.plot(results_ARIMA.fittedvalues, color='red')
plt.title('RSS: %.4f'% sum((results_ARIMA.fittedvalues-ts_log_dif)**2))
```

The output is as follows:

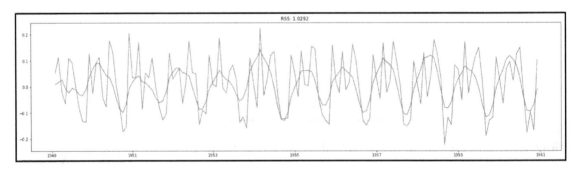

We can experience a dip in the value of RSS from the AR model to ARIMA. Now **RSS= 1.0292**:

```
results_ARIMA.summary()
```

We can see the coefficients of AR1, AR2, MA1, and MA2, and, if we go by *p* values, we can see that all these parameters are significant, as shown in the following screenshot:

ARIMA Model Results

Dep. Variable:	D.#Passengers	No. Observations:	143
Model:	ARIMA(2, 1, 2)	Log Likelihood	149.640
Method:	css-mle	S.D. of innovations	0.084
Date:	Sat, 13 Oct 2018	AIC	-287.281
Time:	07:05:22	BIC	-269.504
Sample:	02-01-1949	HQIC	-280.057
	- 12-01-1960		

	coef	std err	z	P>|z|	[0.025	0.975]
const	0.0096	0.003	3.697	0.000	0.005	0.015
ar.L1.D.#Passengers	1.6293	0.039	41.868	0.000	1.553	1.706
ar.L2.D.#Passengers	-0.8946	0.039	-23.127	0.000	-0.970	-0.819
ma.L1.D.#Passengers	-1.8270	0.036	-51.303	0.000	-1.897	-1.757
ma.L2.D.#Passengers	0.9245	0.036	25.568	0.000	0.854	0.995

0.9106 -0.5372j 1.0573 -0.0848 0.9106 +0.5372j 1.0573 0.0848 0.9881 -0.3245j 1.0400 -0.0505 0.9881 +0.3245j 1.0400 0.0505

Let's turn the predicted values into a series using the following code:

```
predictions_ARIMA_dif= pd.Series(results_ARIMA.fittedvalues, copy=True)
print(predictions_ARIMA_dif.head())
```

We will get the following output:

```
Month
1949-02-01      0.009580
1949-03-01      0.017491
1949-04-01      0.027670
1949-05-01     -0.004521
1949-06-01     -0.023890
dtype: float64
```

The way to convert the differencing to log scale is to add these differences consecutively to the base number. An easy way to do this is to first determine the cumulative sum at the index and then add it to the base number. The cumulative sum can be found using the following code:

```
predictions_ARIMA_dif_cumsum = predictions_ARIMA_dif.cumsum()
print(predictions_ARIMA_dif_cumsum.head())
```

From this, we will get the following output:

```
Month
1949-02-01    0.009580
1949-03-01    0.027071
1949-04-01    0.054742
1949-05-01    0.050221
1949-06-01    0.026331
dtype: float64
```

We will create a series with all values as the base number and add the differences to it in order to add to the base series, as follows:

```
predictions_ARIMA_log = pd.Series(ts_log.ix[0], index=ts_log.index)
predictions_ARIMA_log =
predictions_ARIMA_log.add(predictions_ARIMA_dif_cumsum,fill_value=0)
predictions_ARIMA_log.head()
```

The following shows the output:

```
Month
1949-01-01    4.718499
1949-02-01    4.728079
1949-03-01    4.745570
1949-04-01    4.773241
1949-05-01    4.768720
dtype: float64
```

Let's now find out the forecast using the following code:

```
predictions_ARIMA = np.exp(predictions_ARIMA_log)
plt.plot(ts)
plt.plot(predictions_ARIMA)
plt.title('RMSE: %.4f'% np.sqrt(sum((predictions_ARIMA-ts)**2)/len(ts)))
```

The output can be seen as follows:

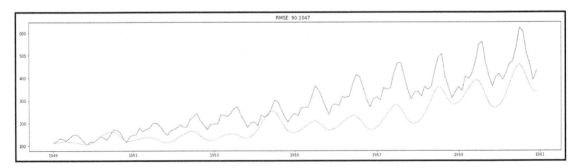

Optimization of parameters

Let's look at how to optimize the parameters of the models.

AR model

```
import statsmodels.tsa.api as smtsa
aic=[]
for ari in range(1, 3):
  obj_arima = smtsa.ARIMA(ts_log_diff, order=(ari,2,0)).fit(maxlag=30,
method='mle', trend='nc')
  aic.append([ari,2,0, obj_arima.aic])
print(aic)

[[1, 2, 0, -76.46506473849644], [2, 2, 0, -116.1112196485397]]
```

Therefore, our model parameters are p=2, d=2, and q=0 in this scenario for the AR model, as the AIC for this combination is the least.

ARIMA model

Even for the ARIMA model, we can optimize the parameters by using the following code:

```
import statsmodels.tsa.api as smtsa
aic=[]
for ari in range(1, 3):
    for maj in range(1,3):
        arima_obj = smtsa.ARIMA(ts_log, order=(ari,1,maj)).fit(maxlag=30,
method='mle', trend='nc')
        aic.append([ari,1, maj, arima_obj.aic])
print(aic)
```

The following is the output you get by executing the preceding code:

```
[[1, 1, 1, -242.6262079840165], [1, 1, 2, -248.8648292320533], [2, 1, 1,
-251.46351037666676], [2, 1, 2, -279.96951163008583]]
```

The combination with the least **Akaike information criterion** (**AIC**) should be chosen.

Anomaly detection

Anomalies are essentially abnormal patterns in a series that are irregular deviations from the expected behavior. For example, many of us have watched a cricket match. One form of getting out in this game is to be caught out, and before the ball travels straight to the hands of a fielder, it has to touch the bat of a batsman. If the stadium is very noisy, sometimes it is too difficult for anyone to judge whether the ball has touched the bat or not. To solve this problem, umpires use a device called the **snickometer** to help them make the call. The snickometer uses the sound from the stump mic to generate a plot of the mic's sound. If the plot is a straight line, then the ball did not make contact with the bat; otherwise, the plot will show a spike. Therefore, a spike is a sign of an anomaly. Another example of an anomaly could be the detection of a malignant tumor in a scan.

Anomaly detection is a technique that we can use to figure out aberrant behavior. An anomaly can also be called an **outlier**. The following list shows several different anomalies:

- **Point anomalies**: A point anomaly is a point that breaches the boundary of a threshold that has been assigned to keep the whole system in check. There is often a system in place to send an alert when this boundary has been breached by a point anomaly. For example, fraud detection in the financial industries can use point anomaly detection to check whether a transaction has taken place from a different city to the card holder's usual location.
- **Contextual anomalies**: Context-specific observations are called **contextual anomalies**. For example, it is commonplace to have lots of traffic on weekdays, but a holiday falling on a Monday may make it look like an anomaly.
- **Collective anomalies**: A set of collective data instances helps in detecting anomalies. Say that someone is unexpectedly trying to copy data form a remote machine to a local host. In this case, this anomaly would be flagged as a potential cyber attack.

In this section, we will focus on contextual anomalies and try to detect them with the help of a simple moving average.

First, let's load all the required libraries as follows:

```
import numpy as np # vectors and matrices
import pandas as pd # tables and data manipulations
import matplotlib.pyplot as plt # plots
import seaborn as sns # more plots
from sklearn.metrics import mean_absolute_error
import warnings # `do not disturb` mode
warnings.filterwarnings('ignore')
%matplotlib inline
```

Next, we read the dataset using the following code. We are keeping the same dataset—namely, `AirPassenger.csv`:

```
data = pd.read_csv('AirPassengers.csv', index_col=['Month'],
parse_dates=['Month'])
 plt.figure(figsize=(20, 10))
 plt.plot(ads)
 plt.title('Trend')
 plt.grid(True)
 plt.show()
```

We get the output as follows:

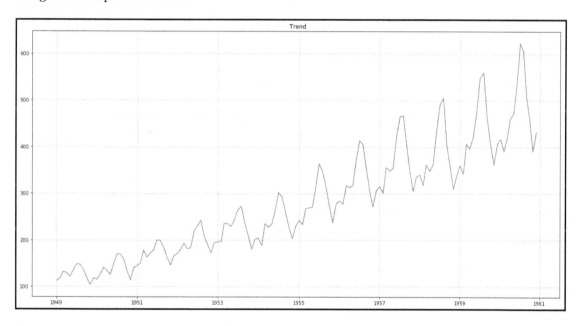

Now we will write a function and create a threshold for detecting the anomalies using the following code:

```
def plotMovingAverage(series, window, plot_intervals=False, scale=1.96,
plot_anomalies=False):
        rolling_mean = series.rolling(window=window).mean()
        plt.figure(figsize=(15,5))
        plt.title("Moving average\n window size = {}".format(window))
        plt.plot(rolling_mean, "g", label="Rolling mean trend")
        # Plot confidence intervals for smoothed values
        if plot_intervals:
            mae = mean_absolute_error(series[window:], rolling_mean[window:])
            deviation = np.std(series[window:] - rolling_mean[window:])
```

```
        lower_bond = rolling_mean - (mae + scale * deviation)
        upper_bond = rolling_mean + (mae + scale * deviation)
        plt.plot(upper_bond, "r--", label="Upper Bond / Lower Bond")
        plt.plot(lower_bond, "r--")
  # Having the intervals, find abnormal values
      if plot_anomalies:
          anomalies = pd.DataFrame(index=series.index,
columns=series.columns)
          anomalies[series<lower_bond] = series[series<lower_bond]
          anomalies[series>upper_bond] = series[series>upper_bond]
          plt.plot(anomalies, "ro", markersize=10)
          plt.plot(series[window:], label="Actual values")
          plt.legend(loc="upper left")
          plt.grid(True)
```

Now, let's introduce anomalies to the series using the following:

```
data_anomaly = data.copy()
data_anomaly.iloc[-20] = data_anomaly.iloc[-20] * 0.2
```

Now, let's plot it to detect the anomalies introduced using the following code:

```
plotMovingAverage(data_anomaly, 4, plot_intervals=True,
plot_anomalies=True)
```

The following diagram shows the output:

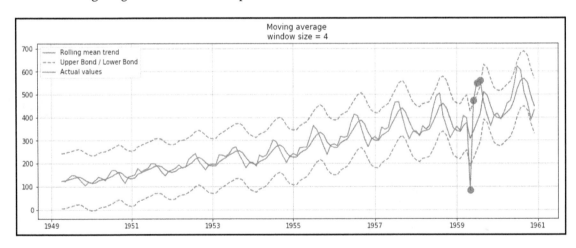

Now, the introduced anomaly can be seen after 1959 as a dip in the number of travelers. It should be noted, however, that this is one of the simpler methods. ARIMA and Holt-Winters can also be used in this scenario.

Summary

In this chapter, we learned about time series analysis and white noise. We were introduced to the concepts of random walk, autoregression, autocorrelation, and stationarity, which describes how to figure out whether data is stationary.

We also learned about differencing, taking the time series data and computing the differences between consecutive observations that lead to the formation of a new series. This chapter also talked about the AR model, which is a part of a stochastic process wherein the specific lagged values of y_t are used as predictor variables and regressed on y_t in order to estimate the values. We also learned two optimization parameters, namely the AR model and ARIMA model.

In the next chapter, we will learn about natural language processing.

6
Natural Language Processing

How fast has the world been changing? Well, technology and data have been changing just as quickly. With the advent of the internet and social media, our entire outlook on data has changed. Initially, the scope of most data analytics revolved around structured data. However, due to so much unstructured data being pumped in through the internet and social media, the spectrum of analytics has broadened. Large amounts of text data, images, sound, and video data are being generated every second. They contain lots of information that needs to be synthesized for business. Natural language processing is a technique through which we enable a machine to understand text or speech. Although unstructured data has a wide range, the scope of this chapter will be to expose you to text analytics.

Structured data is typically made up of fixed observations and fixed columns set up in relational databases or in a spreadsheet, whereas unstructured data doesn't have any structure, and it can't be set up in a relational database; rather, it needs a NoSQL database, example, video, text, and so on.

In this chapter, you will learn about the following topics:

- The document term matrix
- Different approaches to looking at text
- Sentiment analysis
- Topic modeling
- The Bayesian technique

Text corpus

A text corpus is text data that forms out of a single document or group of documents and can come from any language, such as English, German, Hindi, and so on. In today's world, most of the textual data flows from social media, such as Facebook, Twitter, blogging sites, and other platforms. Mobile applications have now been added to the list of such sources. The larger size of a corpus, which is called **corpora,** makes the analytics more accurate.

Sentences

A corpus can be broken into units, which are called **sentences**. Sentences hold the meaning and context of the corpus, once we combine them together. Sentence formation takes place with the help of parts of speech. Every sentence is separated from other sentences by a delimiter, such as a period, which we can make use of to break it up further. This is called **sentence tokenization**.

Words

Words are the smallest unit of corpuses and take the shape of sentences when we put them in order by following the parts of speech. When we break down the sentences into words, it is called **word tokenization**.

Bags of words

When we have text as input data, we can't go ahead and work with raw text. Hence, it's imperative for that text input data to get converted into numbers or vectors of numbers, in order to make it usable for a number of algorithms.

A bag of words model is one of the ways to make the text usable for the algorithms. Essentially, it is a representation of text that works on the occurrence of words in the document. It has nothing to do with the structure, order, and location; this model only looks for the count of the words as a feature.

The thought process behind this model is that having similar content means having a similar document.

The different steps to be taken in the bag of words model are as follows:

- **Building the corpus**: In this step, the documents are collected and combined together to form a corpus. For example, the famous song from the TV series Friends has been used here as a corpus:

> *I will be there for you*
> *When the rain starts to pour*
> *I will be there for you*
> *Like I have been there before*
> *I will be there for you*

Let's consider each line of this song as a separate document.

- **Vocabulary building**: In this step, we figure out the unique words in the corpus and create a list of them:
  - I
  - will
  - be
  - there
  - for
  - you
  - when
  - the
  - rain
  - starts
  - to
  - pour
  - like
  - have
  - been
  - before

- **Document vector creation**: Now, it's time to convert each document of text into a vector.

The simple way to do this is through a Boolean route. This means that raw text will be transformed into a document vector, with the help of the presence/absence of that text in the respective document.

For example, if the first line of the song is turned into a document containing *I will be there for you*, then the document vector will turn out as follows:

	Document vector
I	1
will	1
be	1
there	1
for	1
you	1
when	0
the	0

rain	0
starts	0
to	0
pour	0
like	0
have	0
been	0
before	0

All the words that are present in the document are marked as 1, and the rest are marked as 0.

Hence, the document vector for the first sentence is *[1,1,1,1,1,1,0,0,0,0,0,0,0,0,0,0]*.

Similarly, the document vector for the second sentence is *[0,0,0,0,0,0,1,1,1,1,1,1,0,0,0,0]*.

As the size of the corpus continues to increase, the number of zeros in the document vector will rise, as well. As a result of that, it induces sparsity in the vector and it becomes a sparse vector. Computing a sparse vector becomes really challenging for various algorithms. Data cleansing is one of the ways to counter it, to some extent:

- **Cleansing the text**: This would involve transforming all of the corpus into a single case (either upper (preferably) or lower). The punctuation must be taken out of the corpus. Stemming, which means finding the root words of the text, can be incorporated, and will be able to reduce the unique words in the corpus. Also, removal of stop words, such as *is* and *of*, might be able to abate the pain of sparsity.

- **Count vector**: There is another way to create the document vector, with the help of the frequency of the words appearing in the document. Let's suppose that there is a corpus comprised of N documents and T tokens (words) have been extracted. These T tokens will form our dictionary. Hence, the dimension of the count vector matrix will turn out to be N X T. Every row contains the frequency of tokens (words) in that respective document comprising the dictionary.

For example, let's suppose that we have three documents:

- **N1**: Count vector has got count in it
- **N2**: Is count vector better than the Boolean way of creating feature vector?
- **N3**: Creation of feature vector is very important

After removing `stopwords`, the count vector matrix turns out like the following table:

	count	vector	got	it	better	than	Boolean	way	creating	feature	creation	important
N1	2	1	1	1	0	0	0	0	0	0	0	0
N2	1	2	0	0	1	1	1	1	1	1	0	0
N3	0	1	0	0	0	0	0	0	0	1	1	1

Now, take a look at the matrix dimension carefully; since $N=3$ and $T=12$, that makes this a matrix of 3 x 12.

We will look at how the matrix formation has taken place. For document N1, the number of times the count has occurred in it is 2, the number of times the vector has come is 1, and so on. Taking these frequencies, we enter these values. A similar process has been completed for the other two documents, as well.

However, this has a drawback. A highly frequent word might start to dominate the document, and the corpus, too, which will result in having limited information extracted out of the features. To counter this, **term frequency inverse-document frequency (TF-IDF)** has been introduced.

TF-IDF

As we understood the limitation of count vectorization that a highly frequent word might spoil the party. Hence, the idea is to penalize the frequent words occurring in most of the documents by assigning them a lower weight and increasing the weight of the words that appear in a subset of documents. This is the principle upon which TF-IDF works.

TF-IDF is a measure of how important a term is with respect to a document and the entire corpus (collection of documents):

$$TF\text{-}IDF(term) = TF(term) * IDF(term)$$

Term frequency (TF) is the frequency of the word appearing in the document out of all the words in the same document. For example, if there are 1,000 words in a document and we have to find out the *TF* of a word *NLP* that has appeared 50 times in that very document, we use the following:

$$TF(NLP) = 50/1000 = 0.05$$

Hence, we can conclude the following:

TF(term) = Number of times the term appears in the document/total number of terms in the document

In the preceding example , comprised of three documents, *N1*, *N2*, and *N3*, if the *TF* of the term *count* in the document *N1* needs to be found, it will turn out to be like the following formula:

TF(count) N1= 2/ (2+1+1+1) = 2/5 = 0.4

It indicates the contribution of words to the document.

However, IDF is an indicator of how significant this term is for the entire corpus:

IDF("count") = log(Total number of documents/Number of documents containing the term "count")

IDF("count") = log(3/2)= 0.17

Now, let's calculate the IDF for the term *vector*:

IDF("vector")=log(3/3)= 0

How do we interpret this? It implies that if the same word has appeared in all of the documents, then it is not relevant to a particular document. But, if the word appears only in a subset of documents, this means that it holds some relevance to those documents in which it exists.

Let's calculate the TF-IDF for *count* and *vector*, as follows:

TF-IDF(count) for Document N1= TF(count)*IDF(count)= 0.4 * 0.17 = 0.068

TF-IDF(vector) for Document N1 = TF(vector)* IDF(vector)= (1/5)*0 = 0

It is quite evident that, since it assigns more weight to the *count* in *N1*, it is more important than the *vector*. The higher the weight value, the rarer the term. The smaller the weight, the more common the term. Search engines makes use of TF-IDF to retrieve the relevant documents pertaining to a query.

Now, we will look at how to execute the count vectorizer and TF-IDF vectorizer in Python.

Executing the count vectorizer

The following are the steps for executing the CountVectorizer:

1. Import the library required for the count vectorizer:

   ```
   from sklearn.feature_extraction.text import CountVectorizer
   ```

2. Make a list of the text:

   ```
   text = [" Machine translation automatically translate text from one
   human language to another text"]
   ```

3. Tokenize the list of the text and build the vocabulary:

   ```
   vectorizer.fit(text)
   ```

   You will get the following output:

   ```
   CountVectorizer(analyzer='word', binary=False, decode_error='strict',
           dtype=<class 'numpy.int64'>, encoding='utf-8', input='content',
           lowercase=True, max_df=1.0, max_features=None, min_df=1,
           ngram_range=(1, 1), preprocessor=None, stop_words=None,
           strip_accents=None, token_pattern='(?u)\\b\\w\\w+\\b',
           tokenizer=None, vocabulary=None)
   ```

4. Let's take a look at the vocabulary that was created:

   ```
   print(vectorizer.vocabulary_)
   ```

   We get the following output:

   ```
   {'translation': 10, 'automatically': 1, 'another': 0, 'one': 6, 'machine': 5, 'human': 3, 'from': 2, 'language': 4, 'translate': 9, 'text': 7, 'to': 8}
   ```

5. Now, we have to encode it, as follows:

   ```
   vector = vectorizer.transform(text)
   ```

6. Let's get a summary of the vector and find out the term matrix:

   ```
   print(type(vector))
   print(vector.toarray())
   ```

We get the following output:

```
<class 'scipy.sparse.csr.csr_matrix'>
[[1 1 1 1 1 1 2 1 1 1]]
```

Executing TF-IDF in Python

The following are the steps for executing TF-IDF in Python:

1. Import the library, as follows:

```
from sklearn.feature_extraction.text import TfidfVectorizer
```

2. Let's make a corpus by adding four documents, as follows:

```
corpus = ['First document', 'Second document','Third
document','First and second document' ]
```

3. Let's set up the vectorizer:

```
vectorizer = TfidfVectorizer()
```

4. We extract the features out of the text as follows:

```
X = vectorizer.fit_transform(corpus)
print(vectorizer.get_feature_names())
print(X.shape)
```

The output is as follows:

```
['and', 'document', 'first', 'second', 'third']
(4, 5)
```

5. Here comes the document term matrix; every list indicates a document:

```
X.toarray()
```

We get the following output:

```
array([[ 0.        , 0.55193942, 0.83388421, 0.        , 0.        ],
       [ 0.        , 0.55193942, 0.        , 0.83388421, 0.        ],
       [ 0.        , 0.46263733, 0.        , 0.        , 0.88654763],
       [ 0.6305035 , 0.32902288, 0.4970962 , 0.4970962 , 0.        ]])
```

Sentiment analysis

Sentiment analysis is one of the application areas of natural language processing. It is widely in use across industries and domains, and there is a big need for it in the industry. Every organization is aiming to focus customers and their needs. Hence, to understand voice and sentiment, the customer turns out to be the prime goal, as knowing the pulse of the customers leads to revenue generation. Nowadays, customers voice their sentiments through Twitter, Facebook, or blogs. It takes some work to refine that textual data and make it consumable. Let's look at how to do it in Python.

Here, verbatims of cinegoers have been taken from IMDB. This is shared on GitHub, too.

We will launch the libraries , as follows:

```
import numpy as np
import pandas as pd
import seaborn as sns
import matplotlib.pyplot as plt
sns.set(color_codes=True)
import os
print(os.listdir())
```

We will load the dataset, as follows:

```
data= pd.read_csv("imdb_master.csv",encoding = "ISO-8859-1")
```

Now, let's explore the data and its dimensions:

```
print(data.head())
print(data.shape)
```

We get the following output:

```
   Unnamed: 0  type                                             review label  \
0           0  test  Once again Mr. Costner has dragged out a movie...   neg
1           1  test  This is an example of why the majority of acti...   neg
2           2  test  First of all I hate those moronic rappers, who...   neg
3           3  test  Not even the Beatles could write songs everyon...   neg
4           4  test  Brass pictures (movies is not a fitting word f...   neg

          file
0      0_2.txt
1  10000_4.txt
2  10001_1.txt
3  10002_3.txt
4  10003_3.txt
(100000, 5)
```

We only need two variables, `review` and `label`, to build the model. We will just keep both of them in the data. A new dataframe has been created , as follows:

```
Newdata= data[["review","label"]]
Newdata.shape
```

$$(100000, \ 2)$$

Now, this is the step where we need to check how many categories are in `label`, as we are only interested in keeping the positive and negative ones:

```
g= Newdata.groupby("label")
g.count()
```

The output is as follows:

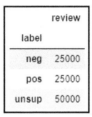

	review
label	
neg	25000
pos	25000
unsup	50000

Now, it's clear that there are three categories and we will get rid of `unsup`, as follows:

```
sent=["neg","pos"]

Newdata = Newdata[Newdata.label.isin(sent)]
Newdata.head()
```

We get the following output:

	review	label
0	Once again Mr. Costner has dragged out a movie...	neg
1	This is an example of why the majority of acti...	neg
2	First of all I hate those moronic rappers, who...	neg
3	Not even the Beatles could write songs everyon...	neg
4	Brass pictures (movies is not a fitting word f...	neg

Our data has now been set up. However, since we got rid of a few rows, we will reset the index of the data, as it sometimes causes some issues:

```
print(len(Newdata))
Newdata=Newdata.reset_index(drop=True) Newdata.head()
```

The output is as follows:

	review	label
0	Once again Mr. Costner has dragged out a movie...	neg
1	This is an example of why the majority of acti...	neg
2	First of all I hate those moronic rappers, who...	neg
3	Not even the Beatles could write songs everyon...	neg
4	Brass pictures (movies is not a fitting word f...	neg

We are done with it. Now, we will encode the `label` variable in order to make it usable for machine learning models. We have to use `LabelEncode` for that, as follows:

```
from sklearn.preprocessing import LabelEncoder
 labelencoder = LabelEncoder()
 Newdata["label"] = labelencoder.fit_transform(Newdata["label"])
```

We have to work on cleansing part of the data, in order to make it clean and standard, as follows:

```
Newdata["Clean_review"]= Newdata['review'].str.replace("[^a-zA-Z#]", " ")

Newdata.head()
```

The output is as follows:

	review	label	Clean_review
0	Once again Mr. Costner has dragged out a movie...	0	Once again Mr Costner has dragged out a movie...
1	This is an example of why the majority of acti...	0	This is an example of why the majority of acti...
2	First of all I hate those moronic rappers, who...	0	First of all I hate those moronic rappers who...
3	Not even the Beatles could write songs everyon...	0	Not even the Beatles could write songs everyon...
4	Brass pictures (movies is not a fitting word f...	0	Brass pictures movies is not a fitting word f...

Here, we are trying to get rid of the words that are less than 3 in length as the idea is that most of the words that are less than 3 in length don't have much of an impact on the meaning:

```
Newdata['Clean_review'] = Newdata['Clean_review'].apply(lambda x: '
'.join([w for w in x.split() if len(w)>3]))
Newdata.shape
```

```
(50000, 3)
```

The tokenization of the data can now take place, as follows:

```
tokenized_data = Newdata['Clean_review'].apply(lambda x: x.split())
tokenized_data.shape
```

```
(50000,)
```

We are making use of stemming, in order to get rid of different variations of the same words. For example, we will look at satisfying, satisfy, and satisfied, as follows:

```
from nltk.stem.porter import *
stemmer = PorterStemmer()
tokenized_data = tokenized_data.apply(lambda x: [stemmer.stem(i) for i in
x])
tokenized_data.head()
```

The output is as follows:

```
0    [onc, again, costner, drag, movi, longer, than...
1    [thi, exampl, major, action, film, same, gener...
2    [first, hate, those, moron, rapper, could, the...
3    [even, beatl, could, write, song, everyon, lik...
4    [brass, pictur, movi, fit, word, them, realli,...
Name: Clean_review, dtype: object
```

After stemming, we have to join the data back, as we are heading towards producing a word cloud:

```
for i in range(len(tokenized_data)):
  tokenized_data[i] = ' '.join(tokenized_data[i])

tokenized_data.head()
```

We get the following output:

```
0    onc again costner drag movi longer than necess...
1    thi exampl major action film same gener bore t...
2    first hate those moron rapper could they press...
3    even beatl could write song everyon like altho...
4    brass pictur movi fit word them realli somewha...
Name: Clean_review, dtype: object
```

Here, the tokenized data has been combined with the old `Newdata` dataframe:

```
Newdata["Clean_review2"]= tokenized_data
 Newdata.head()
```

The following is the output for the preceding code:

	review	label	Clean_review	Clean_review2
0	Once again Mr. Costner has dragged out a movie...	0	Once again Costner dragged movie longer than n...	onc again costner drag movi longer than necess...
1	This is an example of why the majority of acti...	0	This example majority action films same Generi...	thi exampl major action film same gener bore t...
2	First of all I hate those moronic rappers, who...	0	First hate those moronic rappers could they pr...	first hate those moron rapper could they press...
3	Not even the Beatles could write songs everyon...	0	even Beatles could write songs everyone liked ...	even beatl could write song everyon like altho...
4	Brass pictures (movies is not a fitting word f...	0	Brass pictures movies fitting word them really...	brass pictur movi fit word them realli somewha...

A word cloud combining all of the words together has been produced:

```
all_words = ' '.join([str(text) for text in Newdata['Clean_review2']])
 from wordcloud import WordCloud
 wordcloud = WordCloud(width=800, height=500, random_state=21,
max_font_size=110).generate(all_words)
 plt.figure(figsize=(10, 7))
 plt.imshow(wordcloud, interpolation="bilinear")
 plt.axis('off')
 plt.show()
```

The output can be seen as follows:

Now, we will make a word cloud for negative and positive sentiments separately, as follows:

- For `Negative` sentiments, we will use the following:

```
Negative =' '.join([text for text in
Newdata['Clean_review2'][Newdata['label'] == 0]])
 wordcloud1= WordCloud(width=800, height=500, random_state=21,
max_font_size=110).generate(Negative)
 plt.figure(figsize=(10, 7))
 plt.imshow(wordcloud1, interpolation="bilinear")
 plt.title("Word Cloud- Negative")
 plt.axis('off')
 plt.show()
```

The following output shows a word cloud for `Negative` sentiments:

- We will use the following for `Positive` sentiments:

```
Positive=' '.join([text for text in
Newdata['Clean_review2'][Newdata['label'] == 1]])
 wordcloud2 = WordCloud(width=800, height=500, random_state=21,
max_font_size=110).generate(Positive)
 plt.figure(figsize=(10, 7))
 plt.imshow(wordcloud, interpolation="bilinear")
 plt.title("Word Cloud-Positive")
 plt.axis('off')
 plt.show()
```

The following output shows a word cloud for `Positive` sentiments:

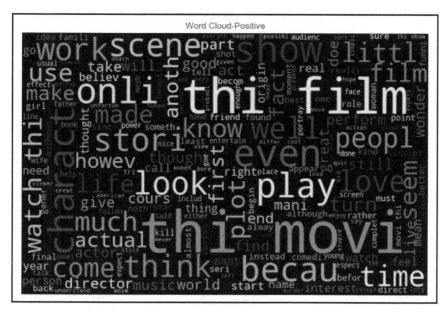

Sentiment classification

We will take two approaches to sentiment classification (positive and negative), as follows:

- TF-IDF
- Count vectorization

Let's see which one gives us the better result.

TF-IDF feature extraction

The following code will provide us with the TF-IDF feature extraction:

```
from sklearn.feature_extraction.text import TfidfVectorizer
tfidf= TfidfVectorizer(max_df=0.9,min_df= 2, max_features=1000,
                       stop_words="english")
tfidfV = tfidf.fit_transform(Newdata['Clean_review2'])

tfidf.vocabulary_
```

We will get the following output:

```
{'mind': 565,
 'self': 764,
 'receiv': 702,
 'festiv': 343,
 'univers': 932,
 'deserv': 235,
 'remind': 715,
 'viewer': 945,
 'certainli': 128,
 'break': 101,
 'boy': 98,
 'moral': 575,
 'battl': 74,
 'book': 94,
 'produc': 675,
 'mood': 574,
 'befor': 80,
 'shot': 781,
 'doubt': 261,
```

Count vectorizer bag of words feature extraction

The following code will show the count vectorizer for a bag of words:

```
from sklearn.feature_extraction.text import CountVectorizer
bow_vectorizer = CountVectorizer(max_df=0.90, min_df=2, max_features=1000,
stop_words='english')
# bag-of-words
bow = bow_vectorizer.fit_transform(Newdata['Clean_review2'])
```

Model building count vectorization

For building count vectorization we can split the data into train and test dataset as follows:

```
from sklearn.linear_model import LogisticRegression
from sklearn.model_selection import train_test_split
from sklearn.metrics import f1_score,accuracy_score
# splitting data into training and validation set
xtrain, xtest, ytrain, ytest = train_test_split(bow, Newdata['label'],
random_state=42, test_size=0.3)
lreg = LogisticRegression()
lreg.fit(xtrain, ytrain) # training the model
prediction = lreg.predict_proba(xtest) # predicting on the validation set
prediction_int = prediction[:,1] >= 0.3 # if prediction is greater than or
equal to 0.3 than 1 else 0
```

```
prediction_int = prediction_int.astype(np.int)
print("F1 Score-",f1_score(ytest, prediction_int))
print("Accuracy-",accuracy_score(ytest,prediction_int))
```

We get the following output:

```
F1 Score- 0.855267194306
Accuracy- 0.842733333333
```

Here, we attain an accuracy of 84%. Let's see how the TF-IDF approach fares:

```
from sklearn.linear_model import LogisticRegression
 # splitting data into training and validation set
 xtraintf, xtesttf, ytraintf, ytesttf = train_test_split(tfidfV,
Newdata['label'], random_state=42, test_size=0.3)
 lreg = LogisticRegression()
 lreg.fit(xtraintf, ytraintf) # training the model
 prediction = lreg.predict_proba(xtesttf) # predicting on the test set
 prediction_int = prediction[:,1] >= 0.3 # if prediction is greater than or
equal to 0.3 than 1 else 0
 prediction_int = prediction_int.astype(np.int)
 print("F1 Score-",f1_score(ytest, prediction_int))
 print("Accuracy-",accuracy_score(ytest,prediction_int))
```

The output is as follows:

```
F1 Score- 0.853920386007
Accuracy- 0.838533333333
```

Here, the accuracy turns out to be 83.8% (a little less than the count vectorizer).

This completes building a model for sentiment classification.

Topic modeling

Modeling is a methodology that's used to identify a topic and derive hidden patterns exhibited by a text corpus. Topic modeling resembles clustering, as we provide the number of topics as a hyperparameter (similar to the one used in clustering), which happens to be the number of clusters (k-means). Through this, we try to extract the number of topics or texts having some weights assigned to them.

The application of modeling lies in the area of document clustering, dimensionality reduction, information retrieval, and feature selection.

There are multiple ways to perform this, as follows:

- **Latent dirichlet allocation** (**LDA**): It's based on probabilistic graphical models
- **Latent semantic analysis** (**LSA**): It works on linear algebra (singular value decomposition)
- **Non-negative matrix factorization**: It's based on linear algebra

We will primarily discuss LDA, which is considered the most popular of all.

LDA is a matrix factorization technique that works on an assumption that documents are formed out of a number of topics, and, in turn, topics are formed out of words.

Having read the previous sections, you should be aware that any corpus can be represented as a document-term matrix. The following matrix shows a corpus of **M** documents and a vocabulary size of **N** words that makes an **M x N matrix**. All of the cells in this matrix have the frequency of the words in that particular document:

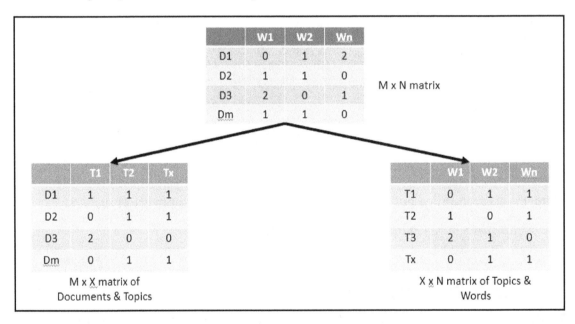

This **M x N matrix of Document & Words** gets translated into two matrices by LDA: **M x X matrix of Documents & Topics** and **X x N matrix of Topics & Words**.

LDA architecture

In the LDA architecture, there are M number of documents having an N number of words, that get processed through the black strip called **LDA**. It delivers **X Topics** with **Cluster of words**. Each topic has psi distribution of words out of topics. Finally, it also comes up with a distribution of topics out of documents, which is denoted by phi.

The following diagram illustrates LDA:

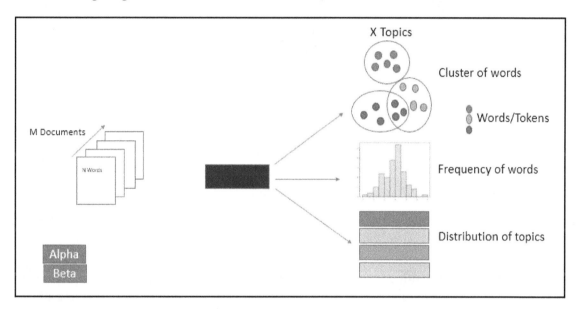

With regard to the **Alpha** and **Beta** hyperparameters: alpha represents document-topic concentration and beta represents topic-word concentration. The higher the value of alpha, the more topics we get out of documents. On the other hand, the higher the value of beta, the more words there are in a topic. These can be tweaked based on the domain knowledge.

LDA iterates through each word of every document and assigns and adjusts a topic for it. A new topic X is assigned to it, on the basis of the product of two probabilities: $p1= (topic\ t/document\ d)$, which means the proportion of the words of a document assigned to topic t, and $p2=(word\ w/topic\ t)$, which refers to the proportion of assignments to topic t spread over all the documents, which has the word w associated with it.

With the number of passes, a good distribution of topic-word and topic-documents is attained.

Let's look at how it's executed in Python:

1. In this step, we are loading `dataset = fetch_20newsgroups`, which comes from `sklearn`:

   ```
   from sklearn.datasets import fetch_20newsgroups
    dataset = fetch_20newsgroups(shuffle=True, random_state=1,
   remove=('headers', 'footers', 'quotes'))
    documents = dataset.data
   ```

2. In this step, we will clean the dataset. In order to do that, the `stopwords` and `WordNetLemmatizer` functions are required. Hence, the relevant libraries are must be loaded, as follows:

   ```
   from nltk.corpus import stopwords
   from nltk.stem.wordnet import WordNetLemmatizer
   import string
   ```

3. Ensure that you have downloaded the following dictionaries:

   ```
   import nltk
   nltk.download("stopwords")
   nltk.download("wordnet")
   ```

4. Here, a `clean` function is created to put the words in lowercase. Remove the `stopwords` and pick the words that have a length greater than 3. Also, it makes it punctuation-free. Finally, lemmatize it , as follows:

   ```
   stop = set(stopwords.words('english'))
   punc = set(string.punctuation)
   lemma = WordNetLemmatizer()
   def clean(doc):
       stopw_free = " ".join([i for i in doc.lower().split() if i not
   in stop and len(i)>3])
       punc_free = ''.join(ch for ch in stop_free if ch not in punc)
       lemmatized = " ".join(lemma.lemmatize(word) for word in
   punc_free.split())
       return lemmatized
    doc_clean = [clean(doc).split() for doc in documents]
   ```

5. Now, we have to make the document term matrix with the help of the `gensim` library. This library will also enable us to carry out LDA:

```
import gensim
from gensim import corpora
```

6. A document term matrix based on a bag of words is created here:

```
corpus = corpora.Dictionary(doc_clean)
 doc_term_matrix = [corpus.doc2bow(doc) for doc in doc_clean]
```

7. Here, a similar matrix is being created with the help of TF-IDF:

```
from gensim import models
tfidf = models.TfidfModel(doc_term_matrix)
corpus_tfidf = tfidf[doc_term_matrix]
```

8. Let's set up the model with a TF-IDF matrix. The number of topics has been given as `10`:

```
lda_model1 = gensim.models.LdaMulticore(corpus_tfidf,
num_topics=10, id2word=corpus, passes=2, workers=2)
```

9. Let's take a look at the topic with words:

```
print(lda_model1.print_topics(num_topics=5, num_words=5))
```

The output is as follows:

```
[(1, '0.001*"game" + 0.001*"team" + 0.001*"player" + 0.001*"play" + 0.001*"season"'), (3, '0.001*"people" + 0.001*"would" + 0.001*"think" + 0.001*"know" + 0.001*"thing"'),
(4, '0.001*"drive" + 0.001*"window" + 0.001*"problem" + 0.001*"maxaxaxaxaxaxaxaxaxaxaxaxaxax" + 0.001*"game"'), (2, '0.001*"mouse" + 0.001*"anyone" + 0.001*"know" + 0.001
*"would" + 0.001*"thanks"'), (6, '0.001*"would" + 0.000*"game" + 0.000*"year" + 0.000*"like" + 0.000*"think"')]
```

10. A similar exercise will be done for the bag of words; later, we will compare it:

```
lda_model2 = gensim.models.LdaMulticore(doc_term_matrix,
num_topics=10, id2word=corpus, passes=2, workers=2)

print(lda_model2.print_topics(num_topics=5, num_words=5))
```

We get the following output:

```
[(8, '0.007*"would" + 0.005*"think" + 0.004*"people" + 0.003*"like" + 0.003*"file"'), (7, '0.008*"file" + 0.006*"entry" + 0.003*"program" + 0.003*"time" + 0.002*"email"'),
(9, '0.034*"maxaxaxaxaxaxaxaxaxaxaxaxaxaxaxax" + 0.003*"year" + 0.003*"also" + 0.003*"would" + 0.002*"space"'), (6, '0.005*"would" + 0.004*"window" + 0.004*"time" + 0.004*"lik
e" + 0.003*"file"'), (5, '0.006*"game" + 0.006*"team" + 0.004*"would" + 0.003*"play" + 0.003*"year"')]
```

Evaluating the model

Log perplexity is a measure of how good an LDA model is. The lower the value of the perplexity, the better the model is:

```
print("lda_model 1- Perplexity:-",lda_model.log_perplexity(corpus_tfidf))
print("lda_model 2- Perplexity:-
",lda_model2.log_perplexity(doc_term_matrix))
```

The output for the log perplexity is as follows:

```
lda_model 1- Perplexity:- -12.8535943147
lda_model 2- Perplexity:- -9.33637689865
```

Visualizing the LDA

In order to visualize the data, we can use the following code:

```
import pyLDAvis
import pyLDAvis.gensim
import matplotlib.pyplot as plt
%matplotlib inline

pyLDAvis.enable_notebook()
visual1= pyLDAvis.gensim.prepare(lda_model, doc_term_matrix, corpus)
visual1
```

The output will be as follows:

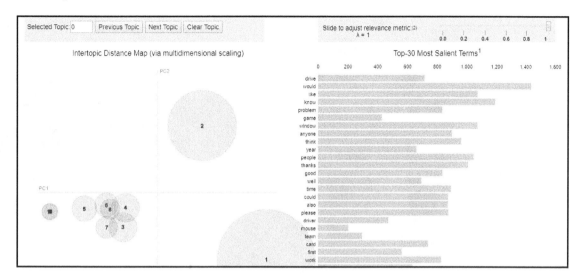

We can enable the notebook here, as follows:

```
pyLDAvis.enable_notebook()
  visual2= pyLDAvis.gensim.prepare(lda_model2, doc_term_matrix, corpus)
  visual2
```

The output is as follows:

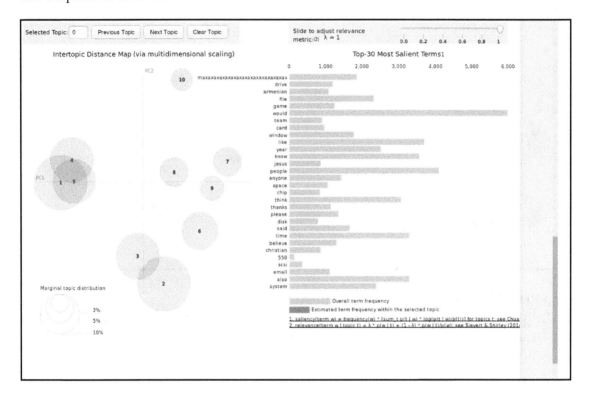

Let's try to interpret this.

On the left hand side, we have the topics, and on the right, we have the terms/words:

- A bigger circle size means more frequent topics.
- Topics that are overlapping or closer to one another are similar.
- Upon selecting a topic, the most representative words for the selected topic can be seen. This reflects how frequent the word is. One can toggle the weight of each property by using the slider.
- Hovering over a topic will provide the contribution of words to the topic on the right and upon clicking on the word, we will see the circle size changing, which reflects how frequent that term is in that topic.

The Naive Bayes technique in text classification

Naive Bayes is a supervised classification algorithm that is based on Bayes theorem. It is a probabilistic algorithm. But, you might be wondering why it is called **Naive**. It is so because this algorithm works on an assumption that all the features are independent of each other. However, we are cognizant of the fact that independence of features might not be there in a real-world scenario. For example, if we are trying to detect whether an email is spam or not, all we look for are the keywords associated with spams such as Lottery, Award, and so on. Based on these, we extract those relevant features from the email and say that if given spam-related features, the email will be classified as spam.

The Bayes theorem

The Bayes theorem helps us in finding posterior probability, given a certain condition:

$$P(A|B) = P(B|A) * P(A)/P(B)$$

A and *B* can be deemed as the target and features, respectively.

Where, $P(A|B)$: posterior probability, which implies the probability of event *A*, given that *B* has taken place:

- $P(B|A)$: The likelihood that implies the probability of feature *B*, given the target *A*
- $P(A)$: The prior probability of target *A*
- $P(B)$: The prior probability of feature *B*

How the Naive Bayes classifier works

We will try to understand all of this by looking at the example of the Titanic. While the Titanic was sinking, a few of the categories had priority over others, in terms of being saved. We have the following dataset (it is a Kaggle dataset):

Person category	Survival chance
Woman	Yes
Kid	Yes
Kid	Yes
Man	No
Woman	Yes
Woman	Yes
Man	No
Man	Yes

Kid	Yes
Woman	No
Kid	No
Woman	No
Man	Yes
Man	No
Woman	Yes

Now, let's prepare a likelihood table for the preceding information:

		Survival chance				
		No	Yes	Grand Total		
Category	Kid	1	3	4	4/15=	0.27
Man	3	2	5	5/15=	0.33	
Woman	2	4	6	6/15=	0.40	
	Grand Total	6	9	15		
		6/15	9/15			
		0.40	0.6			

Let's find out which category of people had the maximum chance of survival:

Kid - P(Yes|Kid)= P(Kid|Yes) * P(Yes)/P(Kid)

P(Kid|Yes) = 3/9= 0.3

P(Yes) = 9/15 =0.6

P(Kid)= 4/15 =0.27

P(Yes|kid) = 0.33 *0.6/0.27=0.73

Woman - P(Yes|Woman)= P(Woman|Yes) * P(Yes)/P(Woman)

P(Woman|Yes) = 4/9= 0.44

P(Yes) = 9/15 =0.6

P(Woman)= 6/15 =0.4

P(Yes|Woman) = 0.44 *0.6/0.4=0.66

Man - P(Yes|Man)= P(Man|Yes) * P(Yes)/P(Man)

P(Man|Yes) = 2/9= 0.22

P(Yes) = 9/15 =0.6

P(Man)= 6/15 =0.33

P(Yes|Man) = 0.22 *0.6/0.33=0.4

So, we can see that a child had the maximum chance of survival and a man the least chance.

Let's perform the sentiment classification with the help of Naive Bayes, and see whether the result is better or worse:

```
from sklearn.naive_bayes import MultinomialNB
# splitting data into training and validation set
xtraintf, xtesttf, ytraintf, ytesttf = train_test_split(tfidfV,
Newdata['label'], random_state=42, test_size=0.3)
NB= MultinomialNB()
NB.fit(xtraintf, ytraintf)
prediction = NB.predict_proba(xtesttf) # predicting on the test set
prediction_int = prediction[:,1] >= 0.3 # if prediction is greater than or
equal to 0.3 than 1 else 0
prediction_int = prediction_int.astype(np.int)
print("F1 Score-",f1_score(ytest, prediction_int))
print("Accuracy-",accuracy_score(ytest,prediction_int))
```

The output is as follows:

```
F1 Score- 0.771008403361
Accuracy- 0.709333333333
```

Here, we can see that our previous results were better than the Naive Bayes results.

Summary

In this chapter, we studied corpus building techniques that consists of sentences and words, which includes a bag of words to make the texts usable for the algorithms. You also learned about TF-IDF and how important a term is with respect to a document and the entire corpus. We went over sentiment analysis, along with classification and TF-IDF feature extraction.

You were also introduced to topic modeling and evaluating models, which includes visualizing LDA. We covered the Bayes theorem and working with the Naive Bayes classifier. In the next chapter, you will learn about temporal and sequential pattern discovery.

7
Temporal and Sequential Pattern Discovery

Many of us have visited retail shops such as Reliance and Walmart for our household needs. Let's say that we are planning to buy an iPhoneX from Reliance Digital. What we would typically do is search for the model by visiting the mobile section of the store, and then select the product and head toward the billing counter.

But, in today's world, the goal of the organization is to increase revenue. Can this be done by pitching just one product at a time to the customer? The answer is a clear **no**. Hence, organizations began mining data relating to frequently bought items. They try to find out associations between different items and products that can be sold together, which gives assisting in right product placement. Typically, it figures out what products are being bought together and organizations can place products in a similar manner.

This is what we are going to talk about in this chapter. How do we come up with such rules by means of machine learning? We will discuss number of techniques here.

In this chapter, we will cover the following topics:

- Association rules
- Frequent pattern growth
- Validation

Association rules

Association rule mining is a technique that focuses upon observing frequently occurring patterns and associations from datasets found in databases such as relational and transactional databases. These rules do not say anything about the preferences of an individual; rather, they rely chiefly on the items within transactions to deduce a certain association. Every transaction is identified by a primary key (distinct ID) called, **transaction ID**. All these transactions are studied as a group and patterns are mined.

Association rules can be thought of as an **if—then** relationship. Just to elaborate on that, we have to come up with a rule: **if** an item **A** is being bought by the customer, **then** the chances of item **B** being picked by the customer too under the same transaction ID (along with item **A**) is found out. You needs to understand here that it's not a causality, rather, it is co-occurrence pattern that comes to the fore.

There are two elements of these rules:

- **Antecedent (if)**: This is an item/group of items that are typically found in the itemsets or datasets
- **Consequent (then)**: This comes along as an item with an antecedent/group of antecedents

Have a look at the following rule:

$$\{Bread, milk\} \Rightarrow \{Butter\}$$

The first part of this rule is called **antecedent** and the second part (after the arrow) is **consequent**. It is able to convey that there is a chance of *Butter* being picked in a transaction if *Bread* and *Milk* are picked earlier. However, the percentage chance for the consequent to be present in an itemset, given the antecedent, is not clear.

Let's look at a few metrics that will help us in getting there:

1. **Support**: This is a measure of the frequency of the itemset in all the transactions. For example, there are two itemsets popping up through the number of transactions for a retail outlet such as Walmart: itemset A = {Milk}, itemset B = {laptop}. Given that support is how frequent the itemset is in all the transactions, we are asked to find out which itemset has got the higher support. We know that itemset A will have higher support because *Milk* features in everyday grocery lists (and, in turn, the transaction) at a greater probability than *laptop*. Let's add another level of association and study with two new itemsets: itemset A= {milk, cornflakes}, itemset B= {milk, USB Drive}. The purchasing frequency of *milk* and *cornflakes* together will be higher than *milk and USB Drive*. It will make the support metric higher for A.

Let's translate this into mathematics:

Support(A, B) = Transactions comprising A and B/Total number of transactions

Here's an example:

- The total number of transactions is 10,000
- Transactions comprising A and B = 500
- Then support (A, B) = 500/10000= 0.05
- 5% of transactions contain A and B together

2. **Confidence**: This indicates how likely item 1 is to be purchased/picked when item 2 is already picked. In other words, it measures the likelihood of the occurrence of consequent transactions given that the antecedent is already there in the transaction. In other words, it is the probability of the occurrence of *Butter* in the transaction if *Bread* has already been part of that transaction. It is quite clear that it is a conditional probability of the occurrence of the consequent while having the antecedent:

- *Confidence(A ⇒ B) = Transactions comprising A and B/Transactions comprising A*
- *Confidence can be transformed in terms of support*
- *Confidence(A ⇒ B) = Support(A, B)/Support(A)*

Here's an example:

- Transactions with the itemset as *milk = 50*
- Transactions with the itemset as *cereal = 30*
- Transactions comprising *milk* and *cereal = 10*
- Total number of transactions = 100
- *Confidence(milk ⇒ Cereal) = 10/(50 +10) = 0.167*

It means that there is 16.7% probability of that event taking place.

A drawback of the confidence is it only accounts for how popular item 1 is, but not item 2. If item 2 is equally frequent, there will be a higher chance that a transaction containing item 1 will also contain item 2. Hence, it will result in an inflated outcome. To account for the frequency of both constituent items, we use a third measure called **lift**.

3. **Lift**: This is an indicator of how likely it is that item B will be picked in the cart/transaction, given that item *A* is already picked, while keeping a tab on the frequency of item *B*. A lift value greater than 1 says that there is a great association between item *A* and item *B*, which implies that there is a good chance that item *B* will be picked if item *A* is already in the cart. A lift value of less than 1 means that the chances are slim that item *B* will be picked if item *A* is already present. If the lift value hits zero, it means no association can be established here.

Lift(A⇒B) = (Transactions comprising A and B/(Transactions comprising A))/fraction of Transaction comprising B

Implies:

$$= Support(A, B)/(Support(A) * Support(B))$$

$$Lift(milk⇒cereal) = (\ 10/(50+10))/0.4$$

$$= 0.416$$

We will see this in a better format here. The probability of having cereal in the cart with the knowledge that milk is already in the cart (which is called **confidence**) = *10/(50+10) = 0.167*.

The probability of having cereal in the cart without the knowledge that milk is in the *cart = (30+10)/100 = 0.4*.

It means that having knowledge that milk is already in the cart reduces the chance of picking cereal from *0.4* to *0.167*. It is a lift of *0.167/0.4= 0.416* and is less than *1*. Hence, the chances of picking cereal while milk is already in the cart are very small.

Apriori algorithm

Apriori is a classical algorithm that is used to mine frequent itemsets to derive various association rules. It will help set up a retail store in a much better way, which will aid revenue generation.

The anti-monotonicity of the support measure is one of the prime concepts around which Apriori revolves. It assumes the following:

- All subsets of a frequent itemset must be frequent
- Similarly, for any infrequent itemset, all its supersets must be infrequent too

Let's look at an example and explain it:

Transaction ID	Milk	Butter	Cereal	Bread	Book
t1	1	1	1	0	0
t2	0	1	1	1	0
t3	0	0	0	1	1
t4	1	1	0	1	0
t5	1	1	1	0	1
t6	1	1	1	1	1

We have got the transaction ID and items such as milk, butter, cereal, bread, and book. 1 denotes that item is part of the transaction and 0 means that it is not.

- We came up with a frequency table for all the items along, with support (division by 6):

Items	Number of transactions	Support
Milk	4	67%
Butter	5	83%
Cereal	4	67%
Bread	4	67%
Book	3	50%

- We will put a threshold of support at 60%, which will filter out the items by frequency as these are the ones that can be addressed as frequent itemsets in this scenario:

Items	Number of transactions
Milk	4
Butter	5
Cereal	4
Bread	4

- Similarly, we form the number of combinations (two at a time, three at a time, and four at a time) with these items and find out frequencies:

Items	Number of transactions
Milk, Butter	4
Milk, Cereal	3
Milk, Bread	2
Butter, Bread	3
Butter, Cereal	4
Cereal, Bread	2

Now, again, we have to find out the support for the preceding examples and filter them by threshold, which is support at 60%

Similarly, the combinations have to be formed with three items at a time (for example, Milk, Butter, and Bread) and support needs to be calculated for them. And, finally, we will filter them out by threshold. The same process needs to be done by doing four items at a time. The step that we have done till now is called **frequent itemset generation**.

Finding association rules

In order to find the association rules, we have to first search for all of the rules that have support greater than the threshold support. But the question arises: how do we find these? A possible way to find this is by brute force, which means to list all the possible association rules and calculate the support and confidence for each rule. Later, remove all the rules that fail the confidence and support thresholds.

Given there are n items in the set I, the total number of possible association rules is $3^n - 2^{n+1} + 1$.

If X is a frequent itemset with k elements, then there are 2^k - 2 association rules.

Let's see how to execute association rules in Python:

```
import numpy as np
import matplotlib.pyplot as plt
import pandas as pd

data = pd.read_csv('association_mining.csv', header = None)

transactions = []
for i in range(0, 7501):
  transactions.append([str(data.values[i,j]) for j in range(0, 20)])
```

If we are asking for an item to appear three times in a day for seven days' time, the support will be 3 x 7/7051. 7051 is the total number of transactions. We will keep the confidence as 20% in the beginning:

```
from apyori import apriori
rules = apriori(transactions, min_support = 0.003, min_confidence = 0.2,
min_lift = 3, min_length = 2)

results = list(rules)
results
```

We can visualize the output by running the `results` command from the preceding code:

```
[RelationRecord(items=frozenset({'chicken', 'light cream'}), support=0.004532728969470737, ordered_statistics=[OrderedS
tatistic(items_base=frozenset({'light cream'}), items_add=frozenset({'chicken'}), confidence=0.29059829059829057, lift=
4.84395061728395)]),
 RelationRecord(items=frozenset({'escalope', 'mushroom cream sauce'}), support=0.005732568990801226, ordered_statistics
=[OrderedStatistic(items_base=frozenset({'mushroom cream sauce'}), items_add=frozenset({'escalope'}), confidence=0.3006
993006993007, lift=3.790852696715049)]),
 RelationRecord(items=frozenset({'escalope', 'pasta'}), support=0.005865584548726837, ordered_statistics=[OrderedStatis
tic(items_base=frozenset({'pasta'}), items_add=frozenset({'escalope'}), confidence=0.3728813559322034, lift=4.700811850
163794)]),
 RelationRecord(items=frozenset({'fromage blanc', 'honey'}), support=0.003332888948140248, ordered_statistics=[OrderedS
tatistic(items_base=frozenset({'fromage blanc'}), items_add=frozenset({'honey'}), confidence=0.2450980392156863, lift=
5.164270764485569)]),
 RelationRecord(items=frozenset({'ground beef', 'herb & pepper'}), support=0.015997866951073192, ordered_statistics=[Or
deredStatistic(items_base=frozenset({'herb & pepper'}), items_add=frozenset({'ground beef'}), confidence=0.323450134770
8895, lift=3.2919938411349285)]),
 RelationRecord(items=frozenset({'ground beef', 'tomato sauce'}), support=0.005332622317024397, ordered_statistics=[Ord
eredStatistic(items_base=frozenset({'tomato sauce'}), items_add=frozenset({'ground beef'}), confidence=0.37735849056603
77, lift=3.840659481324083)]),
 RelationRecord(items=frozenset({'olive oil', 'light cream'}), support=0.003199573390214638, ordered_statistics=[Ordere
dStatistic(items_base=frozenset({'light cream'}), items_add=frozenset({'olive oil'}), confidence=0.20512820512820515, l
ift=3.1147098515519573)]),
 RelationRecord(items=frozenset({'whole wheat pasta', 'olive oil'}), support=0.007998933475536596, ordered_statistics=
[OrderedStatistic(items_base=frozenset({'whole wheat pasta'}), items_add=frozenset({'olive oil'}), confidence=0.2714932
126696833, lift=4.122410097642296)]),
 RelationRecord(items=frozenset({'pasta', 'shrimp'}), support=0.005065991201173177, ordered_statistics=[OrderedStatisti
c(items_base=frozenset({'pasta'}), items_add=frozenset({'shrimp'}), confidence=0.3220338983050847, lift=4.5066721477358
96)]),
 RelationRecord(items=frozenset({'milk', 'spaghetti', 'avocado'}), support=0.003332888948140248, ordered_statistics=[Or
deredStatistic(items_base=frozenset({'spaghetti', 'avocado'}), items_add=frozenset({'milk'}), confidence=0.416666666666
66663, lift=3.215449245541838)]),
```

Frequent pattern growth

Frequent pattern growth (FP-growth) is a frequent itemset generation technique (similar to Apriori). FP-Growth builds a compact-tree structure and uses the tree for frequent itemset mining and generating rules. It is faster than Apriori and can throw results with large datasets.

Let's go through the steps of FP-Growth:

1. **Setting up the transactions**: This step sets up the items by frequency. However, the items are set up vertically, not horizontally. That means transforming input from transaction to items:

t_id	Items
1	(B, C, D, A)
2	(B, C, D)
3	(D, A)
4	(A, B)
5	(A, C, B)

2. **Finding the frequency**: Now we have to find out the frequency of each item individually:

Items	Frequency
A	4
B	4
C	3
D	3

Let's set up the minimum threshold or minimum support as 50%:

- Min Support = (5*50/100) = 2.5
- Ceiling of minimum support = 2.5 ~ 3

3. **Prioritize the items by frequency**: Since all the items have a frequency greater than or equal to minimum support, all the items will be part of it. Also, based on their frequency, priority or rank will be assigned to the items:

Items	Frequency	Rank
A	4	1
B	4	2

C	3	3
D	3	4

The order of the items is: A, B, C, and D (by frequency in descending order)

4. **Ordering the items by priority**: Now the order of items will be set according to the priority given to various items based on frequency. Currently, the order is A, B, C, and D:

t_id	Items	Order by priority
1	(B, C, D, A)	(A, B, C, D)
2	(B, C, D)	(B, C, D)
3	(D, A)	(A, D)
4	(A, B)	(A, B)
5	(A, C, B)	(A, B, C)

Frequent pattern tree growth

We will study the different frequent pattern tree growth from the following rows:

- **Row 1**: Every FP-Tree starts with a null node as a root node. Let's draw the first row of the tree order along with their frequency:

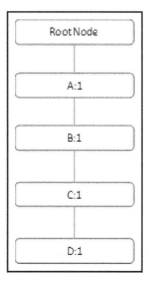

- **Row 2**: It has got *{B,C,D}*. *A* is missing, so we can not merge it with the earlier node. Hence, we will have to create another node, altogether as shown here:

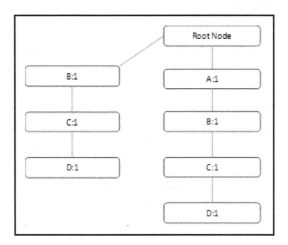

- **Row 3**: It has got *{A,D}*. *B* and *C* are missing, but we can tie it with the earlier node. *A* encounters a repetition, so frequency will change. It becomes 2 now:

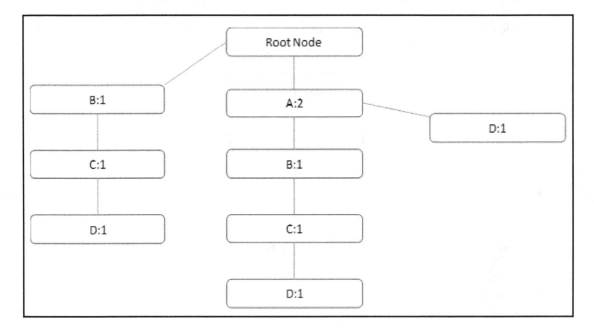

- **Row 4**: It has got *{A,B}*. We can tie it with the earlier node and will traverse on the previous node. *A* and *B* encounters a repetition, so frequency will change for it. It becomes 3 and 2 respectively:

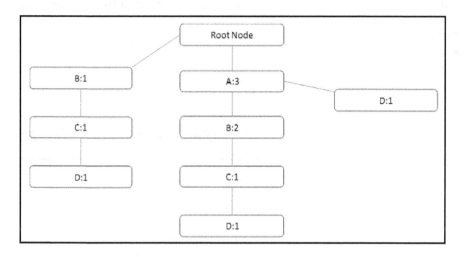

- **Row 5**: It has got *{A,B,C}*. Again, it can be tied with the earlier node and A, B, and C see a repetition, so the frequency will change for them. It becomes 4, 3, and 2 respectively:

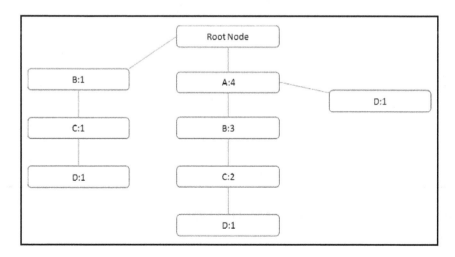

Validation

Now, let's count the frequency of the final tree that we have got and compare the frequency of each item with the table to ensure that we have got the correct frequencies in the table:

- **A:4**
- **B:4**
- **C:3**
- **D:3**

Now we will go from bottom to top. We will find out the branches where D appears:

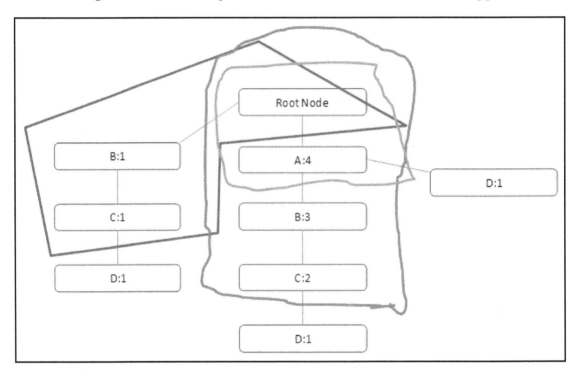

We can see that there are three branches where D appears:

- BC: 1
- ABC: 1
- A: 1

These branches are termed as conditional pattern base for D. While we do this, there are points to be kept in mind:

- Even if we traverse from bottom to top, we write the branches in a top-to-bottom manner
- D is not part of it
- 1 represents the frequency of occurrence of D in each branch

Now, the conditional pattern for D results in the conditional frequencies for A, B, and C, which are 2, 2, and 2. All are less than the minimum support (3). Hence, there can't be any conditional FP- Tree for it.

Now, let's do it for C. C is appears in the following branches:

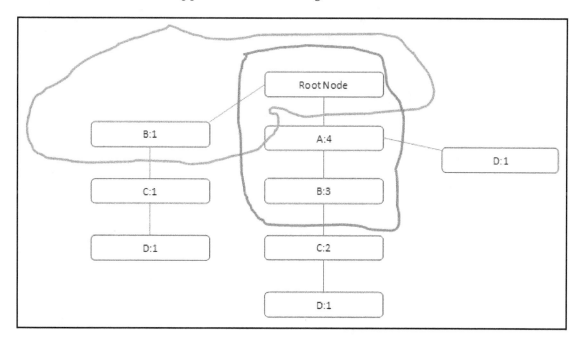

The branches end up like this:

- B:1
- AB:2

It results in A:2 and B:3. So, B fit with the bill in accordance with the minimum support. Now the conditional tree ends up like this:

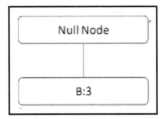

Similarly, conditional pattern finding is done for different combinations. Thus, it sets up the frequent item dataset.

Let's see how it can be done in Python. We will be using a library called pyfpgrowth. Also, we shall create an itemset in the following section.

Importing the library

In order to perform validation we will import the library and build the transactions as shown here:

```
import pyfpgrowth
```

We build our transactions like so:

```
transaction = [["bread", "butter", "cereal"],
 ["butter", "milk"],
 ["bread", "milk"],
 ["butter", "cereal", "milk"],
 ["egg", "bread"],
 ["egg", "butter"],
 ["cereal", "milk"],
 ["bread", "butter", "cereal", "egg"],
 ["cereal", "bread", "butter"]]
```

Minimum support is defined now to find the pattern. find_frequent_patterns(), where transactions are the list of items bought at each transaction, and 2 is the minimum threshold set for support count:

```
patterns = pyfpgrowth.find_frequent_patterns(transaction, 2)
```

Finally, we have to define the confidence to get the rules. Rules are generated based on the patterns and 0.5 is the minimum threshold set for confidence. Then, we store the rules in a dataframe named `rules`. `rules` initially consists of an antecedent, a consequent, and the confidence value:

```
rules = pyfpgrowth.generate_association_rules(patterns, 0.5)
print(rules)
```

We get the output as follows:

```
{('bread',): (('butter',), 0.6),
 ('bread', 'butter'): (('cereal',), 0.6666666666666666),
 ('bread', 'cereal'): (('butter',), 1.0),
 ('butter',): (('bread',), 0.5),
 ('butter', 'cereal'): (('bread',), 0.5),
 ('cereal',): (('butter',), 0.8)}
```

This is how we get the rules. FP-growth tends to have the edge over Apriori as it is faster and more efficient.

Summary

In this chapter, we have studied association rules. We also discussed the Apriori algorithm, which is used for mining frequent itemsets to derive various association rules. We also learned about frequent pattern growth (FP-growth), which is similar to Apriori and about the frequent itemset generation technique, which is similar to the Apriori algorithm. Finally, we saw how FP-growth tends to have an edge over Apriori, as it is faster and more efficient, using an example.

In the next chapter, we will study probabilistic graphical models. We will learn in depth about the Bayesian rules and Bayesian networks.

Probabilistic Graphical Models

8

Before we get into **Bayesian network** (**BN**) concepts, we should be aware of the theories of probability. So, we will try to touch upon them and build the foundation of BNs.

We already know that probability is the degree of certainty/uncertainty of an event occurring. However, it can be also termed as the degree of belief, which is more commonly used when we talk about BN.

When we toss a fair coin, we say that the degree of belief around the event of heads/tails happening is *0.5*. It implies that our belief of heads happening is as strong as tails. The probability can be seen as follows:

$$p(Heads)=p(tails)=0.5$$

In this chapter, we will cover the following topics:

- Bayesian rules
- Bayesian networks

Key concepts

We will cover a few key concepts before moving on to the body of the chapter:

- In the case of discrete distribution, a probability mass function is used to find out the probability, $p(X = x)$, where X is a discrete random variable and x is a real value number.
- In the case of continuous distribution, probability density function is used to find out the probability $p(X <= x)$. In this scenario, a probability curve is plotted and the area under the curve (integration) helps us with the probability.

- Conditional probability is to understand this, a cricket match can be the perfect example. Suppose there is a game scheduled between India and Australia and we are trying to pass on our belief of India triumphing. Do you think that the probability will be impacted by the team selected by India? Will the probability of India winning the match be impacted if *Virat Kohli* and *Rohit Sharma* are part of the team? So, *p(India winning | Rohit and Virat are playing)* denotes the probability of India winning, given that *Rohit* and *Virat* are playing. Essentially, it means that the probability of one event is dependent on the probability of another event. It is called **conditional probability**.

The probability of *x*, given *y*, can be expressed as follows:

$$p(x|y) = \frac{p(x \cap y)}{p(y)}$$

$$\Rightarrow p(x \cap y) = p(y)p(x|y)$$

- The chain rule computes the joint distribution of a set of random variables using their conditional probabilities. From conditional probability, we know that $p(x \cap y) = p(y)p(x|y)$.

It implies that if there are $(x_1, x_2, \ldots, x_n)$ events. The joint probability distribution turns out like this:

$$p(x_1 \cap x_2 \ldots \cap x_n) = p(x_1)p(x_2/x_1) \ldots p(x_n/x_{n-1})$$

Bayes rule

Bayes rule is one of the building blocks of probability theory. It stems from conditional probability and joint probability and extends beyond.

We will explain this in a simple way by again taking an example from cricket. In cricket, pitch condition varies as you go from one place to another and it is one of the factors that can be significant when deciding the team. The outcome can also be dependent upon it.

Let's say the Indian team goes to Australia for a game and we have to predict the belief of an Indian player scoring a century (100 runs) in the game. If that player has got experience of playing in that country, we might say with strong belief that he might score a century. But, there is another player who is a first-timer in this country. What would the the prior belief be for him? Of course, many would have less belief that he would score a century.

However, our prior belief will change as we see the way the player is performing. That is, more data about the player will be at our disposal as more games are played by that player. Based on that, posterior belief will keep getting updated. It changes a lot, largely due to the observations or more data (which is called **likelihood**). Bayes rule is based on these concepts.

Let's say that A_i forms a mutually exhaustive event with B:

$$B = \sum_{i=1}^{n} B \cap A_i$$

The probability of B will be as follows:

$$P(B) = \sum_{i=1}^{n} P(B \cap A_i)$$

We get the probability of B from conditional probability like so:

$$P(B \cap A_i) = P(A_i)P(B|A_i)$$

Hence:

$$P(A_i|B) = \frac{P(A_i \cap B)}{P(B)} .. (1)$$

$$P(B|A_i) = \frac{P(A_i \cap B)}{P(A_i)} .. (2)$$

Now, extracting the value of $P(A_i \cap B)$ from equation 2 and putting it in equation 1, we get this:

$$P(A_i|B) = \frac{P(B|A_i) * P(A_i)}{P(B)} .. (3)$$

After replacing the value of *P(B)* from the preceding equation, we get this:

$$P(A_i|B) = \frac{P(B|A_i) * P(A_i)}{\sum_{i=1}^{n} P(B \cap A_i)} \ldots (4)$$

Have a look at equation 3 first. This is called **Bayes rule**.

P(A|B) is called **posterior**, which needs to be estimated. In the preceding example, this would be the probability of scoring a century given that the player has got the earlier experience of playing there.

P(B|A) is called the **likelihood**, which is the probability of observing the new evidence, given our initial hypothesis. For example, the probability of a player having previous experience in playing cricket get to score a century.

P(A) is called the **prior**, which is the probability of our hypothesis without any additional prior information.

P(B) is called the **marginal likelihood**, which is the total probability of observing the evidence.

Bayes network

Bayes network is a type of probabilistic graphical model that can be used to build models to address business problems. Applications of this are quite wide. For example, it can be used in anomaly detection, predictive modeling, diagnostics, automated insights, and many other applications.

It is totally understandable that a few words used here would have been alien to you till now. For example, what do we mean by graphical here?

A graph forms out of a set of nodes and edges. Nodes are represented by *N={N1,N2.....Nn}*, where independent variables are sitting at every node. Edges are the connectors between nodes. Edges can be denoted by *E={E1, E2.....En}* and can be of two types:

- Directed, represented by $N1 \rightarrow N2$
- Undirected, represented by:

With the help of nodes and edges, a relationship between the variables is exhibited. It can be a conditional independence relationship or a conditional dependence relationship. BN is one a techniques that can introduce causality amongst variables. Although causality is not an essential part of it, having this (causality) in the network can make the structure quite compact.

Let's see it through an example. There are a number of variables, such as waking up late, an accident on the highway, a rainy day, a traffic jam, they will be late for work, and being late for a meeting. If an individual has got up late, it means being late for work. An accident on the highway can cause a traffic jam and, in turn, this will result in being late for work. On a rainy day, the roads can be more prone to accidents and, also, there can be slow-moving traffic that will cause a traffic jam and, in turn, this will result in being late for work. The following diagram explains the example:

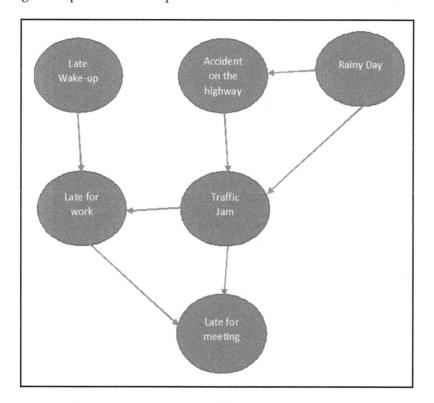

This kind of network is called a **directed acyclic graph**. Acyclic means that there is no cycle in the network. We are talking about a relationship between variables here. For example, waking up late and being late for a meeting are typically not independent. But they are conditionally independent, given being late for work.

Also, it might seem that waking up late has no connection and relationship with an accident on the highway. That is, they may appear to be independent of each other. However, if you know the value of being late for work, then these two can be called conditionally independent.

So, BN allows conditional independence between nodes. At the same time, it is an efficient representation of joint probability distribution, which is enabled by a chain rule.

Let's say that X represents n independent variables or nodes. Arcs or a directed arrow represents the probabilistic dependence or independence amongst variables. An absence of an arc would mean probabilistic independence. The network is a directed acyclic graph wherein the local probability distribution is kept at each node, which is also called the **conditional probability table (CPT)**.

If we talk about the previous network, then we need the probability distribution required to address the whole network. For the purpose of simplicity, we will keep all the nodes as Boolean.

Probabilities of nodes

Let's look at the probability at each node and find out how many probabilities would appear there.

The nodes carrying **Late Wake-up** and **Rainy Day** are the parent nodes as there are no nodes leading to such nodes. The different nodes can be seen in the following points:

1. **Node (Late Wake-up)**: Being one of the parent nodes, we will be looking just to find out the probability of waking up late. Hence, the count of probability to be found out is 1 here.
2. **Node (Rainy Day)**: Like the late wake-up node, the count of probability is 1 here as well.
3. **Node (Accident on the highway)**: As it is a child node of rainy day, it talks about the probability of the accident given the rainy day and the probability of the accident given it's not a rainy day. So, the count of probability is 2 here.
4. **Node (Traffic Jam)**: It has got two parents (rainy day and accident). Rainy day has got two values, which are true and false, the same as accident. Combining both will yield four different combinations. Hence, the count of probability will be 4.
5. **Node (Late for work)** and **Node (Late for meeting)**: A similar explanation applies to these two nodes as well. The count for the probabilities of these is 4:

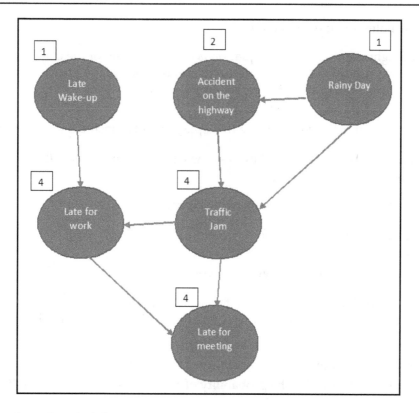

The total number of probabilities are 1 + 2 + 1 + 4 + 4 + 4 = 16.

Had it been just a normal joint probability distribution instead of BN, we would have had 2^6-1 probabilities. Hence, BN makes the network quite compact. Also, another more basic assumption we have to be mindful of is that each node is conditionally independent of its non-descendants given its immediate parents. For example, waking up late and being late for a meeting are conditionally independent in the case that **late for work** is also there. Generally, we can express BN in the following manner, which displays how joint distribution can be translated into a compact structure:

$$P(X1, X2, X3, \ldots \ldots, Xn) = \prod_i P(Xi|Par(Xi))$$

If G is the graph, X_i is a node in the graph G, and P are the parents of the X_i node.

Here are a few notes about the equations:

- The right-hand side of the equation is the application of the chain rule, which exhibits conditional independence relations. It is a graph-structured approximation of the joint probability distribution.
- Of course, the graph has to be acyclic.
- It can provide the convenience to display the relationship among various events.

Now, let's take a simple scenario to showcase the CPT. The following is the combination of three events as shown:

If it rains, the dog starts barking and the man skips work:

- Probability of rain (yes/no)
- Probability that the dog will bark (yes/no)
- Probability that the man will skip work (yes/no)

Let's have the network prepared as a directed acyclic graph. All these nodes reflect an event, and directed arrows are conditional probabilities. We will see here how to read this graph:

- Connector 1 indicates the probability of the dog barking if it rains
- Connector 2 indicates the probability of the man skipping his work if the dog barks

The following diagram shows the flow chart for both the probabilities:

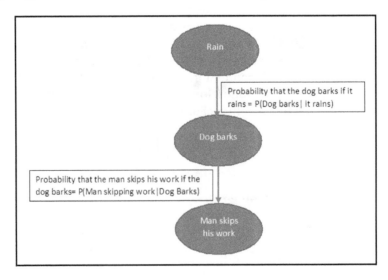

CPT

Let's do the CPT for connector 1:

	The dog barks	The dog doesn't bark	Aggregate
It rains	10	4	14
It doesn't rain	8	5	13
Aggregate	18	9	27

Here, we are talking about the following scenarios:

- Probability *(Dog barks | It rains) = 10/14*
- Probability *(Dog doesn't bark | It rain) = 4/14*
- Probability *(Dog barks | It doesn't rain) = 8/13*
- Probability *(Dog doesn't bark | It doesn't rain) = 5/13*

	The dog barks	The dog doesn't bark
It rains	10/14	4/14
It doesn't rain	8/13	5/13

The following diagram shows the probabilities in detail:

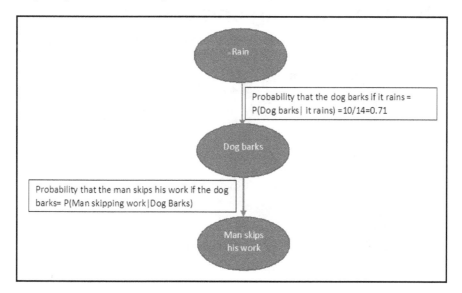

Let's say if the probability of *rain = P(rain) =0.6* then the probability of *no rain = P(no rain) = 0.4*.

Let's say that the CPT for the man skipping work is as follows:

	The man skips work	**The man doesn't skip work**
The dog barks	0.8	0.2
The dog doesn't bark	0.3	0.7

 The probability of every event has to be calculated with respect to the parent node.

And now, we are supposed to find out the probability of *the man skipping work and the dog barks but it doesn't rain = P (Man skips work, the dog barks, it doesn't rain)*:

= P (Man skips work | the dog barks) *P (the dog barks | it doesn't rain) *P(it doesn't rain)

=0.8 * (8/13) *0.4

=0.1969

Example of the training and test set

Let's take a use case and work it out in Python. We are going to use Titanic data from Kaggle.
The data has been split into two groups:

- Training set (train.csv)
- Test set (test.csv)

The data is about the passengers who traveled on the Titanic. It captures their features:

- pclass: Ticket class 1 = 1st, 2 = 2nd, 3 = 3rd
- gender: Gender
- Age: Age in years
- sibsp: Number of siblings/spouses aboard the Titanic
- parch: Number of parents/children aboard the Titanic
- ticket: Ticket number
- fare Passenger: Fare

- `cabin`: Cabin number
- `embarked`: Port of embarkation `C = Cherbourg, Q = Queenstown, and S = Southampton`

We have got to build the model to predict whether or not they survived the sinking of the Titanic. Initially, import the parameters as shown:

```
import pandas as pd
import numpy as np
```

We are loading the datasets here:

```
traindf= pd.read_csv("train.csv")
testdf= pd.read_csv("test.csv")
```

We have to look for the number of unique values for each variable since BNs are discrete models:

```
for k in traindf.keys():
  print('{0}: {1}'.format(k, len(traindf[k].unique())))
```

The output is as follows:

```
PassengerId: 891
Survived: 2
Pclass: 3
Name: 891
Gender: 2
Age: 89
SibSp: 7
Parch: 7
Ticket: 681
Fare: 248
Cabin: 148
Embarked: 4
```

In order to save our system from too much computation and to avoid load on it, we will reduce the number of variables:

```
for k in traindf.keys():
  if len(traindf[k].unique())<=10:
  print(k)
```

We get the following output:

```
Survived
Pclass
Gender
SibSp
Parch
Embarked
```

Now, we are left with six variables.

Also, we have to discretize continuous variables in case they needs to be made part of the model:

```
import math
def forAge(row):
 if row['Age'] < 10:
    return '<10'
 elif math.isnan(row['Age']):
    return "nan"
 else:
    dec = str(int(row['Age']/10))
    return "{0}0's".format(dec)
decade=traindf.apply(forAge, axis=1)
print("Decade: {1}".format(k, len(decade.unique())))
```

The output is as follows:

```
Decade: 10
```

Let's do the pre-processing now:

```
def preprocess(df):
 # create a dataframe with discrete variables (len<10)
 filt=[k for k in df.keys() if len(df[k].unique())<=10]
 filtr2=df[filt].copy()
 forAge = lambda row: int(row['Age']/10) if not math.isnan(row['Age']) else
np.nan
 filtr2['Decade']=df.apply(forAge, axis=1)
 filtr2=filtr2.dropna()
 filtr2['Decade']=filtr2['Decade'].astype('int32')
 return filtr2
```

For `traindf` and `testdf`, we use the following:

```
ptraindf= preprocess(traindf)
ptestdf=preprocess(testdf)
```

We need to save this data, since the `pyAgrum` library accepts only files as inputs:

```
ptraindf.to_csv('post_train.csv', index=False)
ptestdf.to_csv( 'post_test.csv', index=False)

df=pd.read_csv('post_train.csv')
for k in df.keys():
  print("{} : {}".format(k, df[k].unique()))
```

The output can be seen as follows:

```
Survived : [0 1]
Pclass : [3 1 2]
Gender : ['male' 'female']
SibSp : [1 0 3 4 2 5]
Parch : [0 1 2 5 3 4 6]
Embarked : ['S' 'C' 'Q']
Decade : [2 3 5 0 1 4 6 7 8]
```

```
import pyAgrum as gum
import pyAgrum.lib.notebook as gnb
```

Now, it's time to build the model. Here, you need to be watchful while choosing the `RangeVariable` and `LabelizedVariable` variables:

```
template=gum.BayesNet()
template.add(gum.RangeVariable("Survived", "Survived",0,1))
template.add(gum.RangeVariable("Pclass", "Pclass",1,3))
template.add(gum.LabelizedVariable("Gender",
"Gender",0).addLabel("female").addLabel("male"))
template.add(gum.RangeVariable("SibSp", "SibSp",0,8))
template.add(gum.RangeVariable("Parch", "Parch",0,9))
template.add(gum.LabelizedVariable("Embarked",
"Embarked",0).addLabel('').addLabel('C').addLabel('Q').addLabel('S'))
template.add(gum.RangeVariable("Decade", "Calculated decade", 0,9))
gnb.showBN(template)
```

The output can be seen as follows:

For `learnBN()`, we use the following:

```
learner = gum.BNLearner('post_train.csv', template)
bn = learner.learnBN()
bn
```

The following is the output:

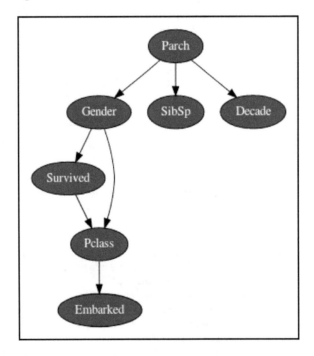

Now that we have the model, let's try to extract the information from it:

```
gnb.showInformation(bn, {}, size="20")
```

We get the output as follows:

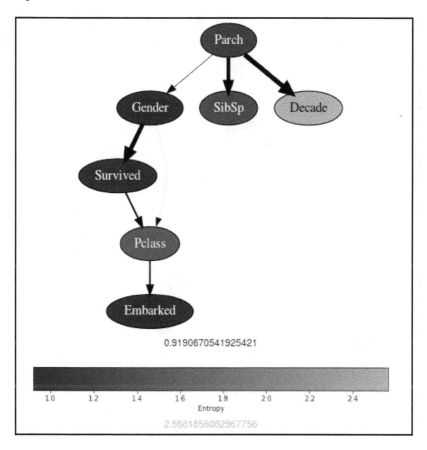

The entropy of a variable means that the greater the value, the more uncertain the variable's marginal probability distribution is. The lower the value of entropy, the lower the uncertainty. The Decade variable has got the highest entropy, which means that it is evenly distributed. Parch has got low entropy and distribution is non-even.

A consequence of how entropy is calculated is that entropy tends to get bigger if the random variable has many modalities.

Finding the inference gives us a view of the marginal probability distribution here:

```
gnb.showInference(bn)
```

The output can be seen as follows:

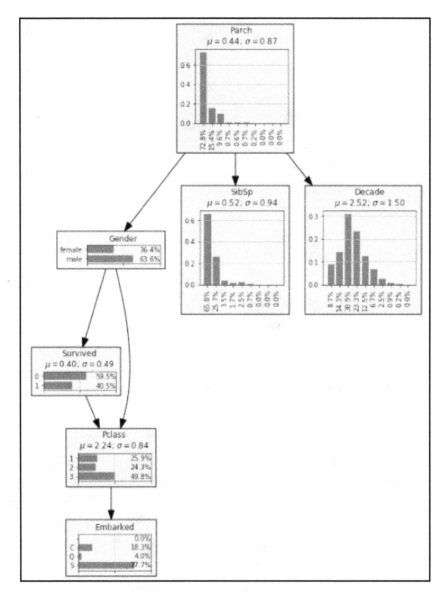

Now, let's see how classification can be done:

```
gnb.showPosterior(bn,evs={},target='Survived')
```

We get the output as follows:

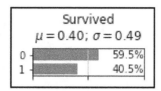

More than 40% of passengers survived here. But, we are not pushing any conditions.

Let's say we want to find out what the chances of a young male surviving are:

```
gnb.showPosterior(bn,evs={"Gender": "male", "Decade": 3},target='Survived')
```

The following is the output:

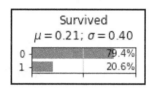

So, the chances are 20.6%.

If we have to find out the chances of an old lady surviving, we go about it as follows:

```
gnb.showPosterior(bn,evs={"Gender": "female", "Decade":
8},target='Survived')
```

The output is as follows:

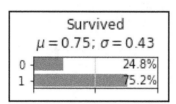

Now, in order to evaluate the model to find out how good it is, we will plot the ROC curve:

```
from pyAgrum.lib.bn2roc import showROC
showROC(bn, 'post_train.csv','Survived',"1",True,True)
```

The following is the output:

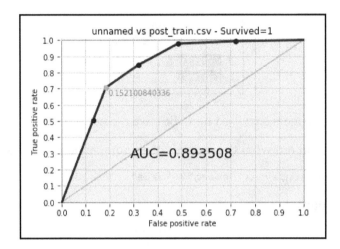

Here, **AUC** comes out to be **0.893508** and it's quite decent.

We are done with the modeling part here. Also, we have learned about probability theory, Bayesian networks, the calculation of CPT, and how to execute it in Python.

Summary

This chapter has given us an understanding of probability theory. Also, the application of probability theory has been put into use. We got an idea of Bayes rule and BNs and how it is formed. We got our hands dirty with the calculation of a CPT. Finally, we looked at a use case to understand how classification can be done with the help of BNs. The readers will now have the skill to have an in-depth knowledge of Bayes rules and BNs.

In the next chapter, we will study selected topics in deep learning.

9
Selected Topics in Deep Learning

In Chapter 4, *Training Neural Networks*, we looked at what an **artificial neural network** (**ANN**) is and how this kind of model is built. You can say that a deep neural network is an elongated version of an ANN; however, it has got its own set of challenges.

In this chapter, we will learn about the following topics:

- What is a deep neural network?
- How to initialize parameters
- Adversarial networks—generative adversarial networks and Bayesian generative adversarial networks
- Deep Gaussian processes
- Hinton's Capsule network

Deep neural networks

Let's recap on what we learned in Chapter 4, *Training Neural Networks*. A neural network is a machine emulation of the human brain that is seen as a set of algorithms that have been set out to extract patterns out of data. It has got three different layers:

- Input layer
- Hidden layer
- Output layer

Sensory numerical data (in the form of a vector) passes through the input layer and then goes through the hidden layers to generate its own set of perceptions and reasoning to yield the final result in the output layer.

Can you recall what we learned in Chapter 4, *Training Neural Networks*, regarding the number of layers in ANN and how we count them? When we have got the layers like the ones shown in the following diagram, can you count the number of layers? Remember, we always count just the hidden layer and the output layer. So, if somebody is asking you how many layers there are in your network, you don't include the input layer while answering:

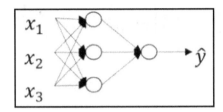

Yes, that's right—there are two layers in the preceding architecture. What about for the following network?

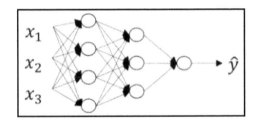

This network has got three layers, which includes two hidden layers. As the layers increase, the model becomes deeper.

Why do we need a deep learning model?

A deep learning model is a highly non-linear model that has got multiple layers with multiple nodes acting in sequence to solve a business problem. Every layer has been assigned a different task.

For example, if we have got a face detection problem, hidden layer 1 finds out which edges are present in the image. Layer 2 finds out the combination of edges, which start taking the shape of eyes, a nose, and other parts. Layer 3 enables the object models, which creates the shape of the face. The following diagram shows the different hidden layers:

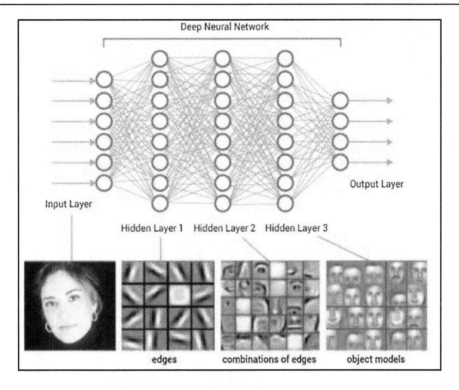

Here, we have got a logistic regression model, also known as a **single layer neural network**. Sometimes, it is also called the most **shallow network**. The second network that can be seen here has got a two-layer network. Again, it's a shallow network, but it's not as shallow as the previous one. The next architecture has got three layers, which is making things more interesting now. The network is getting deep now. The last architecture has got a six layer architecture, which is comprised of five hidden layers. The number of layers is getting even deeper.

Deep neural network notation

The explanation of the notation is as follows:

- l: Number of layers is 4
- $n^{[l]}$: Number of nodes in layer l

For the following architecture, this is as follows:

- $n^{[0]}$: Number of nodes in input layer, that is, 3
- $n^{[1]}$: 5
- $n^{[2]}$: 5
- $n^{[3]}$: 3
- $n^{[4]}$: 1
- $a^{[l]}$: Activations in layer l:

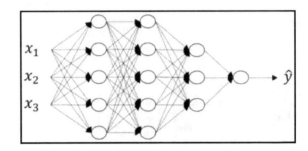

As we already know, the following equation goes through the layers:

$$z = w^T X + b$$

Hence, we get the following results:

- Activation: $a = \sigma(z)$
- $w^{[l]}$: Weight in layer l
- $b^{[l]}$: Bias in layer l

Forward propagation in a deep network

Let's see how these equations set up for layer 1 and layer 2. If the training example set, X is (x1, x2, x3) for the preceding network.

Let's see how the equation comes along for layer 1:

$$z^{[1]} = w^{[1]} x + b^{[1]}$$

The activation function for layer 1 is as follows:

$$a^{[1]} = g^{[1]}\left(w^{[1]}x + b^{[1]}\right) = g^{[1]}\left(z^{[1]}\right)$$

The input can also be expressed as follows:

$$x = a^{[0]}$$

For layer 2, the input will be as follows:

$$z^{[2]} = w^{[2]}a^{[1]} + b^{[2]}$$

The activation function that's applied here is as follows:

$$a^{[2]} = g^{[2]}\left(z^{[2]}\right)$$

Similarly, for layer 3, the input that's applied is as follows:

$$z^{[3]} = w^{[3]}a^{[2]} + b^{[3]}$$

The activation function for the third layer is as follows:

$$a^{[3]} = g^{[3]}\left(z^{[3]}\right)$$

Finally, here's the input for the last layer:

$$z^{[4]} = w^{[4]}a^{[3]} + b^{[4]}$$

This is its activation:

$$a^{[4]} = g^{[4]}\left(z^{[4]}\right) = y$$

Hence, the generalized forward propagation equation turns out to be as follows:

$$z^{[l]} = w^{[l]}a^{[l-1]} + b^{[l]}$$

$$a^{[l]} = g^{[l]}\left(z^{[l]}\right)$$

Parameters W and b

Let's talk about the following architecture. First, let's note down what we learned about in the previous section. Take a look at the following diagram:

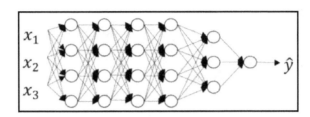

Here, we can see the following:

- l: Number of layers: 6
- $n^{[l]}$: Number of nodes in layer l
- $n^{[0]}$: Number of nodes in input layer: 3 ::
- $n^{[1]}$: Number of nodes in first layer: 4 ::

The equation for this is as follows:

$$n^{[2]} = 4 :: n^{[3]} = 4 :: n^{[4]} = 4 :: n^{[5]} = 3 :: n^{[6]} = 1$$

Implementing forward propagation would mean that hidden layer 1 can be expressed via the following equation:

$$z^{[1]} = w^{[1]}X + b^{[1]} \quad .....(1)$$

Can you determine the dimensions of z, w, and X for forward propagation?

Let's discuss this. X indicates the input layer vectors or nodes, and we know that there are 3 nodes. Can we find out the dimension of the input layer? Well, yes, it's $(n^{[0]}, 1)$ – alternatively, you can say that it is (3,1).

What about for first hidden layer? Since the first hidden layer has got three nodes, the dimension of $z^{[1]}$ will be $(n^{[1]}, 1)$. This means that the dimension will be (4,1).

The dimensions of $z^{[1]}$ and X have been ascertained. By looking at the preceding equation, it is evident that the dimensions of $z^{[1]}$ and $w^{[1]}$X have to be the same (from linear algebra). So, can you come up with the dimension of $w^{[1]}$? We know from linear algebra that matrix multiplication between matrix 1 and 2 is possible only when the number of columns of matrix 1 is equal to the number of rows of matrix 2. So, the number of columns of $w^{[1]}$ has to be equal to the number of rows of matrix X. This will make the number of columns of $w^{[1]}$ 3. However, as we've already discussed, the dimensions of $z^{[1]}$ and $w^{[1]}$X have to be the same, and so the number of rows of the former should be equal to the number of rows of the latter. Hence, the number of rows of $w^{[1]}$ will turn out to be 4. Alright, we have got the dimension of $w^{[1]}$ now, which is (4,3). To make this more general, we can also say that the dimension of $w^{[1]}$ is $(n^{[1]}, n^{[0]})$. Similarly, the dimension of $w^{[2]}$ will be equal to $(n^{[2]}, n^{[1]})$ or (number of nodes of the current layer, number of nodes of the previous layer). It will make the dimension of $w^{[2]}$ (4,4). Let's generalize this. Let's look at the dimension of the following equation:

$$w^{[1]} = (n^{[1]}, n^{[l-1]})$$

What about the dimension of bias $b^{[1]}$? Can you make use of linear algebra and figure that out? This must be a cake walk for you by now. Yes, you would have probably guessed it correctly by now. It is has the same dimension as $z^{[1]}$. Let me explain this, for everyone's benefit. Going by the equation, the dimension of the left-hand side should be equal to the dimension of the right-hand side. Besides, $w^{[1]}$X + $b^{[1]}$ is an addition of two matrices and it is well-known that two matrices can only be added if they have the same dimension; that is, they must have the same number of rows and columns. So, the dimension of $b^{[1]}$ will be equal to $w^{[1]}$X; in turn, it will be equal to $z^{[1]}$ (which is (4,1)).

In terms of generalization, the dimension of $b^{[1]} = (n^{[1]}, 1)$.

For backpropagation, this is as follows:

- Dimension of $dw^{[l]} = (n^{[l]}, n^{[l-1]})$
- Dimension of $db^{[l]} = (n^{[l]}, 1)$

Forward and backward propagation

Let me show you how forward pass and backward pass work with the help of an example.

We have got a network that has got two layers (1 hidden layer and 1 output layer). Every layer (including the input) has got two nodes. It has got bias nodes as well, as shown in the following diagram:

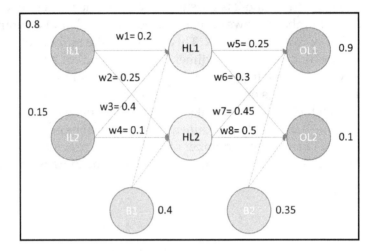

The notations that are used in the preceding diagram are as follows:

- *IL*: Input layer
- *HL*: Hidden layer
- *OL*: Output layer
- *w*: Weight
- *B*: Bias

We have got the values for all of the required fields. Let's feed this into the network and see how it flows. The activation function that's being used here is the sigmoid.

The input that's given to the first node of the hidden layer is as follows:

$$InputHL1 = w1*IL1 + w3*IL2 + B1$$

$$InputHL1= (0.2*0.8)+(0.4*0.15) + 0.4 =0.62$$

The input that's given to the second node of the hidden layer is as follows:

$$InputHL2 = w2*IL1 + w4*IL2 + B1$$

$$InputHL2 = (0.25*0.8) +(0.1*0.15) + 0.4 = 0.615$$

To find out the output, we will use our activation function, like so:

$$OutputHL1 = \frac{1}{1+e^{-Input_H L1}} = 0.650219$$

$$OutputHL2 = \frac{1}{1+e^{-Input_H L2}} = 0.649081$$

Now, these outputs will be passed on to the output layer as input. Let's calculate the value of the input for the nodes in the output layer:

$$InputOL1 = w5*Output\_HL1 + w7*Output\_HL2 + B2 = 0.804641$$

$$InputOL2 = w6*Output\_HL1 + w8*Output\_HL2 + B2 = 0.869606$$

Now, let's compute the output:

$$Output_{OL1} = \frac{1}{1+e^{-Input_O L1}} = 0.690966$$

$$Output_{OL2} = \frac{1}{1+e^{-Input_O L2}} = 0.704664$$

Error computation

We can now calculate the error for each output neuron using the square error function and sum them together to get the total error:

$$Etotal = \sum \frac{1}{2}(target - actual)^2$$

$$EOL1 = \text{Error at first node of output layer} = \frac{1}{2}(target_{OL1} - output_{OL1})^2$$

$$=0.021848$$

$$EOL2 = \text{Error at second node of output layer} = \frac{1}{2}(target_{OL2} - output_{OL2})^2$$

$$=0.182809$$

$$Total\ Error = Etotal= EOL1 + EOL2 = 0.021848 + 0.182809 = 0.204657$$

Backward propagation

The purpose of backpropagation is to update each of the weights in the network so that they cause the actual output to be closer to the target output, thereby minimizing the error for each output neuron and the network as a whole.

Let's focus on an output layer first. We are supposed to find out the impact of change in w5 on the total error.

This will be decided by $\frac{\delta(Etotal)}{\delta w5}$. It is the partial derivative of Etotal with respect to w5.

Let's apply the chain rule here:

$$\frac{\delta(Etotal)}{\delta w5} = \frac{\delta(Etotal)}{\delta Output_{OL1}} * \frac{\delta(Output_{OL1})}{\delta Input_{OL1}} * \frac{\delta Input_{OL1}}{\delta w5}$$

$$Etotal = \frac{1}{2}(target_{OL1} - output_{OL1})^2 + \frac{1}{2}(target_{OL2} - output_{OL2})^2$$

$$\frac{\delta(Etotal)}{\delta Output_{OL1}} = 2 * \frac{1}{2} * (target_{OL1} - target_{OL2}) * (-1) = target_{OL2} - target_{OL1}$$

$$= 0.690966 - 0.9 = -0.209034$$

$$Output_{OL1} = \frac{1}{1 + e^{-Input_{OL1}}}$$

$$\frac{\delta Output_{OL1}}{\delta Input_{OL1}} = \frac{e^{-Input_{OL1}}}{(1 + e^{-Input})^2}$$

$$= 0.213532$$

$$InputOL1 = w5*OutputHL1 + w7*OutputHL2 + B2$$

$$\frac{\delta Input_{OL1}}{\delta w5} = Output_{HL1} = 0.650219$$

Now, let's get back to the old equation:

$$\frac{\delta(Etotal)}{\delta w5} = \frac{\delta(Etotal)}{\delta Output_{OL1}} * \frac{\delta(Output_{OL1})}{\delta Input_{OL1}} * \frac{\delta Input_{OL1}}{\delta w5}$$

$$\frac{\delta(Etotal)}{\delta w5} = (-0.209034) * (0.213532) * (0.650219) = -0.02902$$

To update the weight, we will use the following formula. We have set the learning rate to be $\alpha = 0.1$:

$$⟦w5⟧^{+} = w5 - \alpha * (\delta Etotal)/\delta w5 = 0.25 - (0.1 * -0.02902) = 0.252902$$

Similarly, $⟦w6⟧^{+}$, $⟦w7⟧^{+}$, $⟦w8⟧^{+}$ are supposed to be calculated. The approach remains the same. We will leave this to compute as it will help you in understanding the concepts better.

When it comes down to the hidden layer and computing, the approach still remains the same. However, the formula will change a bit. I will help you with the formula, but the rest of the computation has to be done by you.

We will take *w1* here.

Let's apply the chain rule here:

$$\frac{\delta(Etotal)}{\delta w1} = \frac{\delta(Etotal)}{\delta Output_{HL1}} * \frac{\delta(Output_{HL1})}{\delta Input_{HL1}} * \frac{\delta Input_{HL1}}{\delta w1}$$

This formula has to be utilized for *w2*, *w3*, and *w4*. Please ensure that you are doing partial differentiation of *E_total* with respect to other weights and, in the end, that you are using the learning rate formula to get the updated weight.

Forward propagation equation

We know the equations around it. If the input for this is $a^{[l-1]}$, then the output will be $a^{[l]}$. However, there is a cache part, which is nothing but $z^{[l]}$, as shown in the following diagram:

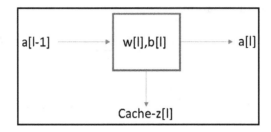

Here, this breaks down into $w^{[1]}a^{[l-1]}+b^{[l]}$ (remember that $a^{[0]}$ is equal to X).

Backward propagation equation

The following equations would be required to execute backward propagation:

$$z^{[l]} = w^{[l]}a^{[l-1]} + b^{[l]}$$

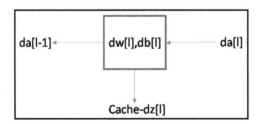

These equations will give you an idea of what is going on behind the scenes. Here, a suffix, *d*, has been added, which is a representation of the partial derivative that acts during backward propagation:

$$dz^{[l]} = dw^{[l]}g^{[l]}(z^{[l]}) + db^{[l]}$$

$$dw^{[l]} = dz^{[l]}(dz^{[l]})$$

Parameters and hyperparameters

While we are getting on with building a deep learning model, you need to know how to keep a tab on both parameters and hyperparameters. But how well do we understand these?

When it comes down to parameters, we have got weights and biases. As we begin to train the network, one of the prime steps is to initialize the parameters.

Bias initialization

It is a common practice to initialize the bias by zero as the symmetrical breaking of neurons is taken care of by the random weights' initialization.

Hyperparameters

Hyperparameters are one of the building blocks of the deep learning network. It is an element that determines the optimal architecture of the network (for example, number of layers) and also a factor that is responsible for ensuring how the network will be trained.

The following are the various hyperparameters of the deep learning network:

- **Learning rate**: This is responsible for determining the pace at which the network is trained. A slow learning rate ensures a smooth convergence, whereas a fast learning rate may not have smooth convergence.
- **Epoch**: The number of epochs is the number of times the whole training data is consumed by the network while training.
- **Number of hidden layers**: This determines the structure of the model, which helps in achieving the optimal capacity of the model.
- **Number of nodes (neurons)**: There should be a trade-off between the number of nodes to be used. It decides whether all of the necessary information has been extracted to produce the required output. Overfitting or underfitting will be decided by the number of nodes. Hence, it is advisable to use it with regularization.
- **Dropout**: Dropout is a regularization technique that's used to increase generalizing power by avoiding overfitting. This was discussed in detail in Chapter 4, *Training Neural Networks*. The dropout value can be between 0.2 and 0.5.

- **Momentum**: This determines the direction of the next step toward convergence. With a value between 0.6 and 0.9, it handles oscillation.
- **Batch size**: This is the number of samples that are fed into the network, after which a parameter update happens. Typically, it is taken as 32, 64, 128, 256.

To find the optimal number of hyperparameters, it is prudent to deploy a grid search or random search.

Use case – digit recognizer

The **Modified National Institute of Standards and Technology** (**MNIST**) is in fact the dataset of computer vision for *hello world*. Considering its release in 1999, this dataset has served as the main fundamental basis for benchmarking classification algorithms.

Our goal is to correctly identify digits from a dataset of tens of thousands of handwritten images. We have curated a set of tutorial-style kernels that cover everything from regression to neural networks:

```python
import numpy as np
import pandas as pd
import matplotlib.pyplot as plt
import matplotlib.image as mpimg
import seaborn as sns
%matplotlib inline
from sklearn.model_selection import train_test_split
import itertools
from keras.utils.np_utils import to_categorical # convert to one-hot-
encoding
from keras.models import Sequential
from keras.layers import Dense, Dropout, Flatten, Conv2D, MaxPool2D
from keras.optimizers import SGD
from keras.preprocessing.image import ImageDataGenerator
sns.set(style='white', context='notebook', palette='deep')
np.random.seed(2)

# Load the data
train = pd.read_csv("train.csv")
test = pd.read_csv("test.csv")

Y_train = train["label"]
# Drop 'label' column
X_train = train.drop(labels = ["label"],axis = 1)

Y_train.value_counts()
```

The output of the preceding code is as follows:

```
1     4684
7     4401
3     4351
9     4188
2     4177
6     4137
0     4132
4     4072
8     4063
5     3795
Name: label, dtype: int64
```

```
X_train.isnull().any().describe()
```

Here, we get the following output:

```
count       784
unique        1
top       False
freq        784
dtype: object
```

```
test.isnull().any().describe()
```

Here, we get the following output:

```
count       784
unique        1
top       False
freq        784
dtype: object
```

```
X_train = X_train / 255.0
test = test / 255.0
```

By reshaping the image into 3 dimensions, we get the following:

```
Reshape image in 3 dimensions (height = 28px, width = 28px, canal = 1)
X_train = X_train.values.reshape(-1,28,28,1)
test = test.values.reshape(-1,28,28,1)

Encode labels to one hot vectors
Y_train = to_categorical(Y_train, num_classes = 10)
```

```
# Split the dataset into train and the validation set
X_train, X_val, Y_train, Y_val = train_test_split(X_train, Y_train,
test_size = 0.1, random_state=2)
```

By executing the following code, we will be able to see the numbered plot:

```
pic = plt.imshow(X_train[9][:,:,0])
```

The output is as follows:

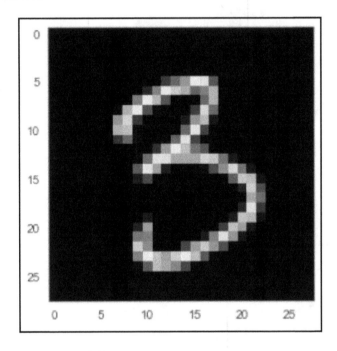

The sequential model is now as follows:

```
model = Sequential()
model.add(Conv2D(filters = 32, kernel_size = (5,5),padding = 'Same',
activation ='relu', input_shape = (28,28,1)))
model.add(Conv2D(filters = 32, kernel_size = (5,5),padding = 'Same',
activation ='relu'))
model.add(MaxPool2D(pool_size=(2,2)))
model.add(Dropout(0.25))
model.add(Conv2D(filters = 64, kernel_size = (3,3),padding = 'Same',
activation ='relu'))
model.add(Conv2D(filters = 64, kernel_size = (3,3),padding = 'Same',
activation ='relu'))
model.add(MaxPool2D(pool_size=(2,2), strides=(2,2)))
model.add(Dropout(0.25))
```

```
model.add(Flatten())
model.add(Dense(256, activation = "relu"))
model.add(Dropout(0.5))
model.add(Dense(10, activation = "softmax"))
```

When we define the optimizer, we get the following output:

```
# Define the optimizer
optimizer = SGD(lr=0.01, momentum=0.0, decay=0.0)
```

When we compile the model, we get the following output:

```
# Compile the model
model.compile(optimizer = optimizer, loss = "categorical_crossentropy",
metrics=["accuracy"])

epochs = 5
batch_size = 64
```

Next, we generate the image generator:

```
datagen = ImageDataGenerator(
  featurewise_center=False, # set input mean to 0 over the dataset
  samplewise_center=False, # set each sample mean to 0
  featurewise_std_normalization=False, # divide inputs by std of the dataset
  samplewise_std_normalization=False, # divide each input by its std
  zca_whitening=False, # apply ZCA whitening
  rotation_range=10, # randomly rotate images in the range (degrees, 0 to
180)
  zoom_range = 0.1, # Randomly zoom image
  width_shift_range=0.1, # randomly shift images horizontally (fraction of
total width)
  height_shift_range=0.1, # randomly shift images vertically (fraction of
total height)
  horizontal_flip=False, # randomly flip images
  vertical_flip=False) # randomly flip images
datagen.fit(X_train)

history = model.fit_generator(datagen.flow(X_train,Y_train,
batch_size=batch_size),
  epochs = epochs, validation_data = (X_val,Y_val),
  verbose = 2, steps_per_epoch=X_train.shape[0] // batch_size)
```

The output can be seen as follows:

```
Epoch 1/5
 - 217s - loss: 1.8641 - acc: 0.3410 - val_loss: 0.5560 - val_acc: 0.8583
Epoch 2/5
 - 218s - loss: 0.7747 - acc: 0.7465 - val_loss: 0.1898 - val_acc: 0.9481
Epoch 3/5
 - 224s - loss: 0.4380 - acc: 0.8618 - val_loss: 0.1323 - val_acc: 0.9605
Epoch 4/5
 - 219s - loss: 0.3300 - acc: 0.8962 - val_loss: 0.1068 - val_acc: 0.9700
Epoch 5/5
 - 233s - loss: 0.2802 - acc: 0.9143 - val_loss: 0.0915 - val_acc: 0.9726
```

We predict the model as follows:

```
results = model.predict(test)
# select with the maximum probability
results = np.argmax(results,axis = 1)
results = pd.Series(results,name="Label")
results
```

The output can be seen as follows:

```
0     2
1     0
2     9
3     0
4     3
5     9
6     0
7     3
8     0
9     3
10    5
11    7
12    4
13    0
14    4
15    3
16    3
17    1
18    9
19    0
20    9
21    1
22    1
23    5
24    7
25    4
26    2
27    7
28    4
29    7
```

Generative adversarial networks

Generative adversarial networks (**GANs**) are another form of deep neural network architecture, and is a combination of two networks that compete and cooperate with each other. It was introduced by Ian Goodfellow and Yoshua Bengio in 2014.

GANs can learn to mimic any distribution of data, which ideally means that GANs can be taught to create an object that's similar to an existing one in any domain, such as images, music, speech, and prose. It can create photos of any object that has never existed before. They are robot artists in a sense, and their output is impressive.

It falls under unsupervised learning wherein both of the networks learn their task upon training. One of the networks is called the **generator** and the other is called the **discriminator**.

To make this more understandable, we can think of a **GAN** as a case of a counterfeiter (generator) and a cop (discriminator). At the outset, the counterfeiter shows the cop fake money. The cop works like a detective and finds out that it is a fake money (you can think of D as a detective too if you want to understand how a discriminator works). The cop passes his feedback to the counterfeiter, explaining why the money is fake. The counterfeiter makes a few adjustments and makes new, fake money based on the feedback it received. The cop says that the money is still fake and he shares his new feedback with the counterfeiter. The counterfeiter then attempts to make new, fake money based on the latest feedback. The cycle continues indefinitely until the cop is fooled by the fake money because it looks real. When a GAN model is being created, the generator and discriminator start to learn from scratch and from each other. It may seem that they are pitted against each other, but they are helping each other learn. The feedback mechanism between these two is helping the model to be more robust.

A discriminator is quite a good learner, since it is capable of learning anything from the real world. That is, if you want it to learn about images of cats and dogs, and its 1,000 different categories where it's asked to differentiate between the images, it will be able to do so without any hassle, like so:

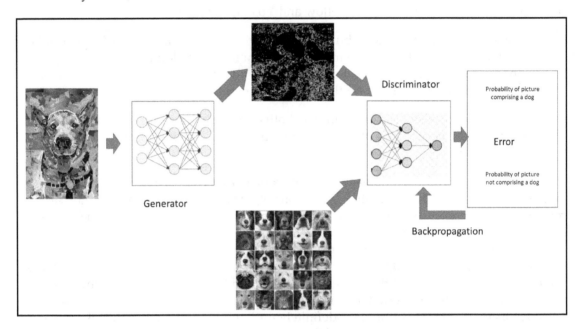

Noise goes into the generator; then, the output of the generator goes through the discriminator and we get an output. Simultaneously, the discriminator is being trained on the images of dogs. However, in the very beginning, even the dog images can be classified by the discriminator as being non-dog images, and it picks up on this error. This error gets back propagated through the network.

Hinton's Capsule network

Geoffrey Hinton, the father of deep learning, created a huge stir in the space of deep learning by introducing a new network. This network was called the **Capsule Network (CapsNet)**. An algorithm to train this network was also brought forth, which is called **dynamic routing between capsules**. For the first time, Hinton spoke about it in 2011 in the paper called **transforming autoencoder**. In 2017 November, a full paper was published by Hinton and his team regarding the Capsule network.

The Capsule Network and convolutional neural networks

The **convolutional neural network (CNN)** has been one of the most important milestones in the area of deep learning. It has got everyone excited and has been the cornerstone for new research, too. But, as they say, *Nothing is perfect in this world.* Nor is our beloved CNN.

Can you recall how CNNs work? The most important job of a CNN is to execute convolution. What this means is that once you pass an image through CNN, the features, such as edges and color gradients, are extracted from image pixels by the convolution layer. Other layers will combine these features into a more complex one. And on top of it, once the dense layer is kept, it enables the network to carry out the classification job. The following diagram shows the image that we are working on:

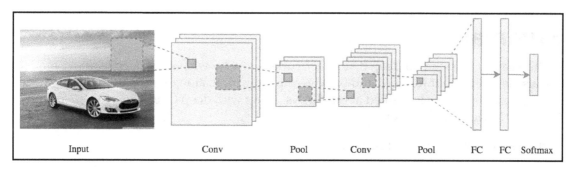

The preceding diagram is a basic CNN network, which is being used to detect the car in the image. The following diagram shows the image of a car that is in perfect order, and a fragmented image of the same:

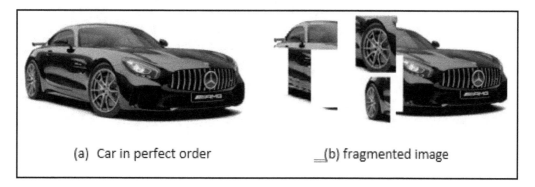

(a) Car in perfect order   (b) fragmented image

Let's say we pass on these two images through the CNN network (to detect the car) – what will be the response of the network for both images? Can you ponder over this and come up with an answer? Just to help you, a car has got a number of components such as wheels, a windshield, a bonnet, and so on, but a car is deemed as a car to human eyes when all of these parts/components are set in order. However, for a CNN, only the features are important. A CNN doesn't take relative positional and orientational relationship into account. So, both of these images will be classified as a car by the network, even though this is not the case to the human eye.

To make amends, CNNs include max-pooling, which helps in increasing the view of a higher layer's neurons, thus making the detection of higher order features possible. Max-pooling makes CNNs work, but at the same time, information loss also takes place. It's a big drawback of CNN.

Summary

In this chapter, we studied deep neural networks and why we need a deep learning model. We also learned about forward and backward prorogation, along with parameters and hyperparameters. We also talked about GANs, along with deep Gaussian processes, the Capsule Network, and CNNs.

In the next chapter, we will study causal inference.

10
Causal Inference

In this final chapter, we will learn about the following topics:

- Granger causality in time series (econometric approach to causality)
- Graphical models causality

Granger causality

In time series, we typically use univariate data. That is, we use a single series to predict its future values. Let's say that we are studying Google's stock price data, and we are asked to forecast the future values of stock prices. In this case, we will need historic data of Google's stock prices. Based on that, we will make predictions.

However, at times, we need multiple time series to make a forecast. But why is it that we need multiple time series? Any guesses?

The following graph shows Google's stock price data:

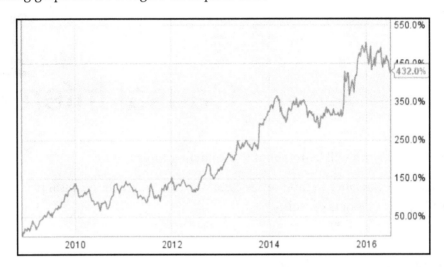

The answer is that we need to understand and explore the relationship between multiple time series as this can improve our forecast. For example, we have got correlated time series of **GDP Deflator: Services** and **WPI: All Commodities**, as follows:

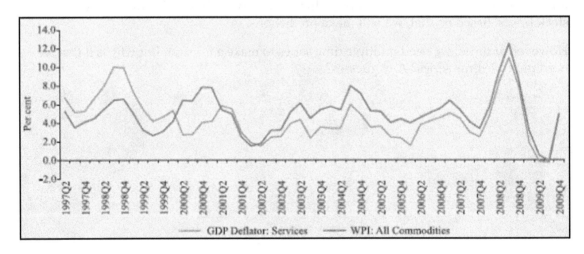

It is quite evident that these two seem to carry a relationship. When we have to forecast **GDP Deflator: Services**, we can use **WPI: All Commodities** time series data as input. This is called **Granger causality**.

To put it more aptly, Granger causality is one of the ways to investigate causality between two variables in a time series. This method is a probabilistic account of causality.

Even though we are talking about causality here, it isn't exactly the same. Typically, causality is associated with a situation where variable *1* is the cause of variable 2 or vice versa. However, with Granger causality, we do not test a true cause and effect relationship. The fundamental reason to know is whether **a particular variable comes before another** in the time series.

You aren't testing a true cause and effect relationship. What you want to know is whether **a particular variable comes before another** in the time series. That is to say, if we find Granger causality in the data, then there isn't any causal link in the true sense of the word.

> When econometricians say cause, what they mean is Granger-cause, although a more appropriate word might be precedence. Granger causality was proposed by a Nobel laureate in Economics, Prof Clive Granger, in 2003.

Let's look at one more example. Here, we have GDP per capita for OECD nations. We can see that the number of OECD countries have a similar growth and pattern in GDP. We can assume that these countries are responsible for each other's GDP growth due to dependencies.

The following is a graph that shows GDP per capita for OECD countries:

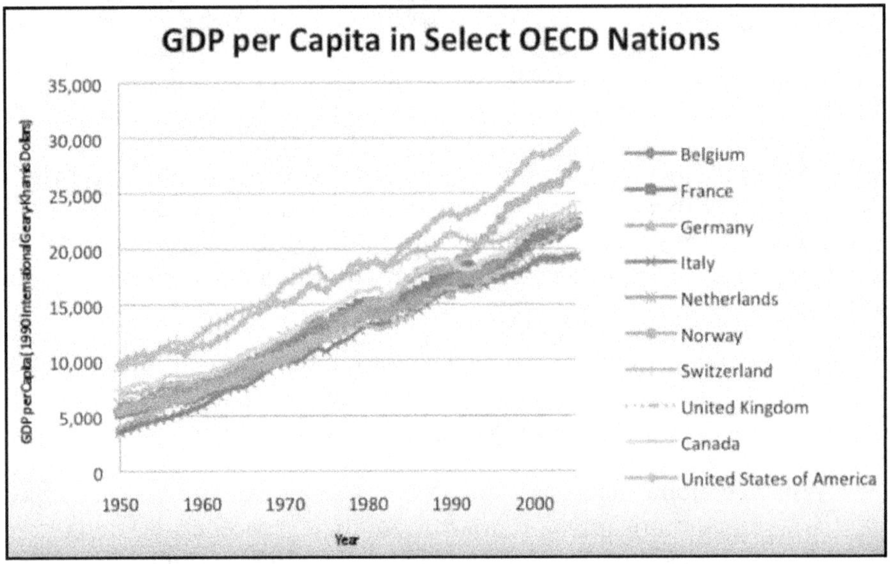

We can utilize the series of one country to forecast for another one. More often than not, this kind of relationship is prevalent more in financial time series. The stock market of India, NSE/BSE, and so on may have an impact on NYSE. Therefore, NYSE indices can be used to make a forecast for NSE indices.

Let's infuse a bit of mathematics into this. Let's say there are two time series, $X(t)$ and $Y(t)$. If the past values of $X(t)$ are helping to predict the future values of $Y(t)$, it is said that $X(t)$ Granger causes $Y(t)$.

So, $Y(t)$ is a function of the lag of $Y(t)$ and also of the lag of $X(t)$. It can be expressed as as follows:

$$Y(t) = f(Yt\text{-}p, Xt\text{-}p)$$

However, this only holds true in the following situations:

- Cause takes place prior to effect. What this means is that $Y(t) = f(Xt-1)$,
- Cause has got significant information about the future values of its effect, for example:

$$Y(t) = a1\ Yt\text{-}1 + b1\ Xt\text{-}1 + error$$

Xt-1 is adding an extra effect on *Y(t)*. The magnitude of effect is decided by *b1*.

Let's say we have two equations:

$$Yt = a0 + a1^* \ Yt\text{-}1$$

$$Yt = a0 + a1^* Yt\text{-}1 + a2^* Xt\text{-}1$$

The null hypothesis here is as follows:

- *H0: a2=0*: What this means is that there is no effect of other series, where *Xt-1* on *Yt*

The alternate hypothesis here is as follows::

- *H1: a2≠ 0*: What this means is that there is a significant effect of other series, where *Xt-1* on *Yt*

We run a t-test to determine whether there is a significant effect of other series of *Xt-1* on *Yt*.

If the null hypothesis is rejected, we can say that it is a case of Granger causality.

F-test

The basic steps for running this test are as follows:

1. Formulate the null hypothesis and its alternative.
2. Choose the lags. These can depend on the amount of data you have. One way to choose lags i and j is to run a model order test. It would be easier to pick up multiple values and run the Granger test to see if the results are the similar for different lag levels.

3. Also identify the f-value. The two equations can be used to find out whether $\beta j = 0$ for all lags j.

Limitations

The different limitations of this approach are as follows:

- Granger causality is not a true causality
- If $X(t)$ affects $Y(t)$ through a third variable, $Z(t)$, then it is difficult to find Granger causality

Use case

Here, we have a multivariate time series dataset called `AirQualityUCI`. We have to test whether NOx has a Granger causality of NO2.

Since we don't have a library in Python for multivariate Granger causality, we will do this in R by using the `lmtest` package.

Load the `lmtest` library. In case the library isn't there, you will need to install it, as follows:

```
install.packages("lmtest")
library(lmtest)
```

Load the data. Then, make use of the `grangertest` function to find out whether there is any significant relationship between NOx and NO2:

```
data= read.csv("AirQualityUCI.csv")
grangertest(NOx.GT. ~ NO2.GT., order = 3, data = data)
```

The output for this is as follows:

```
Granger causality test

Model 1: NOx.GT. ~ Lags(NOx.GT., 1:3) + Lags(NO2.GT., 1:3)
Model 2: NOx.GT. ~ Lags(NOx.GT., 1:3)
  Res.Df Df      F    Pr(>F)
1   9347
2   9350 -3 282.01 < 2.2e-16 ***
---
Signif. codes:  0 '***' 0.001 '**' 0.01 '*' 0.05 '.' 0.1 ' ' 1
```

So, the f-test has become significant, which means that the coefficients of lagged NO2 have a significant impact on NOx.

Graphical causal models

This model was covered in detail in `Chapter 8`, *Probabilistic Graphical Models*. We will also look into it briefly here, too.

Bayesian networks are directed acyclic graphs (DAGs) where the nodes represent variables of interest (for example, the temperature of a device, the gender of a patient, a feature of an object, the occurrence of an event, and so on). Causal influences among the variables are represented using links. The strength of an influence can be potrayed by conditional probabilities that are linked to each cluster of the parent-child nodes in the network. In the following diagram we can see the causal models, that have a node and an edge:

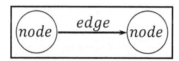

The node represents the variables and the edges stand for conditional relationship between the variables. What we are looking for is full joint probability distribution. Here, the conditional dependency is being spoken. Rain causes the ground to be wet. However, winning the lottery has nothing to do with other variables. It's got conditional independence, as shown in the following diagram:

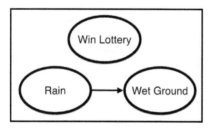

Here, the probability for conditional independence is as follows:

$$P(Lottery, Rain, Wet\ Ground) = P(Lottery)\ P(Rain)\ P(Wet\ Ground \mid Rain)$$

Therefore, we can say that a Bayesian network describes a probability distribution among all variables by putting conditional probability as edges.

Let's look at an example in Python:

1. First, we need to load the library, `CausalGraphicalModel`, as follows:

   ```
   from causalgraphicalmodels import CausalGraphicalModel
   ```

2. Let's set up the model for a condition that if somebody is doing a `Job` and if it's powered by `Smartwork` and `Hardwork`, he/she reaps rewards and eventually, ends up having a promotion:

   ```
   Model = CausalGraphicalModel(
     nodes=["Job", "Smartwork", "Hardwork", "Reward", "Promotion"],
     edges=[
     ("Job", "Smartwork"),
     ("Job", "Hardwork"),
     ("Smartwork", "Reward"),
     ("Hardwork", "Reward"),
     ("Reward", "Promotion")
     ]
   )
   Model.draw()
   ```

   The following is the output of the preceding code:

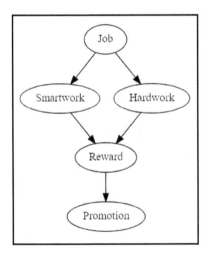

3. Let's obtain the distribution:

   ```
   print(Model.get_distribution())
   ```

Then we will get the following as a output:

```
P(Job)P(Hardwork|Job)P(Smartwork|Job)P(Reward|Smartwork,Hardwork)P(Promotion|Reward)
```

4. Let's extract all of the conditional independence relationships:

```
Model.get_all_independence_relationships()
```

```
[('Job', 'Promotion', {'Reward'}),
 ('Job', 'Promotion', {'Reward', 'Smartwork'}),
 ('Job', 'Promotion', {'Hardwork', 'Smartwork'}),
 ('Job', 'Promotion', {'Hardwork', 'Reward'}),
 ('Job', 'Promotion', {'Hardwork', 'Reward', 'Smartwork'}),
 ('Job', 'Reward', {'Hardwork', 'Smartwork'}),
 ('Job', 'Reward', {'Hardwork', 'Promotion', 'Smartwork'}),
 ('Promotion', 'Smartwork', {'Reward'}),
 ('Promotion', 'Smartwork', {'Job', 'Reward'}),
 ('Promotion', 'Smartwork', {'Hardwork', 'Reward'}),
 ('Promotion', 'Smartwork', {'Hardwork', 'Job', 'Reward'}),
 ('Promotion', 'Hardwork', {'Reward'}),
 ('Promotion', 'Hardwork', {'Job', 'Reward'}),
 ('Promotion', 'Hardwork', {'Reward', 'Smartwork'}),
 ('Promotion', 'Hardwork', {'Job', 'Reward', 'Smartwork'}),
 ('Smartwork', 'Hardwork', {'Job'})]
```

Here, we are able to assess the conditional independence among the variables.

5. Let's mix this in with `Reward`:

```
Intervene = Model.do("Reward")
Intervene.draw()
```

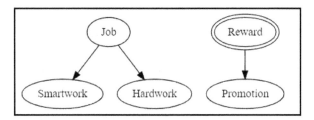

Summary

In this chapter, we studied Granger causality, which is where we use a single time series to predict its future values, along with the different models of graphical causality models. The graphical causality models cover two examples that will give us a basic idea about the graphical causal models.

11
Advanced Methods

We have made it to the final chapter of this book. However, this doesn't mean that we can ignore the topics that we are going to discuss in the upcoming sections. These topics are state of the art and will separate you from the rest.

In this chapter, we will cover the following topics:

- Kernel principal component analysis
- Independent component analysis
- Compressed sensing
- Bayesian multiple imputations
- Self-organizing maps

Introduction

In the previous chapter, we understood what **principal component analysis (PCA)** is, how it works, and when we should be deploying it. However, as a dimensionality reduction technique, do you think that you can put this to use in every scenario? Can you recall the roadblock or the underlying assumption behind it that we discussed?

Yes, the most important assumption behind PCA is that it works for datasets that are linearly separable. However, in the real world, you don't get this kind of dataset very often. We need a method to capture non-linear data patterns.

On the left-hand side, we have got a dataset in which there are two classes. We can see that once we arrive at the projections and establish the components, PCA doesn't have an effect on it and that it is not able to separate it by a line in a 2D dimension. That is, PCA can only function well when we have got low-level dimensions and linearly separable data. The following plot shows the dataset of two classes:

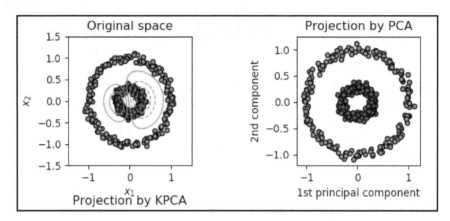

This is why we bring in the kernel method: so that we can merge it with PCA to achieve it.

Just to recap what you learned about the kernel method, we will discuss it and its importance in brief:

- We have got data in a low dimensional space. However, at times, it's difficult to achieve classification (green and red) when we have got non-linear data (as shown in the following diagram). This being said, we do have a clear understanding that having a tool that can map the data from a lower to a higher dimension will result in a proper classification. This tool is called the **kernel method**.
- The same dataset turns out to be linearly separable in the new feature space.

The following diagram shows data in low and high dimensional spaces:

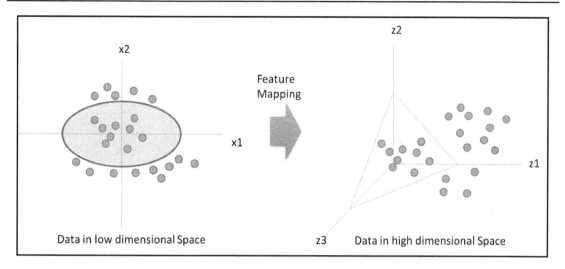

To classify the green and red points in the preceding diagram, the feature mapping function has to take the data and change is from being 2D to 3D, that is, $\Phi = R^2 \rightarrow R^3$. The equation for this is as follows:

$$(x_1, x_2) \rightarrow (z_1, z_2, z_3) = (x1^2, \sqrt{2}x_1x_2, x2^2)$$

The goal of the kernel method is to figure out and choose kernel function K. This is so that we can find the geometry feature in the new dimension and classify data patterns. Let's see how this is done:

$$\Phi(x)^T \Phi(z) = (x_1^2, \sqrt{2}x_1x_2, x_2^2)^T (z_1^2, \sqrt{2}z_1z_2, z_1^2)$$

$$= x_1^2 z_1^2 + x_2^2 z_2^2 + 2x_1x_2z_1z_2$$

$$= (x_1z_1 + x_2z_2)^2$$

$$= (x^T z)^2$$

$$= K(x, z)$$

Here, Phi is a feature mapping function. But do we always need to know the feature mapping function? Not really. Kernel function K does the trick. With a given kernel function, K, we can come up with a feature space, H. Two of the popular kernel functions are Gaussian and polynomial kernel functions.

Picking an apt kernel function will enable us to figure out the characteristics of the data in the new feature space quite well.

Now that we have made ourselves familiar with the kernel trick, let's move on to the Kernel PCA.

Kernel PCA

The Kernel PCA is an algorithm that not only keeps the main spirit of PCA as it is, but goes a step further to make use of the kernel trick so that it is operational for non-linear data:

1. Let's define the covariance matrix of the data in the feature space, which is the product of the mapping function and the transpose of the mapping function:

$$C_F = \frac{1}{N} \sum_{i=1}^{N} \phi(x_i)\phi(x_i)^T$$

It is similar to the one we used for PCA.

2. The next step is to solve the following equation so that we can compute principal components:

$$C_F v = \lambda v$$

Here, C_F is the covariance matrix of the data in feature space, v is the eigenvector, and λ (lambda) is the eigenvalues.

3. Let's put the value of *step 1* into *step 2* – that is, the value of C_F in the equation of *step 2*. The eigenvector will be as follows:

$$v = \frac{1}{N\lambda} \sum_{i=1}^{N} \phi(x_i)\phi(x_i)^T v = C_F = \sum_{i=1}^{N} \frac{\phi(x_i)^T v}{N\lambda}\phi(x_i) = \sum_{i=1}^{N} \alpha_i \phi(x_i)$$

Here, $\alpha_i = \dfrac{\phi(x_i)^T v}{N\lambda}$ is a scalar number.

4. Now, let's add the kernel function into the equation. Let's multiply $\Phi(x_k)$ on both sides of the formula, $\lambda v = C_F v$:

$$\Rightarrow \lambda[\phi(x_k)v] = [\phi(x_k)C_F v]$$

5. Let's put the value of v from the equation in *step 3* into the equation of *step 4*, as follows:

$$\Rightarrow \lambda \sum_{i=1}^{N} \alpha_i \phi(x_i)\phi(x_k) = \frac{1}{N} \sum_{i=1}^{N} \alpha_i (\phi(x_k) \sum_{j=1}^{N} \phi(x_j))(\phi(x_i)\phi(x_j))$$

6. Now, we call K $K = (\phi(x_i) \cdot \phi(x_j))$. Upon simplifying the equation from *step 5* by keying in the value of K, we get the following:

$$N\lambda K\alpha = K^2 \alpha$$

On doing eigen decomposition, we get the following:

$$\Rightarrow N\lambda\alpha = K\alpha$$

On normalizing the feature space for centering, we get the following result:

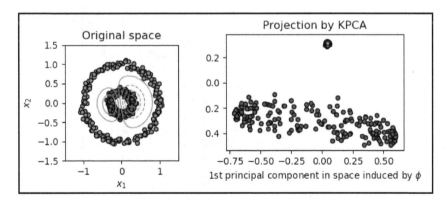

Now, let's execute the Kernel PCA in Python. We will keep this simple and work on the Iris dataset. We will also see how we can utilize the new compressed dimension in the model:

1. Let's load the libraries:

```
import numpy as np # linear algebra
import pandas as pd # data processing
import matplotlib.pyplot as plt
from sklearn import datasets
```

2. Then, load the data and create separate objects for the explanatory and target variables:

```
iris = datasets.load_iris()
X = iris.data
y = iris.target
```

3. Let's have a look at the explanatory data:

```
X
```

```
array([[ 5.1,  3.5,  1.4,  0.2],
       [ 4.9,  3. ,  1.4,  0.2],
       [ 4.7,  3.2,  1.3,  0.2],
       [ 4.6,  3.1,  1.5,  0.2],
       [ 5. ,  3.6,  1.4,  0.2],
       [ 5.4,  3.9,  1.7,  0.4],
       [ 4.6,  3.4,  1.4,  0.3],
       [ 5. ,  3.4,  1.5,  0.2],
       [ 4.4,  2.9,  1.4,  0.2],
       [ 4.9,  3.1,  1.5,  0.1],
       [ 5.4,  3.7,  1.5,  0.2],
       [ 4.8,  3.4,  1.6,  0.2],
       [ 4.8,  3. ,  1.4,  0.1],
       [ 4.3,  3. ,  1.1,  0.1],
       [ 5.8,  4. ,  1.2,  0.2],
       [ 5.7,  4.4,  1.5,  0.4],
       [ 5.4,  3.9,  1.3,  0.4],
       [ 5.1,  3.5,  1.4,  0.3],
       [ 5.7,  3.8,  1.7,  0.3],
```

4. Let's split the data into train and test sets, as follows:

```
from sklearn.model_selection import train_test_split
X_train, X_test, y_train, y_test = train_test_split(X, y, test_size
= 0.25, random_state = 0)
```

5. Now, we can standardize the data:

```
from sklearn.preprocessing import StandardScaler
sc = StandardScaler()
X_train = sc.fit_transform(X_train)
X_test = sc.transform(X_test)
```

6. Let's have a look at X_train:

```
X_train
```

The output is as follows:

```
array([[  1.54399532e-02,  -1.19254753e-01,   2.25126850e-01,
          3.56381749e-01],
       [ -9.98450310e-02,  -1.04039491e+00,   1.13559562e-01,
         -2.86480506e-02],
       [  1.05300481e+00,  -1.19254753e-01,   9.50314227e-01,
          1.12644135e+00],
       [ -1.36797986e+00,   3.41315328e-01,  -1.39259884e+00,
         -1.31208072e+00],
       [  1.16828980e+00,   1.11030287e-01,   7.27179649e-01,
          1.38312788e+00],
       [ -1.02212490e+00,   1.03217045e+00,  -1.22524790e+00,
         -7.98707650e-01],
       [ -5.60984968e-01,   1.49274053e+00,  -1.28103155e+00,
         -1.31208072e+00],
       [ -1.02212490e+00,  -2.42210516e+00,  -1.65358660e-01,
         -2.85334584e-01],
       [  7.07149859e-01,  -1.19254753e-01,   9.50314227e-01,
          7.41411549e-01],
       [  9.37719827e-01,   5.71600368e-01,   1.06188152e+00,
```

7. Now, let's apply the kernel PCA on this. Here, we are trying to condense the data into just two components. The kernel that's been chosen here is the radial basis function:

```
from sklearn.decomposition import KernelPCA
kpca = KernelPCA(n_components = 2, kernel = 'rbf')
X_train2 = kpca.fit_transform(X_train)
X_test2 = kpca.transform(X_test)
```

We have got the new train and test data with the help of the kernel PCA.

8. Let's see what the data looks like:

```
X_train2
```

We get the following as output:

```
array([[ -3.37725246e-01,  -2.67929399e-01],
       [ -2.28159618e-01,  -6.42964823e-01],
       [ -5.42657970e-01,   4.00470428e-01],
       [  7.68893086e-01,   4.93146060e-02],
       [ -4.94431455e-01,   4.74938667e-01],
       [  7.26835183e-01,   1.08946020e-01],
       [  6.93412746e-01,   1.93039625e-01],
       [  2.71518785e-02,  -4.56605659e-01],
       [ -5.56008764e-01,   2.08040974e-01],
       [ -4.15727350e-01,   5.35959232e-01],
       [ -2.33820327e-01,  -4.91624713e-01],
       [ -4.12615994e-01,  -2.79420859e-02],
       [ -1.42346326e-01,  -6.98291047e-01],
       [ -3.19744482e-01,   5.23774154e-01],
       [ -3.91565822e-01,   1.76538163e-01],
       [ -1.06099524e-01,  -7.01543477e-01],
       [ -5.02349236e-01,  -1.80419722e-01],
       [ -4.93355128e-01,  -1.85187916e-01],
       [ -1.27684052e-01,  -5.40426177e-01],
```

Now, we've got two components here. Earlier, X_train showed us four variables. Now, the data has been shrunk into two fields.

Independent component analysis

Independent component analysis (ICA) is similar to PCA in terms of dimensionality reduction. However, it originated from the signal processing world wherein they had this problem that multiple signals were being transmitted from a number of sources, and there were a number of devices set up to capture it. However, the problem was that the captured signal by the device was not very clear as it happened to be a mix of a number of sources. They needed to have clear and independent reception for the different devices that gave birth to ICA. Heralt and Jutten came up with this in.

The difference between PCA and ICA is that PCA focuses upon finding uncorrelated factors, whereas ICA is all about deriving independent factors. Confused? Let me help you. Uncorrelated factors imply that there is no linear relationship between them, whereas independence means that two factors have got no bearing on each other. For example, scoring good marks in mathematics is independent of which state you live in.

An underlying assumption for this algorithm is that the variables are linear mixtures of unknown latent and independent variables.

The data $x_i(t)$ is modeled using hidden variables $s_i(t)$:

$$x_i(t) = \sum_{j=1}^{m} a_{ij} s_j(t)$$

Here, i= 1,2,3..........n.

It can also be written in the form of matrix decomposition as **x=As**:

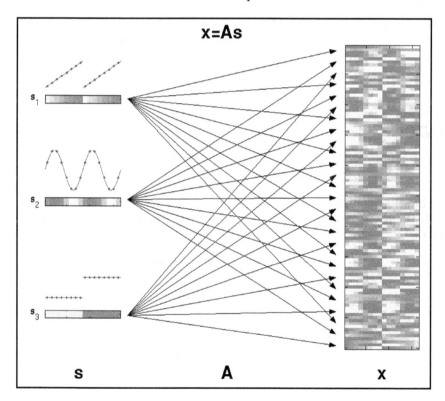

Here, we have the following:

- **A**: Constant mixing matrix
- **s**: Latent factor matrices, which are independent of each other

We have to estimate the values of both **A** and **s** while we have got **X**.

In other words, our goal is to find W, which is $W = A^{-1}$, which is an unmixing matrix.

Here, s_{ij} has to be statistically independent of and non-Gaussian (not following normal distribution).

Preprocessing for ICA

The preprocessing of ICA can be done as follows:

- **Centering**: The first step is to center x. That is, we need to subtract its mean vector from x so as to make x a zero-mean variable.
- **Whitening**: Before putting the data through ICA, we are supposed to whiten the data. This means that the data has to be uncorrelated. Geometrically speaking, it tends to restore the initial shape of the data and only the resultant matrix needs to be rotated.

Approach

To find out what unmixing matrices are independent, we have to bank upon non-Gaussianity. Let's see how we can do this.

Here, we will need to maximize the kurtosis, which will turn the distribution into a non-Gaussian. This will result in independent components. The following diagram shows an image of fast ICA:

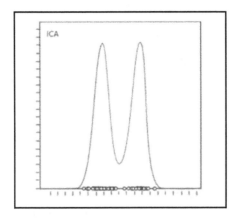

For this, we have the `FastICA` library in Python.

Let's look at how we can execute this in Python. We will work with the same Iris data. This might not be an ideal dataset for executing ICA, but this is being done for directional purposes. To execute the code in Python, we will need to perform the following steps:

1. First, we need to load the library:

```
import numpy as np # linear algebra
import pandas as pd # data processing
import matplotlib.pyplot as plt
from sklearn import datasets
```

2. Now, we need to load the data:

```
iris = datasets.load_iris()
X = iris.data
y = iris.target
```

3. Let's partition the data into train and test sets:

```
from sklearn.model_selection import train_test_split
X_train, X_test, y_train, y_test = train_test_split(X, y, test_size
= 0.25, random_state = 0)
```

4. Let's make the data a standard scalar:

```
from sklearn.preprocessing import StandardScaler
sc = StandardScaler()
X_train = sc.fit_transform(X_train)
X_test = sc.transform(X_test)
```

5. Now, we need to load in the ICA library:

```
from sklearn.decomposition import FastICA
```

6. We carry out ICA as follows. We will stick to three components here:

```
ICA = FastICA(n_components=3, random_state=10,whiten= True)
X=ICA.fit_transform(X_train)
```

7. We will then plot the results, as follows:

```
plt.figure(figsize=(8,10))
plt.title('ICA Components')
plt.scatter(X[:,0], X[:,1])
plt.scatter(X[:,1], X[:,2])
plt.scatter(X[:,2], X[:,0])
```

The output for this is as follows:

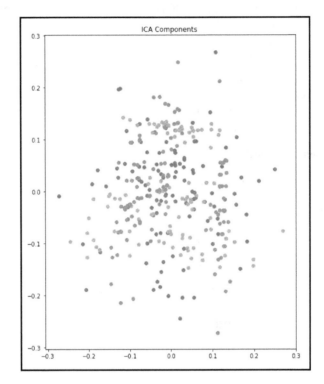

We can see the three different components here (by color).

Compressed sensing

Compressed sensing is one of the easiest problems to solve in the area of information theory and signal processing. It is a signal acquisition and reconstruction technique where the signal is compressible. The signal must be sparse. Compressed sensing tries to fit samples of a signal to functions, and it has a preference to use as few basic functions as possible to match the samples. This is described in the following diagram:

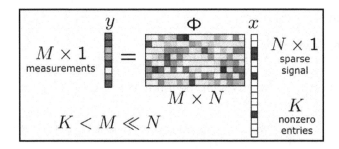

This is one of the prime equations that we see in linear algebra, where **y** is a **M x 1** matrix, phi is a **M x N** matrix that has got a number of columns that is higher than the number of rows, and **x** is a **N x 1** matrix comprising **k** non-zero entries. There are so many unknowns, which is expressed as an **N** length vector and **M** measurements, wherein **M << N**. In this type of equation, we know that many solutions are possible since the null space of this matrix is non-trivial. Hence, this equation can accommodate many solutions.

Our goal

Our goal is to find out the solution with a least possible non-zero entry of all of the solutions. That is, the solution should give us as few non-zeros as possible. Are you wondering where this can be applied? There are plenty of applications for it. The areas where it can be applied are as follows:

- Signal representation
- Medical imaging
- Sparse channel estimation

Let's say that we have got a time signal. This signal is highly sparse, but we know a little bit about it as it has a few frequencies. Can you sense what it is from the earlier equation? Yes, it can be deemed as X.

Let's call this **unknown** signal X. Now, even though we don't know the whole signal, we can still make observations about it, or samples, as shown in the following code:

```
import numpy as np
import matplotlib as mpl
import matplotlib.pyplot as plt
import scipy.optimize as spopt
import scipy.fftpack as spfft
import scipy.ndimage as spimg
import cvxpy as cvx
```

This will form a random equation:

```
x = np.sort(np.random.uniform(0, 15, 30))
y = 5 + 0.5 * x + 0.1 * np.random.randn(len(x))
```

Now, we need to fit the l1 norm. We get the following output:

```
l1 = lambda x0, x, y: np.sum(np.abs(x0[0] * x + x0[1] - y))
opt1 = spopt.fmin(func=l1, x0=[1, 1], args=(x, y))
```

Then, we need to fit the l2 norm. We get the following output:

```
l2 = lambda x0, x, y: np.sum(np.power(x0[0] * x + x0[1] - y, 2))
opt2 = spopt.fmin(func=l2, x0=[1, 1], args=(x, y))

y2 = y.copy()
y2[3] += 5
y2[13] -= 10
xopt12 = spopt.fmin(func=l1, x0=[1, 1], args=(x, y2))
xopt22 = spopt.fmin(func=l2, x0=[1, 1], args=(x, y2))
```

By summing up the two sinusoids, we get the following output:

```
n = 10000
t = np.linspace(0, 1/5, n)
y = np.sin(1250 * np.pi * t) + np.sin(3000 * np.pi * t)
yt = spfft.dct(y, norm='ortho')
plt.figure(figsize=[10,5])
plt.plot(t,y)
plt.title('Original signal')
plt.xlabel('Time (s)')
plt.ylabel('y')
```

Now, let's take the sample out of n:

```
m = 1000 # 10% sample
ran = np.random.choice(n, m, replace=False) # random sample of indices
t2 = t[ran]
y2 = y[ran]
```

Let's create the idct matrix operator:

```
# create idct matrix operator
A = spfft.idct(np.identity(n), norm='ortho', axis=0)
A = A[ran]
# do L1 optimization
vx = cvx.Variable(n)
objective = cvx.Minimize(cvx.norm(vx, 1))
```

```
constraints = [A*vx == y2]
prob = cvx.Problem(objective, constraints)
result = prob.solve(verbose=True)
```

The output for this is as follows:

```
ECOS 2.0.4 - (C) embotech GmbH, Zurich Switzerland, 2012-15. Web: www.embotech.com/ECOS

It    pcost       dcost      gap    pres   dres   k/t    mu     step    sigma    IR    |   BT
 0  +0.000e+00  +4.986e-22  +6e+04  1e+00  1e-02  1e+00  3e+00   ---     ---    1  1  - | - -
 1  +1.843e+02  +1.844e+02  +3e+04  9e-01  5e-03  6e-01  1e+00  0.6016  1e-01  1  1  1 | 0 0
 2  +2.368e+02  +2.371e+02  +2e+04  8e-01  4e-03  7e-01  1e+00  0.3928  6e-01  2  1  0 | 0 0
 3  +3.080e+02  +3.083e+02  +2e+04  6e-01  3e-03  5e-01  8e-01  0.5850  4e-01  1  1  1 | 0 0
 4  +3.660e+02  +3.662e+02  +9e+03  4e-01  2e-03  3e-01  5e-01  0.5546  3e-01  1  1  1 | 0 0
 5  +4.180e+02  +4.181e+02  +5e+03  2e-01  1e-03  2e-01  3e-01  0.5174  2e-01  1  1  1 | 0 0
 6  +4.659e+02  +4.660e+02  +3e+03  1e-01  5e-04  1e-01  2e-01  0.5998  3e-01  1  1  1 | 0 0
 7  +5.209e+02  +5.209e+02  +2e+03  6e-02  3e-04  7e-02  8e-02  0.6191  2e-01  1  1  1 | 0 0
 8  +5.643e+02  +5.643e+02  +7e+02  3e-02  1e-04  3e-02  3e-02  0.7787  3e-01  1  1  1 | 0 0
 9  +5.851e+02  +5.851e+02  +3e+02  1e-02  6e-05  2e-02  2e-02  0.7366  3e-01  1  1  1 | 0 0
10  +5.956e+02  +5.956e+02  +2e+02  7e-03  3e-05  8e-03  8e-03  0.7063  3e-01  1  1  1 | 0 0
11  +6.001e+02  +6.001e+02  +9e+01  4e-03  1e-05  4e-03  4e-03  0.5765  2e-01  1  1  1 | 0 0
12  +6.027e+02  +6.027e+02  +4e+01  2e-03  7e-06  2e-03  2e-03  0.7119  3e-01  1  1  1 | 0 0
13  +6.042e+02  +6.042e+02  +2e+01  8e-04  3e-06  9e-04  1e-03  0.7316  2e-01  1  1  1 | 0 0
14  +6.048e+02  +6.048e+02  +1e+01  4e-04  2e-06  5e-04  5e-04  0.6762  3e-01  1  1  1 | 0 0
15  +6.051e+02  +6.051e+02  +5e+00  2e-04  8e-07  2e-04  2e-04  0.7416  2e-01  1  1  1 | 0 0
16  +6.053e+02  +6.053e+02  +2e+00  8e-05  3e-07  1e-04  1e-04  0.6391  1e-01  1  1  1 | 0 0
17  +6.054e+02  +6.054e+02  +9e-01  4e-05  2e-07  4e-05  4e-05  0.7088  2e-01  1  1  1 | 0 0
18  +6.054e+02  +6.054e+02  +4e-01  2e-05  7e-08  2e-05  2e-05  0.9890  5e-01  1  1  1 | 0 0
19  +6.054e+02  +6.054e+02  +1e-01  5e-06  2e-08  6e-06  6e-06  0.7531  5e-02  1  1  1 | 0 0
20  +6.054e+02  +6.054e+02  +6e-02  2e-06  1e-08  3e-06  3e-06  0.6106  2e-01  1  1  1 | 0 0
21  +6.054e+02  +6.054e+02  +2e-02  7e-07  3e-09  9e-07  9e-07  0.8765  2e-01  1  1  1 | 0 0
22  +6.054e+02  +6.054e+02  +5e-03  2e-07  8e-10  2e-07  2e-07  0.7680  4e-02  1  1  1 | 0 0
23  +6.054e+02  +6.054e+02  +1e-03  6e-08  2e-10  6e-08  7e-08  0.7542  5e-02  1  1  1 | 0 0
24  +6.054e+02  +6.054e+02  +3e-04  1e-08  6e-11  2e-08  2e-08  0.8159  7e-02  1  1  1 | 0 0
25  +6.054e+02  +6.054e+02  +9e-06  4e-10  2e-12  5e-10  5e-10  0.9854  1e-02  1  1  1 | 0 0
26  +6.054e+02  +6.054e+02  +1e-07  4e-12  5e-14  5e-12  5e-12  0.9890  1e-04  1  1  1 | 0 0

OPTIMAL (within feastol=4.3e-12, reltol=1.7e-10, abstol=1.0e-07).
```

To reconstruct the signal, we must do the following:

```
x = np.array(vx.value)
x = np.squeeze(x)
signal = spfft.idct(x, norm='ortho', axis=0)
```

That is how we reconstruct the signal.

Self-organizing maps

Self-organizing maps (SOM) were invented by Teuvo Kohonen in the 1980s. Sometimes, they are known as **Kohonen maps**. So, why do they exist? The prime motive for these kind of maps is to reduce dimensionality through a neural network. The following diagram shows the different 2D patterns from the input layers:

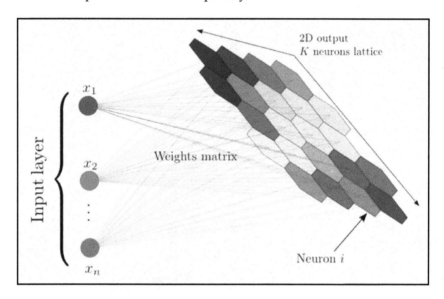

They take the number of columns as input. As we can see from the 2D output, it transforms and reduces the amount of columns in the dataset into 2D.

The following link leads to the the 2D output: `https://www.cs.hmc.edu/~kpang/nn/som.html`

The depiction of the preceding diagram in 2D talks about a health of the country based on various factors. That is, it shows whether they are rich or poor. Some other factors that are taken into account are education, quality of life, sanitation, inflation, and health. Therefore, it forms a huge set of columns or dimensions. Countries such as Belgium and Sweden seem to show similar traits, depicting that they have got a good score on the health indicator.

Since this is an unsupervised learning technique, the data wasn't labeled. Based on patterns alone, the neural network is able to understand which country should be placed where.

Similar to the situation we just covered, opportunities are aplenty where self-organizing maps can be utilized. It can be thought as being similar in nature to K-means clustering.

SOM

Let's go through process of how SOMs learn:

1. Each node's weights are initialized by small standardized random values. These act like coordinates for different output nodes.
2. The first row's input (taking the first row from all of the variables) is fed into the first node.
3. Now, we have got two vectors. If V is the current input vector and W is the node's weight vector, then we calculate the Euclidean distance, like so:

$$D = \sqrt{\sum_{i=0}^{n}(V_i - W_i)^2}$$

4. The node that has a weight vector closest to the input vector is tagged as the **best-matching unit (BMU)**.
5. A similar operation is carried out for all the rows of input and weight vectors. BMUs are found for all.
6. Once the BMU has been determined for every iteration, the other nodes within the BMU's neighborhood are computed. Nodes within the same radius will have their weights updated. A green arrow indicates the radius. Slowly, the neighborhood will shrink to the size of just one node, as shown in the following diagram:

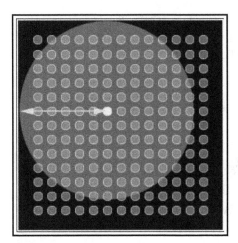

7. The most interesting part of the Kohonen algorithm is that the radius of the neighborhood keeps on shrinking. It takes place through the exponential decay function. The value of lambda is dependent on sigma. The number of iterations that have been chosen for the algorithm to run is given by the following equation:

$$\sigma(t) = \sigma_0 exp(-\frac{t}{\lambda})$$

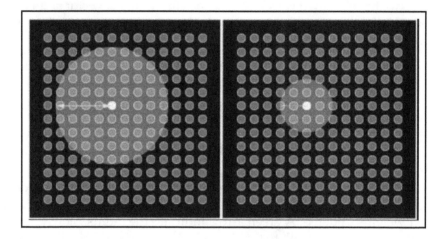

8. The weights get updated via the following equation:

$$W(t+1) = W(t) + \theta(t)L(t)(V(t) - W(t))$$

Here, this is as follows:

$$\theta(t) = exp(-\frac{D^2}{2\sigma^2(t)})$$

t= 1, 2... can be explained as follows:

-   *L(t)*: Learning rate
-   *D*: Distance of a node from BMU
-   σ: Width of the function

Now, let's carry out one use case of this in Python. We will try to detect fraud in a credit card dataset:

1. Let's load the libraries:

```
import numpy as np
import matplotlib.pyplot as plt
import pandas as pd
```

2. Now, it's time to load the data:

```
data = pd.read_csv('Credit_Card_Applications.csv')
X = data.iloc[:, :-1].values
y = data.iloc[:, -1].values
```

3. Next, we will standardize the data:

```
from sklearn.preprocessing import MinMaxScaler
sc = MinMaxScaler(feature_range = (0, 1))
X = sc.fit_transform(X)
```

4. Let's import the `minisom` library and key in the hyperparameters, that is, learning rate, sigma, length, and number of iterations:

```
from minisom import MiniSom
som = MiniSom(x = 10, y = 10, input_len = 15, sigma = 1.0,
learning_rate = 0.5)
som.random_weights_init(X)
som.train_random(data = X, num_iteration = 100)
```

5. Let's visualize the results:

```
from pylab import bone, pcolor, colorbar, plot, show
bone()
pcolor(som.distance_map().T)
colorbar()
markers = ['o', 's']
colors = ['r', 'g']
for i, x in enumerate(X):
 w = som.winner(x)
 plot(w[0] + 0.5,
 w[1] + 0.5,
 markers[y[i]],
 markeredgecolor = colors[y[i]],
 markerfacecolor = 'None',
 markersize = 10,
 markeredgewidth = 2)
show()
```

The following output will be generated from the preceding code:

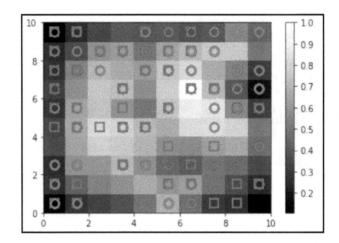

We can see that the nodes that have a propensity toward fraud have got white backgrounds. This means that we can track down those customers with the help of those nodes:

```
mappings = som.win_map(X)
frauds = np.concatenate((mappings[(8,1)], mappings[(6,8)]), axis = 0)
frauds = sc.inverse_transform(frauds)
```

This will give you the pattern of frauds.

Bayesian multiple imputation

Bayesian multiple imputation has got the spirit of the Bayesian framework. It is required to specify a parametric model for the complete data and a prior distribution over unknown model parameters, θ. Subsequently, m independent trials are drawn from the missing data, as given by the observed data using Bayes' Theorem. Markov Chain Monte Carlo can be used to simulate the entire joint posterior distribution of the missing data. BMI follows a normal distribution while generating imputations for the missing values.

Let's say that the data is as follows:

$$Y = (Yobs, Ymiss),$$

Here, *Yobs* is the observed *Y* and *Ymiss* is the missing *Y*.

If $P(Y|\theta)$ is the parametric model, the parameter θ is the mean and the covariance matrix that parameterizes a normal distribution. If this is the case, let $P(\theta)$ be the prior:

$$Posterior\ Predictive\ Distribution = P(Ymiss|Yobs) = \int P(Ymis|Yobs,\theta)P(\theta|Yobs)d\theta$$

Let's make use of the `Amelia` package in R and execute this:

```
library(foreign)
dataset = read.spss("World95.sav", to.data.frame=TRUE)

library(Amelia)

myvars <- names(dataset) %in% c("COUNTRY", "RELIGION", "REGION","CLIMATE")
newdata <- dataset[!myvars]
```

Now, let's make the imputation:

```
impute.out <- amelia(newdata, m=4)
```

Summary

In this chapter, we have studied the Kernel PCA, along with ICA. We also studied compressed sensing, the goals of compressed sensing, and self-organizing maps and how they work. Finally, we concluded with Bayesian multiple imputations.

Other Books You May Enjoy

If you enjoyed this book, you may be interested in these other books by Packt:

Python Machine Learning - Second Edition
Sebastian Raschka, Vahid Mirjalili

ISBN: 9781787125933

- Understand the key frameworks in data science, machine learning, and deep learning
- Harness the power of the latest Python open source libraries in machine learning
- Master machine learning techniques using challenging real-world data
- Master deep neural network implementation using the TensorFlow library
- Ask new questions of your data through machine learning models and neural networks
- Learn the mechanics of classification algorithms to implement the best tool for the job
- Predict continuous target outcomes using regression analysis
- Uncover hidden patterns and structures in data with clustering
- Delve deeper into textual and social media data using sentiment analysis

TensorFlow Machine Learning Cookbook
Nick McClure

ISBN: 9781786462169

- Become familiar with the basics of the TensorFlow machine learning library
- Get to know Linear Regression techniques with TensorFlow
- Learn SVMs with hands-on recipes
- Implement neural networks and improve predictions
- Apply NLP and sentiment analysis to your data
- Master CNN and RNN through practical recipes
- Take TensorFlow into production

Leave a review - let other readers know what you think

Please share your thoughts on this book with others by leaving a review on the site that you bought it from. If you purchased the book from Amazon, please leave us an honest review on this book's Amazon page. This is vital so that other potential readers can see and use your unbiased opinion to make purchasing decisions, we can understand what our customers think about our products, and our authors can see your feedback on the title that they have worked with Packt to create. It will only take a few minutes of your time, but is valuable to other potential customers, our authors, and Packt. Thank you!

Index

C

Capsule Network (CapsNet) 236, 237, 238
Classification and regression trees (CART) 75
collective anomalies 148
compressed sensing
  about 260, 261
  goal 261, 263
computation, neural networks
  activation for H1,calculating 105, 106
conditional probability 200
conditional probability table (CPT) 204, 207, 208
confidence 186
confusion matrix
  about 31, 33
  False Negative (FN) 32
  False Positive (FP) 32
  True Negative (TN) 32
  True Positive (TP) 32
contextual anomalies 148
convolutional neural network (CNN) 237, 238
corpora 153
count vectorizer
  executing 159
cross-validation
  about 27
  used, for model selection 29
curve fitting
  about 15, 16, 18
  residual 19

D

data sets, model building
  about 21
  development set 21
  test set 22
  training set 21
Decision Node 74
decision tree
  about 72, 73
  branch 74
  Decision Node 74
  Leaf Node 74
  Root Node 74
  tree splitting 75, 76

deep learning model
  need for 218, 219
deep neural network
  about 217, 218
  backward propagation 223, 225
  error computation 225
  forward propagation 220, 221, 223, 225
  notation 219, 220
  parameter b 222, 223
  parameter W 222, 223
development set
  about 21
  size 22
digit recognizer 230, 233
dimensionality reduction 37, 39
directed acyclic graph 203
discriminator 235
dot product 44
dynamic routing between capsules 236

E

electrical energy output (PE) 12
elements, association rules
  antecedent (if) 184
  consequent (then) 184
elements, autoregressive integrated moving
    average (ARIMA) model
  autoregressive operator 139
  integration operator 139
  moving average operator 139
elements, backpropagation
  dataset 110
  feed-forward network 110
  loss function 110
ensemble learning 66
ensemble model
  about 65, 67
  building, methods 67
entropy 76
error computation 225
errors, bias-variance trade off
  development error 23
  training error 23